Fighting the Somme

To my beautiful granddaughter
Evelyn Rose Wesson (Evie)
With love and hope for the future.

By the same author:

The German Army on the Somme 1914 – 1916
The German Army at Passchendaele
The German Army on Vimy Ridge 1914 – 1917
The German Army at Cambrai
The German Army at Ypres 1914
The German Army on the Western Front 1915
The German Army in the Spring Offensives 1917
The Germans at Beaumont Hamel
The Germans at Thiepval

With Nigel Cave:

The Battle for Vimy Ridge 1917
Le Cateau
Ypres 1914: Langemarck
Ypres 1914: Messines
Ypres 1914: Menin Road

Fighting the Somme

German Challenges,
Dilemmas and Solutions

Jack Sheldon

Pen & Sword
MILITARY

First published in Great Britain in 2017 by
Pen & Sword Military
an imprint of
Pen & Sword Books Ltd
47 Church Street
Barnsley
South Yorkshire
S70 2AS

ISBN 978 1 47388 199 0

Typeset in Ehrhardt by
Mac Style Ltd, Bridlington, East Yorkshire
Printed and bound in the Malta by Gutenberg Press Ltd.

Pen & Sword Books Ltd incorporates the imprints of Pen & Sword
Archaeology, Atlas, Aviation, Battleground, Discovery, Family
History, History, Maritime, Military, Naval, Politics, Railways,
Select, Transport, True Crime, Fiction, Frontline Books, Leo Cooper,
Praetorian Press, Seaforth Publishing and Wharncliffe.

For a complete list of Pen & Sword titles please contact
PEN & SWORD BOOKS LIMITED
47 Church Street, Barnsley, South Yorkshire, S70 2AS, England
E-mail: enquiries@pen-and-sword.co.uk
Website: www.pen-and-sword.co.uk

Contents

Introduction

It is now over ten years since *The German Army on the Somme 1914–1916* appeared; ten years in which extensive research in the surviving German archives has continued. These archives, especially the unweeded *Kriegsarchiv* in Munich, contain material in far larger quantities than is generally realised. This work has yielded a great deal of information that throws further light on a range of matters associated with the fighting in that region, particularly during the major 1916 offensive. This book is not meant to be read as a complete or even partial history of the Battle of the Somme 1916, nor is it a replacement for the earlier book, whose focus was on the tactical level. Rather, it is intended as an expansion of what was previously published, in particular as far as issues of command and control and the relationships between senior commanders and between commanders and the Great General Staff were concerned.

In other words, this is a study of several linked themes that help to explain why from the German perspective events unfolded as they did. To that end, it begins with an examination of the continuous thread which ran through German military theory and practice for one hundred years from the early part of the Nineteenth Century. This casts light on the influence of Clausewitz and the other Prussian reformers; explaining the crucial role played by the concept of the *Schwerpunkt*, why successive generations strived to bring about battles of annihilation and how the Great General Staff emerged as a dominant force within the army. All these matters are examined in detail in later chapters.

There is a natural human tendency to think that there is something inevitable about the way great events play out, but that was certainly not the case with this battle. Falkenhayn, who succeeded Moltke the Younger as chief of the general staff when the attempted war of annihilation against France failed on the Marne in autumn 1914, found himself thereafter forced to conduct a war of attrition on highly unfavourable terms. However, his obsession with Verdun in 1916 blinded him to the threat which was building up astride the Somme and almost led to catastrophe. Another man in charge could well have handled matters quite differently, so instead of the battle getting off to a terrible start for the German army and continuing in a hand to mouth way, the Allies might have been confronted by an initial check, followed by a massive counteroffensive with untold consequences.

In this context it is important to be aware of the scale of these potential operations as visualised by men such as Oberst von Loßberg and General von

Gallwitz when their proposals were put to Falkenhayn. Sixth Army, in planning a possible attack north and south of Arras in March 1916, for example, calmly requested reinforcements of '300 heavy batteries and ten corps [twenty divisions]', so this would not have been a matter of the odd division here and there but, the Battle of Verdun halted, of the concentration of a huge force with genuine battle-altering ability. These men were bold, decisive and thought big. One of the natural consequences of this, of course, was the fact that they also had big egos, were highly opinionated and tended to be confrontational and dismissive of others.

In other words, they needed unambiguous, strong direction and a clear chain of command; but that is precisely what Falkenhayn did not provide when the expansion of the numbers of formations committed to the battle forced a division of command responsibility between a newly formed First Army under Below and a Second Army commanded by Gallwitz. Some sort of high level coordinating function was obviously needed but, shrinking from the creation of an army group headquarters and faced with a flat refusal by Gallwitz to be directed by Below, Falkenhayn appointed Gallwitz both commander Second Army and, simultaneously, of an 'Army Group Gallwitz'. The arrangement was doomed from the start. Below, equally touchy, was insulted by the implied criticism of his ability and the two headquarters were at once at daggers drawn. Mutual suspicion, arguments, disputes, staff manoeuvrings and rows overshadowed the command and control of the battle dangerously for six critical weeks until 28 August when, not before time, Crown Prince Rupprecht was made the army group commander.

For this and a succession of other dubious judgement calls, Falkenhayn was replaced at the end of August by Hindenburg as chief of the general staff, with Ludendorff in the role of 'First Quartermaster General' and *de facto* the man with executive control of the battle. Matters slowly began to improve, especially with regard to the air battle and provision of additional artillery, but it was by then impossible to change radically the way the battle was fought. Resources had to be provided for the war against Romania and the Battle of Verdun rumbled on, making it hard to maintain even minimum force levels, in particular of high grade troops, on the Somme front. A major part of the book is taken up, therefore, with an attempt to quantify, through exploitation of surviving primary sources, how great the strain on the German army really was, how close the Allies came to breakthrough, what the overall cost was and how, drawing on experiences gained during the battle, the German army prepared itself for the offensives they knew would occur in spring 1917.

Jack Sheldon
Vercors, France
December 2016

Acknowledgements

O nce more I am grateful for the assistance of others who have helped me with the eighth volume of my books concerning the activities of the German army from 1914–1918. I received excellent service from the staff of the *Kriegsarchiv* in Munich during the week I spent there in December 2015. Their willingness to supply me with far more bundles of files per day than their rules normally permit enabled me to get through a great deal of work in a short time. I wish to express particular thanks to Till Poser for permission to quote from the unpublished Great War memoir of Jochimsen Johannes Jürgen: *Herz im Feuer 1914–1921.* Nigel Cave, my editor and regular co-author was his usual helpful self; much of the scope and structure of the book came about as a result of numerous conversations with him. Finally and most importantly, I am grateful to Laurie, my wife, who draws my maps and is a constant source of help and loving encouragement to me whilst I am engaged in the lengthy process of writing.

Author's Note

By fortunate chance the German defenders at certain key places and times during the Battle of the Somme were from Bavaria or Württemberg, so it has been possible to base much of this study on primary source material from Munich or Stuttgart. Furthermore, the fact that from the end of August 1916 the army group on the northern sector of the Western Front was commanded by Crown Prince Rupprecht of Bavaria means that large amounts of correspondence between Supreme Army Headquarters and its subordinate headquarters after August 1916 are still available for study, despite the loss of most of the Prussian archives in 1945. As usual in this series, extensive use has been made of material published in Germany during the interwar period and as usual the same caveats apply: use with caution and seek corroboration.

German time, which was one hour ahead of Allied time, is used throughout the book.

Every effort has been made to avoid infringing copyright. Should this have occurred accidently, I should be grateful if the holder would contact me via the publisher.

Maps

CHAPTER 1

In the Beginning were the Prussian Reformers

It may seem strange to begin an account of the methods employed by the German army to fight a battle in 1916 by starting with the work of the Prussian reformers at the beginning of the 19th Century, but there is logic and a sound reason for it. In the wake of defeat in the field by the armies of Napoleon and the harsh terms of the 1808 Treaty of Paris, which was designed to emasculate Prussia by limiting the size of its army to 42,000 long service volunteers and banning all reserve forces or militias, five men nevertheless created something new and potent from the ashes. Those particularly involved were Scharnhorst, Gneisenau, Grolman, Boyen and Clausewitz. Of these Scharnhorst was the most important, until his untimely demise as a result of a minor wound sustained at the Battle of Lützen in 1813 that led to septicaemia and his death. Initially frustrated by their inability to introduce a systematic approach to conscription or to develop detailed mobilisation plans, nevertheless the reformers were determined to change the entire relationship between army, the state of Prussia and its king.

They had, it must be said, mixed success. Officer training was opened to non-noble applicants and they created the *Landwehr*, effectively local militias, that played a useful role in the Wars of Liberation against Napoleon. With the coming of peace, however, the reformers found themselves sidelined and, by 1820, many of the old ways were reintroduced, fortunately not before the Defence Law of 1814 and the *Landwehr* Law of 1815 had been enacted. Under the first, the principle of conscription of all able bodied men from the age of twenty was introduced and the second made possible the creation of a great many reservists without the necessity to maintain an expensive large-scale standing army. The other institution whose origins can be traced back to the original reformers is the Great General Staff, so although the Prussian army largely stagnated for forty years from 1820, it contained within itself the foundations of the mechanisms which would see it expand and improve so as to become the most powerfully effective military force in Europe.

All armies require guiding principles and it was Clausewitz through his unfinished book *On War* who provided the philosophical underpinning, not only of the work of the reformers but also their successors right up to the present day. According to him, the critical matter in war was – and remains – to determine what he called the *centra gravitatis* [centre of gravity].[1] Just as important today to campaign planners as it was in the mid nineteenth century, definition of the enemy's centre of gravity enables staffs to work out a line of operations which will lead up to that point and victory. What did Clausewitz mean by this term? In essence, for him it was that element of the entire make up of an enemy which, once defeated or neutralised, will lead inevitably to fatal weakness and collapse.

Fundamentally, he equated this with total destruction of an opponent's army. In order to prevail, the winning side had, 'To conquer and destroy the armed power of the enemy'. For him war was an arena where acts of extreme violence were to be brought to bear with total ruthlessness to produce a swift effect on the enemy's armed forces and so achieve a victory of annihilation. Not for him a slow, attritional, approach to operations. The decisive battle was of key importance. 'The military forces of the enemy must be destroyed, that is reduced to such a state as not to be able to prosecute the war.'[2] Of course it must be borne in mind that during the Napoleonic era there were plenty of 'decisive battles' to provide examples from history. Matters became much less clear cut as armies increased in size and outcomes less than total destruction of the enemy became thinkable.

Nevertheless, it was an outcome engineered by Helmuth von Moltke (Moltke the Elder) when he sealed the fate of the French armies at Sedan on 1–2 September 1870. Having outmanoeuvered Marshal de MacMahon's men and trapped them against the frontier with Belgium, Moltke, during a visit to Third Army on 31 August, stated, accurately, 'Now we have them in a mousetrap'. In resigned agreement with this assessment, General Ducrot who, briefly, was to succeed to the command on 1 September after the wounding of MacMahon, on observing the fires of the encircling German troops, marked up his map and remarked sardonically, *Nous sommes dans un pot de chambre, et nous y serons emmerdés.* Pulling his cloak tightly around him, he sat by a fire of one of his Zouave regiments awaiting the morning and the French army's inevitable fate.[3] By nightfall on 1 September the French had lost almost 40,000 men killed, wounded or captured, against total Prussian losses of around 9,000; and the following day Napoleon III surrendered the entire army.

This was a Clausewitzian victory of annihilation in the truest sense of the word. 'The best strategy is always to be very strong, above all in an absolute sense, but at least at the decisive point … There is no higher or simpler rule of strategy than concentrating force. Absolutely nothing should be taken away from the main force unless it is absolutely essential to serve a most urgent purpose.'[4] This was precisely what Moltke had done. Ignoring all other calls for men, he assembled half a million troops and launched them against the 300,000 the French could muster. It was a classic case of achieving total numerical superiority in support of his operational *Schwerpunkt* [point of main effort]. Moltke summarised what he had done in this way. 'The concentration of all our forces in the Pfalz protected both the lower as well as the upper Rhine and allowed an offensive into enemy territory which, timed carefully, meant that it forestalled any attempt by the French to set foot on German territory.'[5] This culminated in Sedan and opened the way to Paris, the *centra gravitatis* of the French.

By achieving this stunning victory, Moltke had demonstrated that it was still possible in an era of large scale armies and increasingly sophisticated weaponry to pursue a *Niederwerfungstrategie* [strategy of annihilation] via swift, decisive, military action. This suited Germany, whose unfavourable geographical location and shortage of resources militated against long drawn out wars of attrition (which could take many forms, including economic warfare and blockade). As a result, this thread runs through German military thinking throughout the nineteenth century and beyond. The adoption of universal conscription to facilitate the development of mass armies with plentiful reserves served to make one of Clausewitz's principal points a reality, but Germany's potential opponents were also moving forward.

By the early years of the twentieth century the French, for example, were conscripting almost every single available man for military service. In contrast the Germans, limited until 1912 to an active army that did not exceed one per cent of the population, never called up more than about thirty five percent of each year group (including the *Ersatz Reserve*), so never again would Germany be able to muster an absolute numerical superiority over its French neighbours, despite the fact that the 1905 change in the period of conscription in France from three years to two meant that the fourth battalions of sixty infantry regiments had to be disbanded and there were serious consequences for the French technical troops, cavalry and horse artillery.[6] In any case the change was short-lived and was reversed in 1912.

At the outbreak of the Great War, of the 67.8 million German citizens, the German mobilised army comprised a total of about 120,000 officers and 3.7 million other ranks, but there were also almost 5.5 million untrained, but fit, men still in Germany. Almost 10.5 million men were liable for conscription in Germany but in 1914 only 36.5% were serving so, in addition to the untrained group, a further 1.2 million trained men were not called up for duty.[7] If Germany had called up the same percentage of conscripts as France did, its army would have numbered well over six million men when hostilities began, though quite how an army of that size would have been paid for remains an open question. As an aside, it was this initially untapped potential which carried the German army through the first two years of war. It was not until summer 1916 that manpower began to become critical.

The challenge for Moltke the Elder's successors, however, was to attempt, in a clear extension of this line of thought, to make a *Niederwerfungstrategie* possible despite the changed circumstances and, especially, in the face of the two front risk created as a result of the disastrous failure in 1890 by Germany to renew the 'Reinsurance Treaty' with Russia. The closest Germany came to solving the problem was primarily through the work of Alfred Graf von Schlieffen, Chief of the General Staff from 1891 – 1906. All his war planning and preparation was marked by a clear inclination towards a campaign of annihilation. Repeatedly, echoes of the Clausewitzian preference for the destruction of the enemy's armed forces as 'the superior and more effectual means to which all others must give way'[8] appear in his writings. As a follower of Clausewitz he was well aware of the need to develop a wide, if sceptical, knowledge of military history, subscribing to the view that, 'military principles could only be derived, second hand as it were, from a critical analysis of history [because] historians exaggerated and manipulated the history of military affairs in order to glorify their own countries or provide factual support for their theories.'[9] As Clausewitz put it, his principles, 'should educate the mind of the future leader in war, or rather guide him in his self-instruction, but not accompany him to the field of battle'.[10]

In pursuit of this approach, Schlieffen laid great stress on the study of military history and he himself when in high office and despite his enormous workload found time to research and then write about the Battle of Cannae, at which Hannibal prevailed by means of a bold double envelopment. This became his inspiration as he wrestled with the problem of bringing about the swift defeat of France by annihilating its armies in decisive battle. In his introduction to a post war English edition of Cannae, General Hugo Freiherr von Freytag-Loringhoven, who had served under Schlieffen as a major on the Great General Staff, wrote,

"Strictly, the Cannae studies of Count Schlieffen are not presentations from military history. They comprise, rather, a conversational document of instruction. Just as the field marshal, in his activity as chief of the general staff of the army, always endeavoured during the long period of peace to keep alive in the General Staff, and thus in the army at large, the idea of a war of annihilation, so, likewise, is this expressed in his writings. Germany's situation demanded a quick decision. Though the Count set great store on the efficiency of the German army he was, nevertheless, always preoccupied with thoughts of how our leaders would acquit themselves when the time came. Hence, in his writings he often attributes his own ideas to the leaders of the past – among them Moltke – when he wishes to prove that to achieve a decisive victory of annihilation outflanking – preferably from two or three sides – must be resorted to, as Hannibal did at Cannae. In everything which Count Schlieffen wrote, the two-front war which threatened Germany hovered before him. In such a war we would be victorious only if soon after its outbreak we succeeded in obtaining an annihilating defeat of France. Modern battles Count Schlieffen characterises even more than earlier battles as a 'struggle for the flanks'. Therefore, he stresses the necessity, in case parts of an army have made contact with the enemy, that the neighbouring columns be allowed to march further so that they may be able to turn against flank and rear. In this method of presentation, the Count is not always just to the actors of war history, especially the subordinate leaders of our own army of 1866 and 1870–71. However, he explains their conduct as born of the Napoleonic traditions in the absence of war experience by their own generation. Notwithstanding the severity of his judgement, the writings of the field marshal show a real appreciation of true military art, for within him abided an incomparable military fire. The reckless urge to the offensive of our infantry he emphasizes as the prerequisite to victory."[11]

It is ironic that Schlieffen chose Cannae (216 BC) as his model battle – though he had tended previously to favour study of Frederick the Great's famous victory at Leuthen (5 December 1757) and, later, Napoleon's victory at the Battle of Ulm (16–19 October 1805). Napoleon captured, at negligible cost, an entire Austrian army commanded by Karl Freiherr Mack von Leiberich, whereas at Cannae, despite it being a crushing victory for Hannibal, the overall strategy was a failure. The Second Punic War dragged on until 201 BC, Hannibal lacked the means to take Rome and the Romans showed themselves capable of raising conscript armies repeatedly until Hannibal was defeated in 202 BC at Zama. It was, after all, not perhaps the best example to follow.

Though Schlieffen was known primarily as a strategic thinker and military planner, he was fully aware of the need to produce an army that was, in its fighting power, head and shoulders above any potential enemy. Faced with the enormous financial demands of the Tirpitz Plan of major naval construction, which left relatively small amounts for the army, Schlieffen devoted much of his time to matters of training and military education in the broadest sense, coupled with the introduction (suitably adapted if required) of all modern technological developments. He made great use of war gaming, map exercises and staff rides to train and test the General Staff and he piled work on its members constantly, even to the extent of disrupting their brief break over Christmas. General der Infanterie Hermann von Kuhl remembered,

"For several years the doorbell to my quarters would ring on Christmas Eve and his Christmas gift to me would be handed over by special messenger. It would be a large scale war situation that he had devised and the task was to hand back an operational plan. He would have been truly astounded if it had not been completed and been back in his hands by the evening of Christmas Day. On Boxing Day would be delivered the development of the situation which he had written, accompanied by a further task. Sundays and holidays were, in his opinion, ideal for carrying out the larger jobs, which required long and calm consideration, undisturbed by the interruptions encountered during the normal working day.'[12]

As far as producing a solution to the conundrum posed by a future war to be fought simultaneously in east and west was concerned, Schlieffen devoted much thought to the problem and finally came down firmly in favour of a lightning strike against France in the first phase of operations. Although doubts about its feasibility were raised at the time and have gone on being debated ever since, a broader question has recently been posed about whether Schlieffen really did bequeath his successors a ready made plan for the invasion of France.[13] This work produced a sharp reaction from other historians and led to the publication of a robust rebuttal by leading scholars in the field.[14] Regardless of the absolute truth, one thing remains certain, such was the influence of Schlieffen, drawing on the Clausewitzian principle of annihilation, that the actual war plan as directed by Moltke drew heavily on the former's concepts, which he had developed in response to the two front threat, *viz*:

- Not to stand on the reactive defensive but to pursue offensive action in order to seize the initiative.
- Through the exploitation of interior lines, solve the problem of a two front war by transforming it into two single front wars to be conducted sequentially.
- The *Schwerpunkt* to be placed on an offensive in the west, whilst a delay battle was fought in the east.
- A swift battle of annihilation by means of a strong right flank which would envelop the French system of fortresses and a successful march through the territories of Belgium and Luxembourg ...
- After victory in the west, immediate transport by railway of the greater part of the victorious formations to the Eastern Front, there to destroy the enemy which up until then had merely been delayed.[15]

What is also definitely the case is that somewhere between 1905 and 1914 sight was lost of Schlieffen's insistence on total concentration of force. 'Frederick the Great', wrote Schlieffen, 'was ultimately of the opinion that it was better to sacrifice a province than split up the army with which one seeks and must achieve victory. The <u>whole</u> of Germany must throw itself on <u>one</u>[16] enemy – the strongest, most powerful, most dangerous enemy and that can only be the Anglo-

French!'[17] Leaving aside any consideration about the overall logistical viability of the campaign against France, to reduce the size of the right wing to a little over half of the army, when Schlieffen had specified at least three quarters, to strip out at a critical moment and send east two corps (where they arrived too late to play any part at Tannenberg), was bound to have an effect. For these and other reasons, the entire plan as finally conducted foundered on the Marne, the race for an open flank to the north ended at Nieuwpoort on the Belgian coast and the German army found itself thereafter engaged in battles of attrition in entirely unfavourable circumstances.

How did this army, imbued from top to bottom with the philosophy of Clausewitz and wedded firmly to a *Niederwerfungstrategie*, for which it had planned and trained for decades, react and so adjust to the new situation that it was able to continue the war for a full four more years, sinking to defeat only once its resources in manpower and materiel had been ground down by a lengthy blockade and overwhelming odds? It was an immense challenge and is a subject that is inextricably associated with the performance of the General Staff and its relationship to both higher commanders and the troops subordinate to them. 'It must be admitted', wrote General der Infanterie von Kuhl after the war, 'that we had not foreseen a war lasting for years along a static front stretching from the sea to Switzerland. We had placed our entire emphasis on a war of manoeuvre, believing that that offered the best route to success.'[18]

The Great General Staff occupied a dominant position in the German army during the Great War; dominance which, as has been mentioned, may be traced right back to the earliest days of the Prussian reformers. Well aware that commands would inevitably be given to men because of their connections to royalty or the aristocracy, rather than because of their suitability or training in military matters, they decided that what was needed was a permanent and robust arrangement that would enable armies to be commanded and battles to be won, despite any deficiencies in their titular heads. Scharnhorst, aware of the sensitivities involved and picking his words forcefully, but carefully, wrote,

"Normally it is not possible for an army simply to dismiss incompetent generals. The very authority which their office bestows upon generals is the first reason for this. Moreover, the generals form a clique, tenaciously supporting one another, all convinced that they are the best possible representatives of the army. But we can at least give them capable assistants. Thus the General Staff officers are those who support incompetent generals, providing the talents that might otherwise be wanting among leaders and commanders."[19]

It seems apparent that this viewpoint, or a slight variation on it, was widely held amongst the ranks of the Prussian reformers, because Clausewitz himself referred to the matter in Book II of *On War*. Comparing the sending of an army into battle with a river system emptying into the sea, he remarked that a commander required only that slight knowledge necessary to initiate and then direct operations.

> "Only those activities emptying themselves directly into the sea of war have to be studied by him who is to conduct its operations ... Only thus is explained how so often men have made their appearance with great success in war, and indeed in the higher ranks, even in supreme command, whose pursuits had been previously of a totally different nature; indeed how, as a rule, the most distinguished generals have never risen from the very learned or erudite class of officers, but have been mostly men who, from the circumstances of their position, could not have attained to any great amount of knowledge. On that account those who have considered it necessary or even beneficial to commence the education of a future general by instruction in all details have always been ridiculed as absurd pedants."[20]

In terms of providing a template for the future, in many ways Gneisenau came the closest of the original reformers to operating as a modern chief of staff would. He it was, for example, who encouraged Blücher at Waterloo to march to the aid of Wellington at a critical moment; and certainly Blücher acknowledged the debt he owed him. Receiving an honorary doctorate at the University of Oxford, Blücher stated that, 'If he was to be a doctor, Gneisenau should be an apothecary because Gneisenau mixed the potions which [he] administered'.[21]

The seeds of a successful, efficient, General Staff may have been sown by the early reformers, but it was not until the middle of the nineteenth century that further reform of the Prussian army was accompanied by a much clearer definition of the duties and responsibilities of the General Staff. These were laid down and consolidated during the thirty years from 1857 that Moltke the Elder, as Chief of the General Staff, imposed his thinking and methodology on the army to great effect. This was not just reform for the sake of it. Moltke had seen that the expansion of armies and the fact that the advent of the electric telegraph and the railways, which in Germany had always been laid down to serve a strategic purpose, meant their dispersal into smaller groupings and rapid concentration was now a fact to be reckoned with. He also realised that command and control was henceforth to be a matter for highly trained and dedicated professional specialists. The day of manoeuvre in massed armies led by enthusiastic amateurs were now over. Commanders needed, just as Scharnhorst had recognised, expert advice and guidance.

On the modern battlefield the army commander might be located at some considerable distance from the forward corps, so it was also essential that there should be commonality of thought and reaction to rapidly changing situations. This could not be guaranteed among the subordinate commanders, but talented and hardworking staff officers could be trained and practised intensely to carry out the wishes of the supreme commander, even though he himself was not personally present to impose his personality on events. The objective, therefore, was to create a staff within which each officer, confronted with the same set of factors, would come to the same conclusion and act in furtherance of previously received higher direction. Out of this stemmed the system of *Auftragstaktik* [mission command], whereby subordinates were given a detailed description of what the higher commander was trying to achieve, but were left to decide how best to achieve it. Not only that, they were trained to know when to take a completely different decision if the situation had changed so as to demand swift and positive action.

"A favourable situation", wrote Moltke, "will never be exploited if commanders wait for orders. The highest commander and youngest soldier must always be conscious of the fact that omission and inactivity are worse than resorting to the wrong expedient."[22]

Responding to a protestation from an officer on an exercise that he had been ordered to carry out a certain action which turned into a tactical error because of a change in the battle situation, Prince Friedrich Karl of Prussia, a nephew of Kaiser Wilhelm I and a soldier of considerable ability, memorably dressed him down with the words, 'His Majesty made you a major because he believed you would know when not to obey his orders'. This was a favourite anecdote of Moltke's and it became a guiding principle throughout the Prussian army. That said, Moltke did not invent the concept of *Auftragstaktik*. Once more its origin dates back to Scharnhorst and Gneisenau; but Moltke was the first to practise it on a wide scale and to test its applicability during the Austro-Prussian War of 1866 and the Franco-Prussian War of 1870/71.[23] The term itself was of even more recent origin, first appearing in the military literature in an article in the *Militär-Wochenblatt* in early 1892.[24]

Out of the need for the highest standards of staff work, Moltke insisted on nothing but total dedication from those involved. His General Staff officers were drawn from the very best of each year's intake at the *Kriegsakademie*. Only one hundred and twenty officers per year would sit the entrance examination. Of these Moltke would choose the twelve he considered most suitable; but even then they were on probation, risking a return to troop duties if their performance fell below the accepted standard in any respect. In any case each time they came up for promotion they had to return to a period of duty with a unit or formation. This ensured that best practice was spread throughout the army and that the staff did not become detached from the broader army. This criticism was subsequently levelled at it during the Great War, though in fact there was a well-known example of this policy when General von Freytag-Loringhoven was given leave of absence from his appointment as Deputy Chief of the General Staff to act simultaneously as Commander 17th Reserve Division and IX Reserve Corps at Vimy Ridge in spring 1916 during Operation Schleswig Holstein and thus gained current operational experience in command.

It had one more important effect. The General Staff, which later became the Great General Staff, was always very small and élite, with strongly established loyalty to the Chief of the General Staff, who was in a position to give clear, unambiguous orders to his subordinates on the staff, knowing that they would be obeyed. This was of great importance, because he was in a different position vis-à-vis the commanders. They were unlikely to be trained to the same extent as the staff. In many cases they were senior to the Chief of the General Staff and, at times, they could actually be hostile towards him. Out of this grew the system of two separate command structures – which in turn led to great tension and controversy during the Great War as the Great General Staff gained in influence and power.

A major factor in the way the situation developed from 1914 was the personality of the Kaiser. *De jure* he was the supreme commander and in his vanity he was going to play that role to the full. It was an extension of the way he had performed in peacetime, when he always wore uniform in public, gloried in all forms of military spectacle and even held back the development of arms such as the cavalry through his insistence on time wasting activities that did nothing to prepare that arm for its vital role in manoeuvre warfare. *De facto*, whilst nominally retaining his position as the head of the armed forces, he in fact did not act as a commander in chief, delegating responsibility for overall command to, successively, Moltke the Younger, Falkenhayn and the duumvirate of Hindenburg and Ludendorff. Prey to depression, which was worsened by the setbacks of autumn 1914, the Kaiser, wallowing in self-pity, was heard by Alexander von Müller, head of his Naval Cabinet, to complain on one occasion, 'If people in Germany think I am the Supreme Warlord, they are grossly mistaken. The General Staff tells me nothing and never asks my advice.'[25]

The problems to which the position of the Kaiser could lead had been debated (discreetly) before the war. Was it still appropriate in the modern age for the head of state in a monarchical system to exercise supreme command? The general consensus was that the answer would depend upon the training, inclination and ability of the monarch in question. If he had been absorbed into the military from a young age, if he had matured within it and been so trained that he felt himself capable of taking key decisions at moment of crisis, then it would make sense because from the appointment would flow full unity of command. Furthermore, orders emanating from the monarch would have far greater resonance and power than those issued by a professional commander in chief. The relationship between the monarch and his senior military adviser was at the same time both crucial but also problematical. Forty years previously ambiguities in the precise separation of responsibilities and numerous unhelpful interventions by Bismarck meant that Moltke the Elder repeatedly had to resolve differences of opinion during both the campaigns of 1866 and 1870; and also had to harmonise and integrate the work of his stripped down Field General Staff and the comparatively large Royal Staff that accompanied Wilhelm on campaign. This produced friction and cost precious time precisely when that was at a premium. It was generally felt that because of this it was on the whole better, if the monarch did not intend or was not able to fulfil the role of commander in chief, for him to keep well clear of the Supreme Army Headquarters.

If he chose to be present, this could only have a negative effect on the working of the headquarters, because it would always be impossible to avoid the necessity for the monarch to have his voice heard and his views taken into consideration when matters of the first importance were being examined. In addition, there would always be the temptation for the monarch, regardless of the agreed methods of working, to want, or feel it his duty, to intervene in, say, existential questions. There was, of course, never the slightest chance that Kaiser Wilhelm II would agree to do anything other than play the role of Supreme Warlord, even though he relied entirely on his Chiefs of the General Staff and, carrying that concept on further down the chain of command, he ordered his son always to do precisely what his chief of staff advised. Fortunately, throughout the nineteenth century, but especially from the time of Moltke the Elder, the essential trust the monarch had to have in his chief was formalised so that, in order for the professional head of the army to be able carry out his duties efficiently, he and he alone advised the monarch. There were a few exceptions to this rule and the role played by *Immediatrecht*, the right of certain individuals to bypass the Chief of the General Staff and address the Kaiser in private, in the change of command from Falkenhayn to Hindenburg and Ludendorff will be discussed later, in Chapter 5.

Quite aside from any other consideration, from the time of Frederick the Great it had been recognised that councils of war, debates for and against action, led to timid decisions or a 'wait and see' attitude, when what was wanted was decisive action. In order to facilitate this, Clausewitz had defined the role of the General Staff in this way: 'It is the task of the General Staff to turn the commander's concepts into orders; not only assuming responsibility for their transmission to the troops but even more importantly working through all matters of detail and so relieving the General of the responsibility for this tedious task.'[26] However, given the Kaiser's attitude to the exercise of command, it is obvious that, first, the scope of the role of the Chief of the General Staff and his subordinates could not be restricted to technical matters and, secondly, that to this semi-abdication of responsibility could be attributed the extraordinary influence of the General Staff during the war.

Ultimately its dominance in the military field was further expanded into political manoeuvrings prior to the forced resignation of the Foreign Minister, Gottlieb von Jagow, in November 1916, then the Chancellor, Theobald von Bethmann-Hollweg, on 13 July 1917 – though well before that the General Staff had begun to cut him out of the overall picture. At the end of May 1917, he attempted to carry out a wide ranging visit to assess the situation on the Western Front for himself, but achieved little. On 30 May a furious Ludendorff telephoned General von Kuhl at Army Group Crown Prince Rupprecht, stating, 'The Chancellor is travelling without the knowledge of *OHL*. A telegram is on its way. Give him no military information! It is to be treated as a private journey!'[27] From July onwards, therefore, Hindenburg and Ludendorff dominated all aspects of political and military life in Germany during what amounted to military dictatorship. How had it come to this?

As has been noted, over time systems came into being that made certain that the General Staff became the preserve of a very small minority of highly motivated men, who had dedicated themselves to the study and practice of their profession, were talented militarily and were possessed of an enormous capacity for hard work and long hours. Bound together by an obsessively secretive approach to their, admittedly exacting, duties, their self-belief was so marked that it came across frequently as aloofness and a disregard for other parts of the army they deemed to be inferior to themselves. This manifested itself as the war went on in increasing manipulation of the system of dual command that was developed to the greatest extent along the Western Front. Commanders always had to take full responsibility for all decisions they made but, inevitably, many such would have been reached after advice or persuasion from their chiefs of staff.

There is nothing inherently sinister in this method of working. In fact, the more senior the headquarters and the broader the span of responsibility, the more important it was and remains for the preliminary analysis to be completed by subject matter specialists and then to be presented by the chief of staff to the commander as a series of options and a final recommendation. In general, unless there was an emergency, there would be two main briefings per day to the commander: an information briefing in the morning to bring him up to date with the latest situation and for the commander to issue any instructions to his staff then, in the evening, he would receive a *Lagevortrag zur Vorbereitung einer Entscheidung* [situation briefing to prepare for a decision]. This was where the scope for staff manipulation was at its greatest, especially if time was short and the decision pressing. Towards the end of the briefing the chief of staff would go through the possibilities, point the commander towards the staff-preferred option and indicate the urgency of the decision, so that orders could be issued in a timely manner.

Interesting to note, von Kuhl stated later, in his personal experience as chief of staff to Crown Prince Rupprecht for three years, that,

"The Crown Prince was extremely industrious, maintained battle maps in his office that showed the exact situation, worked his way systematically through all signals, letters, reports and orders and was constantly superbly informed. It was, therefore, straightforward to brief the situation and decision to him. He was always quick to appreciate the situation and personally weighed up the options for decision."[28]

There is no reason to doubt that this was the case, though in Ludendorff's opinion Duke Albrecht of Württemberg possessed more clearly defined soldierly qualities than either of the Crown Princes.[29] However, even if the interactions within first, Sixth Army and later Army Group Bavarian Crown Prince were as harmonious as Kuhl states, he himself, as will be seen in later chapters, was positively Machiavellian in his plotting and scheming within the General Staff chain of command.

Naturally the commander did not have to take the advice or accept the preferred option proposed. However, if he chose to reject the advice, usually after a further private discussion with his chief of staff with all other officers excluded, he would be well aware that the matter would not rest there. The first thing that would happen is that his decision would be written out in full in the war diary then, that done, the chief of staff would record his personal decision, complete with all the reasoning that led to it. This would demonstrate, especially if things went awry subsequently, that the commander had taken this particular decision against the fully worked out advice of his staff and accepted total responsibility for the consequences. This done, either next, or simultaneously, the chief of staff would be on the telephone to report up the staff chain of command what was happening. In the case of the chiefs of staffs of the armies or army groups, they were granted access to, initially, Falkenhayn and later Ludendorff at any time of the day or night;[30] and given that these two had the power to veto or override all decisions, this knowledge must have given pause for thought to any commander tempted to go his own way – even assuming that he had a sufficiently good overview and grasp of the facts to be able to come to an independent decision.

Overall, the way that command was exercised on a day to day basis was by telephone and signal. From the departure of Falkenhayn at the end of August

1916, the chiefs of staff at army group and army level spoke to Ludendorff by telephone every day and briefed the situation to him. There were consequences of course. Ludendorff was 'only' the First Quartermaster General. The commander in chief, the Supreme Warlord, was the Kaiser, with Hindenburg in the role of Chief of the General Staff, to whom was granted the power to issue orders in the name of the Kaiser, the latter generally keeping clear of the exercise of command and only giving the most important orders personally. The execution of all orders was Ludendorff's job and because he did not have overall power of command, i.e. over the actual commanders, he dealt primarily down the staff chain of command with the key staff officers, though naturally he maintained close links to the commanders as appropriate. This procedure was followed at lower levels all the way down to divisional headquarters, so it is easy to see why the General Staff was open to the accusation that it gradually effectively hijacked the running of the war.

It was of course the availability for the first time in military history of telephone trunk networks that made it possible for the General Staff to place a stranglehold over much of the conduct of the defensive battle and it was this which was criticised severely, both within the army and from outside sources. Writing after the war, a civilian member of the Reichstag even complained,

> 'The army was split into two sharply differing parts, that had almost nothing in common. On the one hand there was the battlefront, the officers and men who actually fought the war; on the other was the staff ... who knew nothing of the true needs of the front. The front and staff were divided by an opaque, impermeable wall.'[31]

As with all such criticism, it overstated the case. Nevertheless, there was a case to answer, so General der Infanterie Hermann von Kuhl lost no time in publishing, in 1920, a book with the title *Der deutsche Generalstab in Vorbereitung und Durchführung des Weltkrieges* [The German General Staff in the Preparation and Conduct of the World War]. His was a robust defence of the staff and its methods of working. That said, senior army officers often expressed similar criticisms. Generalleutnant von Moser, commander during the Battle of the Somme of the highly regarded 27th Infantry Division, which defended the Guillemont sector for most of August 1916, and later of XIV Reserve Corps, was quite certain – and was quite outspoken about it in his post war memoirs – that the General Staff had developed the habit of exploiting the telephone system not just to promote operational efficiency but also to manoeuvre behind the backs of commanders.

> "I had the feeling', he wrote subsequently, 'that misuse of the telephone system was in full swing ... It appeared to me that one of my General

Staff officers was more than keen to participate in this. The officer had occupied exactly the same position since the beginning of the war. As a result, his attitude to all around him and, indeed, to the fighting troops, was insufferably high handed. He had become accustomed to thinking that he was quite infallible. I discussed this matter in serious terms with my chief of staff and directed that this officer was to be posted without delay to a front line unit ... Quite rightly, the endless retention of totally fit and able unwounded General Staff officers in the higher level staffs was the source of much ill feeling in the army."[32]

He did not restrict his criticism to the actions of individual staff officers either. He was fundamentally opposed to the way the staff chain of command operated.

"... the most important tactical matters dealt with from army chief of staff down to the General Staff officer of a division', he wrote, 'are often thrashed out totally over the telephone, or so arranged that, when the commander gets to hear about them subsequently, he can hardly do other than agree to what has been decided ... The climate of mistrust, the patronizing system and the way the General Staff operates, unavoidably damages the authority of the corps and divisional commanders ... Complaints about this are general because it encourages the impression, in fact it is often expressed that, as far as tactical operations are concerned, not only is this not exclusively the responsibility of the commander but rather it is due in equal, if not greater, measure of the General Staff officer."[33]

At the root of the problem was the pressure under which the staff had to operate. There was little time to take into consideration the bruised feelings of those who felt themselves wronged or sidelined. In addition, the fact remains that there was a war to be fought against the odds and semi-dictatorial methods may well have been the only way of staving off early defeat. So it came about that the Battle of the Somme was effectively conducted on the German side by the Great General Staff and for much of the time the direction came from one man, namely the defensive expert Oberst Fritz von Loßberg. Loßberg began the war as chief of staff to XIII (Royal Württemberg) Corps, commanded by General der Infanterie von Fabeck, who is remembered primarily for his role in the later stages of the First Battle of Ypres, when his corps secured the Messines ridge but failed to break through. Having been involved on both the Western and Eastern Fronts, by January 1915 Loßberg was summoned to the staff of *OHL* [Supreme Army Headquarters], where his outstanding ability in the role of deputy head of the Operational Branch was quickly recognised.

However, he really began to make his reputation when he was posted from there at the Kaiser's personal command at the end of September 1915 as chief of staff Third Army, sent to resolve a major crisis during the autumn battle in Champagne. From there he was later posted to Second (later First) Army on the Somme, Sixth Army at Arras and Fourth Army in Flanders, prior to finishing the war as chief of staff to Army Group Duke Albrecht of Württemberg. It was some achievement, especially because in every case he had to stabilise a threatening situation. He was a man of supreme self-confidence, who combined this with great tactical acumen. He had a will of iron, a strong constitution, good stamina and a huge capacity for work. He was especially noted for his skill in being able to cut through the complexities of a confused battle situation to get directly to the heart of the matter and then to act in a bold and decisive way.

As an oberst, he was junior to all the commanders with whom he dealt, but his authority stemmed from his appointment, not his rank, so, having been granted complete power of command by the army commander, General von Below, wherever he went he issued instructions, directions and orders that were received and acted upon as though they were from the general himself. He was also renowned for the pressure he exerted up the chain of command in order to obtain all the resources he needed for the fulfilment of his mission. This did not always sit well with his fellow chiefs of staff but, because he was usually operating at the point of maximum danger and could effectively be guaranteed to get good results, he tended to be given every consideration in this regard. There were times, however, when even von Kuhl, who was generally his first point of contact, became exasperated with his demands. One of Kuhl's diary entries reads, 'Loßberg is excellent, but he always wants everything exactly as he specifies, regardless of whether or not it is possible'.[34] It goes without saying that he required at all times the complete support and backing of all the staff officers in his headquarters, regardless of their rank or seniority and naturally and, invariably, he was given it. Quite apart from anything else, each individual would have known that if he gave the Loßberg the slightest cause for dissatisfaction with the way he carried out his duties he would at once have been posted away and replaced.

As has already been discussed, the German army that fought the Great War was totally steeped in the philosophical writings of Clausewitz; hence the emphasis placed pre-war on a strategy of annihilation and the decisive battle brought about by large scale, bold, manoeuvre. In the situation which now obtained, with complex trench systems which offered no flanks a fact of life the full length of the Western Front, some other guiding principle was required. Here again it was a broader development of the thinking of Clausewitz, one which predated the Great War by several decades, which came to the rescue.

So far only the concept of *centra gravitatis* has been mentioned, together with its application at the strategic level, but this term translates into German as *Schwerpunkt* and it was soon realised that this was an extremely useful conceptual tool, applicable to all levels of command from the operational to the tactical because it provided a sure fire method of determining priorities. To understand, for example, the way that the defence was first laid out and then conducted on the Somme, it is crucial to understand what the term meant to the German army and how it was applied because, once this is grasped, matters such as the allocation and deployment of forces and other scarce resources at once becomes clear. The first point to make is that the concept influenced every single aspect of the German military. The word *Schwerpunkt* may be translated in different ways. These include 'centre of gravity', 'crucial' or 'focal' point but, as far as its use by the army is concerned, the most helpful version is 'point of main effort', a term which, though correct, barely hints at its all-embracing applicability. Every level of command, from *OHL* to infantry company or artillery battery, identified a *Schwerpunkt*; but so did the entire system of service support, so at any given moment a decision maker would know at once where to place his priorities and why. In order to give absolute priority to a particular course of action, the entire army was trained to be ruthless and to run considerable risks elsewhere if necessary in support of the main effort. Given this principle, it is fairly straightforward to work out the placement of the *Schwerpunkt* in any particular set of circumstances – especially with the benefit of hindsight. So, for example, in 1915, the *OHL Schwerpunkt* was centred on the Eastern Front and, as a result, the Western Front spent the entire year on the strategic defensive, while all twenty two of the newly raised divisions were sent east – not always to good effect, as demonstrated by the way the first eight were frittered away in a winter campaign that gained a great deal of territory but achieved little or nothing strategically.

In the first eight months of 1916 the *Schwerpunkt* was placed at Verdun in support of General von Falkenhayn's plan to 'bleed the French army white'. Meanwhile, the rest of the Western Front was kept short of reinforcements and stripped of almost all its modern heavy artillery and ammunition. This had serious consequences for the German Second Army, commanded by General der Infanterie Fritz von Below, which was fully engaged in the preparations to meet the major forthcoming offensive astride the River Somme and will be examined in detail in Chapter 2, followed in Chapter 3 by a description of how the German chain of command reacted as one when the Second Army defensive *Schwerpunkt* was very nearly lost on 1 July.

So the army that fought the Somme was the fruit of one hundred years of intellectual and practical development. It had been brought up to train for a battle of annihilation; when that failed in 1914, its doctrinal background and adaptability, coupled with the genius of key members of its élite Great General Staff, enabled it to conduct a fundamentally defensive war of attrition for four years against increasingly overwhelming odds. How and why it tackled the problem of the Somme in the way it did is the subject of the remainder of the book.

Notes

1. Clausewitz *On War Book III* Quoted Leonard *A Short Guide to Clausewitz on War* p. 15.
2. Clausewitz *op. cit.* Book 1 Chapter 2 p. 123.
3. Howard *The Franco-Prussian War* pp. 207–208.
4. Clausewitz *op. cit. Book III, Ch 11* Quoted Cochenhausen *Gedanken von Clausewitz* p. 74.
5. Gehre *Die deutsche Kräfteverteilung* pp. 15–16.
6. Kuhl *Der deutsche Generalstab* p. 9.
7. Afflerbach *Bis zum letzten Mann und letzten Groschen?* In Foerster (Hrsg) *Die Wehrpflicht* pp. 75–76.
8. Clausewitz *op. cit.* Book 1 Chapter 2 p. 134.
9. Leonard *op. cit.* p. 6.
10. Clausewitz *op. cit.* Quoted Cochenhausen *op. cit.* p. 20.
11. Schlieffen *Cannae*, quoted Dupuy *A Genius for War* p. 133.
12. Kuhl *op. cit.* p. 132.
13. Zuber *Inventing the Schlieffen Plan*
14. Ehlert (Ed) *Der Schlieffenplan*
15. Ehlert *op. cit.* pp. 159–160
16. Schlieffen's emphasis.
17. Quoted from Ritter Gerhard *The Schlieffen Plan* New York 1958 in Dupuy *op. cit.* p139.
18. Kuhl *op. cit.* p. 129.
19. Quoted in Hohn Reinhard *Scharnhorsts Vermächtnis* pp. 312–313.
20. Clausewitz *op. cit.* Book 2 Chapter 2 p. 196.
21. Görlitz *The German General Staff* p. vi.
22. Moltke Quoted in Dupuy *op. cit.* p. 116.
23. Ilsemann Carl-Gero von *Das operative Denken des älteren Moltke* in *Operatives Denken* MGFA (Hrsg) pp. 22–23.
24. The article was *Neuen Studien* über *die Schlacht bei Werth* by Generalleutnant z.D. Albert von Boguslawski and was cited in Leistenschneider *Auftragstatik im preußisch-deutschen Heer* p. 101.
25. Müller diary in Görlitz *Regierte der Kaiser.* Quoted Brose *The Kaiser's Army* p. 231.
26. Schreibershofen *Das deutsche Heer* p. 122.
27. Kuhl *Persönliches Kriegstagebuch* 30 May 17.
28. Kuhl *op. cit.* p. 197.
29. Ludendorff *Meine Kriegserinnerungen* p. 216.
30. Kuhl *op. cit.* p. 195.
31. Gothein Georg *Warum verloren wir den Krieg?* p 33. Quoted Kuhl *Der deutsche Generalstab* p. 200.
32. Moser General Otto von *Feldzugsaufzeichnungen* pp. 306–307.
33. *ibid.* pp. 308–309.
34. BA./MA. RH61/50652 Kuhl *Persönliches Kriegstagebuch* 3 Aug 17.

THE SOMME BATTLEFIELD JULY – NOVEMBER 1916

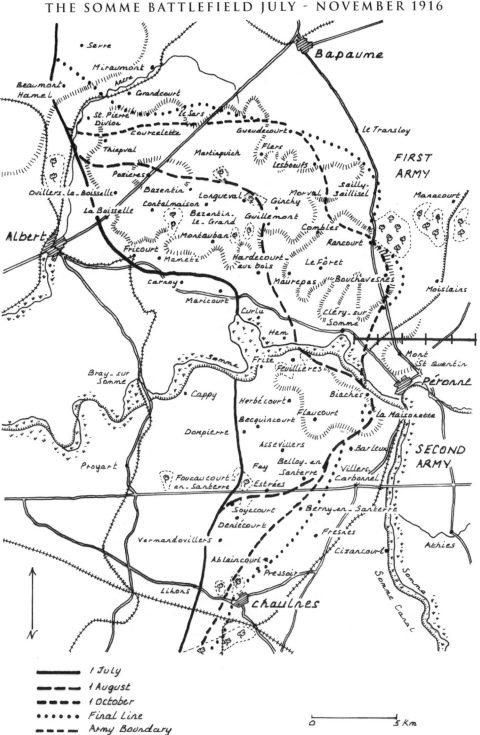

Serre • Miraumont • Ancre • Grandcourt • Beaumont Hamel • St. Pierre Divion • le Sars • Courcelette • Gueudecourt • le Transloy • FIRST ARMY • Thiepval • Martinpuich • Flers • Lesbœufs • Pozières • Sailly-Saillisel • Morval • Ovillers-la-Boisselle • Bazentin • Longueval • Ginchy • Contalmaison • Bazentin-le-Grand • Guillemont • La Boisselle • Montauban • Combles • Rancourt • Maricourt • Fricourt • Mametz • Hardecourt-aux-bois • Le Forêt • Albert • Carnoy • Maurepas • Bouchavesnes • Maricourt • Curlu • Cléry-sur-Somme • Hem • Moislains • Somme • Frise • Feuillières • Mont St. Quentin • Bray-sur-Somme • Cappy • Herbécourt • Biaches • Péronne • Becquincourt • Flaucourt • La Maisonette • Dompierre • Asssevillers • SECOND ARMY • Proyart • Belloy-en-Santerre • Barleux • Fay • Villers-Carbonnel • Foucaucourt-en-Santerre • Estrées • Soyecourt • Berny-en-Santerre • Denicourt • Fresnes • Athies • Vermandovillers • Cizancourt • Ablaincourt • Pressoir • Somme Canal • Lihons • Chaulnes

————	1 July
– – –	1 August
– · – ·	1 October
· · · · ·	Final Line
– – –	Army Boundary

0   5 Km

CHAPTER 2

Falkenhayn's Folly:
Sleepwalking to Near Disaster

Given that the *Schwerpunkt* was central in German military theory and practice and in order to understand how the Battle of the Somme was prepared and then conducted, it is essential to know how the concept was applied at the strategic (*OHL*), operational (army/army group) and tactical (corps and below) levels. In 1916 the strategic *Schwerpunkt* was clearly centred on Verdun. This had considerable and far reaching consequences elsewhere, because the remainder of the Western Front was systematically and, in the case of the Somme, dangerously, starved of men and matériel to sustain the attacks in that area. This process began early in the year; one immediate negative effect being the withdrawal of almost all modern heavy artillery pieces from the armies deployed elsewhere and moved to Verdun in support of the coming offensive. As early as 7 January the Sixth Army war diary recorded the fact that,

> "The new high angle batteries which have been allocated to replace the army artillery batteries are not equipped with modern captured equipment. Instead they are old German heavy howitzers. That is a great disappointment. They are *Landsturm* batteries, so from that viewpoint as well they cannot be spoken of as replacements of the same value. According to a report by the commander, the 200 mm Russian guns are currently neither manned nor equipped sufficiently to enable them to be deployed at the front. That will be all right, provided that heavy fighting does not break out."[1]

Interesting to note, in allocating troops to tasks prior to the opening of operations at Verdun, Falkenhayn provided a further example of the frequently eccentric command style that was eventually to lead to his removal. His chief of operations at *OHL*, Generalmajor Tappen, urged him to attack simultaneously on both banks of the Meuse, but allegedly only elicited this response: 'I am not going to do it. It is my responsibility. I do not wish to find myself in the situation I was in in Champagne in autumn 1915. I must keep hold of strong reserves.'[2] Apart from the consequences for the way the offensive at Verdun developed, this also had considerable implications later for Second Army once it began the preparations to meet the major offensive astride the River Somme.

As 1916 opened, Second Army, commanded by General der Infanterie Fritz von Below, was engaged in positional warfare in the Somme region, in what was at that time a quiet front. On 28 January it did, nevertheless, contribute to deception operations in support of the forthcoming Verdun offensive by launching a limited strike with 11th Infantry Division against the French army at Frise, south of the Somme. This successful one day operation culminated in the capture of over 1,300 prisoners, together with numerous machine guns and large quantities of matériel. At one officer and four men killed plus eighty wounded, the cost to the attackers was remarkably small.[3] Sixth Army in the Vimy area was also involved in similar operations, the so-called 'Rupprecht Operations I–IV', which were more costly and, given that the start of the Verdun campaign was delayed, largely irrelevant in diversionary terms.[4] Its commander, Crown Prince Rupprecht, unimpressed by the entire approach, made a scathing diary entry about it on 2 February.

"Request received today by telegraph from Army Group Crown Prince Wilhelm to launch diversionary attacks from 8 February, because the attack on Verdun is due to begin on 12 February. I really do not know how we shall be able to meet this requirement, or why it is that we were not informed in good time about the postponement of the offensive and why, despite our repeated submissions on the subject, we were ordered by *OHL* to begin diversionary attacks during the last week of January. Now they and all the attendant sacrifices were in vain!"[5]

Nevertheless, all this activity involving armies deployed well away from Fifth Army at Verdun does illustrate how Falkenhayn harnessed his forces up and down the Western Front in support of his *Schwerpunkt*; and he himself was subsequently adamant that they had served a useful purpose.

"Extensive preparations for feint attacks had been made according to instructions in Upper Alsace by Gaede's Army Detachment, for the purpose of misleading enemies and friends alike and the same thing, though on a smaller scale, was done by Fourth, Fifth, Sixth and Third Armies. These operations were continued when the preparations for the operations in the Meuse region started in earnest after Christmas 1915. In this way we succeeded in keeping the enemy for a long time in uncertainty as to the sector to be chosen for attack."[6]

Once into February Falkenhayn was in repeated contact with his subordinate headquarters to gauge reaction to the forthcoming operation. A coded signal concerning the overall appreciation of the situation, together with a request for information about the availability of its reserves, arrived at Sixth Army on 3 February. Because of its importance its contents were summarised in the war diary.

> "In contrast to army headquarters, *OHL* believes that an enemy attack or a significant thinning out of the enemy to the north of the Somme is highly likely once the Verdun attack is fully developed. The British cannot leave the French to struggle.
>
> "How [easily] Sixth Army could make available its reserves for an attack or a counter-attack elsewhere cannot yet be determined. The assumption is that the six divisions could arrive at the front in three to four days, as could the necessary supports and matériel (less labour battalions)."[7]

Responding to a written request for an opinion concerning possible enemy action on the Sixth Army front, Generalleutnant von Kuhl, chief of staff Sixth Army, despatched a signal on 7 February which he summarised in his diary as, 'British attack not likely; possibly they will take over sectors of the French front'. Returning to the topic in a telephone conversation with Falkenhayn the following day, Kuhl noted down his view that, 'Perhaps the British will take over parts of the French front to release French forces. But they certainly will not send troops to Verdun ... I cannot associate myself with Falkenhayn's opinion that the enemy will either attack us or weaken themselves so much that we can attack them.'[8]

A very short time after these exchanges and within days of agreement being reached by the French and British for an attack astride the Somme, the Germans began to pick up intelligence indicators which pointed in that direction. Three days before the offensive at Verdun opened, Joffre confirmed this intention in writing to Haig, 'Main aim, breakthrough of the German army by means of joint offensive by Franco-British forces on the front of Army Group North (General Foch). The attack will be carried out astride the Somme, with the French army operating on both banks. Everything must be ready by 1 July ...'[9] Of course numerous aspects of this plan went by the board as the Verdun campaign gained momentum, but preparations began more or less at once. German reconnaissance aircraft began to spot extensive temporary barracks being constructed opposite XIV Reserve Corps, for example, whilst, simultaneously, Second Army was beginning to discover signs that the British Army was preparing an attack north of the Somme and against its right flank.[10]

This was a source of concern because, although its positions were strongly developed along most of their length, with only a total of eleven divisions under command, Second Army was not well placed to meet a serious offensive. So, as early as March, it began pressing for permission to carry the attack to the Allies rather than wait until they had been able to make all their preparations without disturbance. On 2 March, for example, Below sent several suggestions to *OHL* for consideration, emphasising that, 'For the time being there is no intention to attempt a major offensive with distant objectives'; rather, what was being considered were operations intended, 'to lead to great, but geographically limited successes'. One such was designed to straighten out the line from St Pierre Divion to Fay via Maricourt. For this there would be a need for reinforcement by twelve divisions and 130 heavy artillery batteries.[11]

The plan received short shrift from Falkenhayn. 'No!', he wrote in the margin, and also dismissed two other subsequent Second Army proposals. As far as he was concerned nothing was going to dilute the offensive *Schwerpunkt* at Verdun. However, he did drive to see Crown Prince Rupprecht at Sixth Army on 8 March and there conducted a lengthy meeting about possible attacks in the Arras area. Responding to Rupprecht's suggestion that to be viable any such attack would have to be conducted on a twenty kilometre front and would require the service of 300 heavy artillery batteries and ten infantry corps, Falkenhayn advocated a ten kilometre front. This, Rupprecht warned, would be far too narrow and would carry great risks of being taken on either flank. He also added, when questioned, that any such attack would require preparation time of one month. In a subsequent diary entry Rupprecht noted, 'I had the impression that his sole reason for coming was to persuade me to reduce considerably the size of force we had specified in our plans. He appeared only to have glanced at our paper concerning the breakthrough. His constant travelling to all the various fronts makes uninterrupted work problematic. In complaining about points of detail, he loses sight of what is important.'[12]

The situation continued to be monitored and reports flowed up to *OHL*, together with further plans for offensive operations near Arras, none of which came to fruition, though Falkenhayn did speak to Crown Prince Rupprecht about Arras once more on 6 April. This time he was willing to release greater quantities of artillery, but only four divisions. This irritated Rupprecht, who felt that it would be better and would save a great deal of time and effort for the staff if Falkenhayn would simply admit that the attack around Arras would have to be cancelled due to lack of resources.[13] In mid April Sixth Army reported yet again that, 'The overall situation is unchanged. The enemy is mining actively [but] … otherwise there are no indications anywhere of an intention to attack. They are working busily at improving their positions, especially those recently taken over from the French. This applies especially to the front line trenches.'[14] Meanwhile, despite previous rebuffs, planning continued for the potential Operation *Hubertus*, a simultaneous attack to be launched north and south of Arras in a bid to pinch it out. On 16 April the Army war diary recorded the essence of a message to *OHL* (Ia No. 301 geh. [secret]):

"In connection with the plans for the double attack at Arras, army headquarters has requested the use of fifty four batteries of heavy and twenty two batteries of super heavy howitzers. In addition, to facilitate the capture of the centre of Arras and the well protected batteries located within the city, an urgent request has been placed for the allocation of two batteries of the very heaviest howitzers. The justification for the additional demands beyond that placed in the bid of 23.3.16 (No. 284 Ia) lies in the fundamental change in circumstances; that is to say they have been raised in response to the move forward by the British of additional forces and the vigorous construction or refurbishment of the enemy positions. If the requested equipment in support of the attack is not available, the operation will have to be postponed. *OHL* has been requested to make a decision in order that the preliminaries may be correctly directed."[15]

There was obviously no swift reply to the above message because two days later Sixth Army returned to the subject – not that it received a satisfactory response.

"According to reports by agents, it cannot be ruled out that the British will go over to the offensive in May. In view of the overall situation this is quite possible. If the conduct of *Hubertus* is delayed for so long that we can be pre-empted by the British attacking at another place, it will be necessary to release the work forces brought together from other corps for preparatory work on *H*. The positions, which have suffered considerably during the unusually wet period of weather, urgently need to be improved. Ia No. 303 geh. has been sent to *OHL* requesting a decision, because the withdrawal of the work force for other tasks is of equal importance as the preliminary work in connection with *Hubertus*."[16]

Potential diversions of effort from the *Schwerpunkt* at Verdun were never well received at *OHL* and all suggestions, such as that made by the German Crown Prince when Falkenhayn visited Headquarters Fifth Army on 13 May, to suspend operations there completely, were ignored. In fact, following further discussion between Falkenhayn and the Fifth Army chief of staff, General Schmidt von Knobelsdorf, orders were given that, 'At Verdun local attacks are to continue on both banks of the Meuse to improve the lines'.[17] Elsewhere, there were so many examples of nugatory planning of limited assaults in the weeks leading up to 1 July that it would appear that armies were either being encouraged, or at least tacitly permitted, to conduct repeated planning exercises for operations that had no chance of being carried out. This could have served a joint purpose. First, to keep them occupied with contingency planning and, second, to enable them to cling on to the idea that there might at some point be a change of heart at the top, which would enable them either to counter Allied preparations or at least allow them to build up forces and matériel, the better to parry the blow when it fell. Falkenhayn's motivation for acting as he did is difficult to judge. He left little in the way of evidence. Habitually, he tended to keep his cards close to his chest and frequently did not share his thoughts even with his principal staff officers.

As summer approached it was not only on the Sixth Army front where the continuing build-up of Allied forces was causing concern and, in early May, General von Stein, commanding XIV Reserve Corps, Second Army, concluded a report to *OHL* by stating, 'Enemy infantry superiority to our front is currently approximately three to one; artillery superiority very considerable'.[18] Then, on 26 May, General von Below sent a fully worked out, 'Proposal for an Attack Astride the Somme'[19] to *OHL*, suggesting a limited attack to be launched from St Pierre Divion, north of the Somme, to Foucaucourt en Santerre. This plan was an expansion and development of the 2 March scheme. The aim was not breakthrough but to advance up to twenty kilometres on a twenty five kilometre front, to capture a considerable slice of territory and so disrupt Allied plans, while improving the German situation. In recognition of the fact that resources would be hard to find, the plan was to attack in sequential phases; first, north of the river on the army right flank, to achieve a break in, followed by an operation to the south. Detailed staff checks led to calculations that thirteen divisions and 250 heavy artillery batteries would have to be made available if the operation was to be conducted all at once; hence the proposal to split it into phases. The idea was to attack north of the river and then to redeploy forces with a view to resuming the attack south of the Somme some six weeks later.

> "As far as the timing of the offensive, to be split into two or three phases, is concerned, it cannot begin too soon. The British have been so reinforced north of the Somme that there can be no doubt at all that they intend to launch an offensive … whether they intend to attack in the very near future or if they are waiting for additional reinforcements or to improve the training of their troops cannot be determined. If we can launch a thrust north of the Somme in the next few weeks, it is quite possible that we may pre-empt the British offensive and ruin their plans."[20]

There had still been no reply from *OHL* to this proposal when Second Army became aware of a considerable increase in the threat to its right flank. The assessment now was that a major British offensive north of the Somme was increasingly likely and that it could be launched at almost any time. In response Below sent another appeal to *OHL* stating, 'If, however, it is still not possible for this major offensive to be launched, the British attack plans could still be disrupted by a thrust as far as the Ancre on a frontage a few kilometres wide from St Pierre Divion to Ovillers.' This plan would only require an additional division, thirty heavy and super heavy howitzers and a few 100 mm batteries. There was no doubt, not even at *OHL*, that Second Army was about to be attacked. Falkenhayn even went so far as to describe it as 'long-expected and hoped-for'.[21] It may well have been 'long expected'; it is extremely unlikely that it was 'hoped-for'. All Below's requests for permission to launch a pre-emptive attack, including this modest latest one to interfere with British preparations and for reinforcements of manpower, aircraft and artillery as the moment of the attack approached, were turned down flat by *OHL*.

The notably successful opening of the Brussilov offensive on the Eastern Front on 4 June, which meant that reserves had to be rushed to the threatened area, finally put paid to all thoughts of pre-emptive action or even reinforcement of the Somme region; or at least that is what Falkenhayn maintained at the time and subsequently in his memoirs.

> "There is no doubt that even so limited a withdrawal of reserves made the situation on the Western Front much less favourable. The intention of nipping in the bud, by means of a heavy counter-attack, the offensive then being prepared by the English had to be dropped. The reserves of men and ammunition which were being held in readiness for this were too seriously reduced by the claims of the East. We could, however, rely on our brave troops in the West to weather the gathering storm even without this help."[22]

As has been noted, there is precious little evidence that Falkenhayn was ever completely serious about launching one or more pre-emptive attacks during the months leading up to 1 July and plenty that he would brook no distraction from the Verdun campaign, so his statement, seen in that light, is actually a case of special pleading to excuse the fact that the Battle of the Somme opened with the defence at such a huge disadvantage. It is of course arguable that had offensive operations at Verdun been halted as soon as the threat astride the Somme had been identified, it might still have been possible to have generated sufficient reserves to have given Second Army a better chance of properly countering the offensive when it opened but, in point of fact, 'The Battle of Verdun ... raged on with unreduced bitterness on both banks of the Meuse'.[23]

This imbalance of forces, this total lack of realistic operational reserves, was a matter of the gravest concern at both Second and Sixth Armies as June wore on. It is true that a little earlier there had been certain limited allocations of troops, most significantly the deployment of 2nd Guards Reserve Division in May, but, although Falkenhayn claimed that this meant that Second Army had been 'materially strengthened',[24] they were dismissed by everyone else as 'a drop of water on a hot stone'.[25] Even the official historian commented unfavourably on it subsequently. 'Despite the clearly approaching serious danger in the Somme area, *OHL* restricted its assistance to the allocation of only slight reinforcements to Second Army, even though this had a far wider sector to defend than Sixth Army and had fewer forces at its disposal.'[26] The situation was tracked closely by Generalleutnant von Kuhl at Sixth Army throughout the first half of June and was noted in his diary. His sense of increasing concern is readily observable.

"1 Jun 16 The 111th Division believes that it is threatened because a British attack is expected to be directed against the right flank of Second Army.

3 Jun 16 The British are now prepared for battle. It must be assumed that there will be a British attack on the Somme ... It is noticeable that the French have brought no new forces onto the Verdun front. Rather they have established fresh reserves behind the left flank south of the Somme. Are they intending to participate in the planned British attack?

7 Jun 16 Yesterday Second Army reported that aerial observers had spotted an increase in digging and new battery positions north of the Somme. Something is clearly happening there. I spoke to Grünert [Chief of Staff Second Army] this morning. There is no doubt that there are French [troops] north of the Somme around Maricourt.

9 Jun 16 There is strikingly heavy air activity in front of the right wing of Second Army. It is all rather suspicious. Apparently the French civilian population have been evacuated from the Maricourt area. Civilians loaded down with personal possessions have been seen. That would certainly be another indicator. Several reports by agents have spoken of a British attack after Whitsun.

11 Jun 16 Yesterday evening Second Army reported the presence of large tented areas south of Albert, but north of the Somme. There is heavy traffic on the Amiens-Rosières railway. During the past few days, networks of trenches have appeared in several places astride the Roye-Montdidier railway. It would appear that an attack on both sides[27] of the Somme is ever more probable. Will the French just create diversions south of the Somme, or launch a subsidiary attack (next to the main British attack north of the Somme) or even launch a major attack? ... At any rate it is high time we prepared ourselves."[28]

On 15 June the Kaiser, accompanied by Falkenhayn, visited first Sixth Army and then moved on to Second Army at St Quentin, where the party stayed overnight. Generalleutnant von Kuhl, who presumably gave the Sixth Army briefing, made only a short reference to the meeting in his diary. 'Note from the briefing to the Kaiser. So far there are no signs of a frontal attack against us, though there certainly are to the front of Second Army and apparently against our left flank. The artillery of 111st Division has been reinforced.'[29] However, Crown Prince Rupprecht recorded a much more detailed and interesting account of the meeting, which provides another insight into Falkenhayn's sometimes eccentric reasoning.

> "This morning the Kaiser and General von Falkenhayn arrived at my headquarters. I learned that, as before, the intention is still to wear down the French army at Verdun! According to Falkenhayn, the German Verdun initiative caused the cancellation of a planned spring offensive by the enemy. The French and British would probably now undertake an operation against Alsace-Lorraine. In reply to my objection that I did not think it likely that the British would join in on an operation to be launched so far from their operational bases on the coast and that I was much more inclined to think in terms of an attack against Second Army, he countered by saying that he could not imagine why precisely Second Army should be attacked ... the desire to spare northern France or Belgium would cause our opponents to launch an offensive against German territory.
>
> "I replied by saying that the French regarded Alsace-Lorraine as French territory and in any case the British would be indifferent to the prospect of Belgium or any other region being devastated. In some ways Falkenhayn's conception of war reminds me of a certain 18th Century strategist ...
>
> "Operations Branch of *OHL* is of the opinion that we must accept the possibility of a subsidiary attack around Lens. Why Lens exactly? In our considered opinion there is no reason whatever to justify such an assumption."[30]

As mentioned, later that day the Kaiser's party moved on to Headquarters Second Army. Falkenhayn, having listened to a briefing by General von Below concerning the increasingly threatening situation, would still not commit to the latter's urgent request, 'to earmark to him at least a few divisions as a reserve'. Even worse, the following morning over breakfast, when news arrived of a new threat to the Eastern Front, Falkenhayn stated that he would have to withdraw 11th Infantry Division from Second Army reserve. According to Below's biographer, the following exchange then occurred. Below requested him not to do so, at which the Kaiser asked Falkenhayn, 'What do you make of that?' To this came the reply,

'I trust the Prussian grenadier to hold his position'. Below retorted, 'I have no doubt about that; nevertheless, it is our duty to take precautions.'[31] In the event – and fortunately for Second Army and the integrity of the defence during the early desperate battles – 11th Infantry Division remained where it was.

During the next few days intelligence concerning the forthcoming offensive continued to arrive at Headquarters Second Army, where it was processed and redistributed up and down the chain of command and to both flanks. Commenting in his diary, Crown Prince Rupprecht remarked,

> "Second Army reports that opposite them the French have not expanded their frontage. However, they believe that they have observed increases in the overall trench network. Headquarters XIV Reserve Corps, deployed on the right flank of Second Army, expects an attack in the very near future. It is striking that recently the enemy has increased the amount of fire directed at the normally quiet right flank of the [Sixth] Army. Perhaps this increase in battle activity is merely intended as deception and to disguise from us the fact that strong enemy forces and reserves have been withdrawn.
>
> "According to reports which have just arrived from Second Army, it appears that, bit by bit, the British have actually withdrawn four divisions that were opposite the northern flank of Sixth Army and redeployed them on the Second Army front. In addition to the French XX Corps that is deployed along the Somme and apparently is tasked with maintaining contact with the British, the French XXX Corps, which previously was deployed in the area of Belfort, has appeared opposite Second Army south of the Somme, near to Lihons. It is said that Joffre visited XX Corps before it arrived at the front. In view of all this there can no longer be any doubt that a major French offensive against Second Army is imminent."[32]

On 20 June, Second Army itself reported to *OHL* that, 'It is no longer possible to harbour any doubt that a very powerful attack, which has been prepared with the utmost care, is imminent, now that French reinforcements have been identified south of the Somme.'[33] Then, three days later, General von Stein, commanding XIV Reserve Corps, added, 'I expect the enemy to attack the entire front. Enemy air formations are patrolling forward as far as the Arras – Bapaume – Péronne road and even beyond it. The enemy has air superiority.'[34] To the north, strenuous and extensive patrolling activity and careful monitoring of enemy artillery fire had revealed the northern limit of the forthcoming attack and yielded the information that a blow was definitely going to fall on Second Army. As General von Kuhl's diary reveals, the possible threat to Sixth Army had faded away and there was no longer any need for significant reserves to be held to its rear.

"20 Jun 16. Numerous patrols sent forward by 111th Division have discovered that there are no Russian saps or other attack preparations such as have been spotted opposite Second Army.

"22 Jun 16 The situation is becoming ever clearer. The British are deploying to attack the right wing of Second Army. Nothing is happening to our front.

"23 Jun 16 Gradually the situation is becoming clear. The right flank of the British attack is definitely Gommecourt. Second Army is requesting artillery support. Tappen [Generalmajor, Chief of Operations Branch *OHL*] told me that privately arranged moves are not desirable; *OHL* would lose oversight … The enemy artillery is reasonably active all along the Sixth Army front, but in many places only one or two guns are firing, so the impression is deception fire! Bombs have been dropped from the air in numerous places. The whole gives the impression of being one great diversion."[35]

Despite the accumulating evidence of enemy intentions, as late as the eve of the preliminary bombardment and for the week that it lasted, it was obvious to those most closely faced with the impending assault that all pleas for assistance would be met with deaf ears, that nothing would be forthcoming from the Verdun front, where the situation around Fort Souville was still seen as critical, and that the reserves held to the north in the Sixth Army sector were not going to be made available. It remains a mystery why Falkenhayn continued to be fixated by a possible threat on the Sixth Army front, when all the intelligence on the ground pointed in a different direction. As late as 23 June, when attack preparations astride the Somme were being pushed forward vigorously, the Sixth Army evening report included the facts that,

"111th Infantry Division reports that there are still <u>no saps or attack preparations observable to their front</u>.[36]
    "A prisoner from the British 51st Division states that <u>there is no intention to attack in the Arras area, but on the other hand there will be, both to the south (namely on the Second Army front) and also to the north</u>."[37]

Based on the appreciation of the situation and whilst accepting that secondary or diversionary attacks on its front remained a possibility, Sixth Army continued to withdraw heavy guns into army reserve, which suggest that the risk was not considered to be great. There seems to be a suggestion that one explanation of Falkenhayn's position was that he feared a subsidiary attack in the Lens area with a possible thrust towards Lille. Responding in 1934 to a request by the *Reichsarchiv* for information on this subject, Crown Prince Rupprecht wrote that Falkenhayn had based this assumption on reports from agents. However, according to the official historian there was no archival evidence of any such thing.[38] What remains indisputable is that Falkenhayn maintained his position on this and blocked all and any attempts by Sixth Army to pass unneeded formations and matériel to Second Army.

In the circumstances there was no other option open to Second Army and its subordinate formations but to make best use of what was already available or could be obtained from sources other than *OHL*. Pinning down the placement of the Second Army operational *Schwerpunkt* helps to explain the action taken. The most obvious indication that it was to the north of the River Somme was the distribution of its guns, with the greatest allocation going to XIV Reserve Corps and the redeployment of 10th Bavarian Infantry Division from the XVII Corps sector south of the river in late June 1916 into reserve behind XIV Reserve Corps. It is important in this context to be aware that this action was taken even though the concomitant risks were self-evident. The actual order for its move, issued by Bavarian Reserve Infantry Regiment 8, on 24 June stated, 'It has been established from reports by agents that an attack by British and French formations is to be expected shortly on both banks of the Somme. A wing of German aircraft fought its way across enemy lines south of Arras on 23 June and then forced its way on a reconnaissance flight behind enemy lines right down to the south of the Somme, everywhere detecting extremely heavy traffic on all routes to the rear.'[39] Once the Bavarians were pulled out of the line, the already weakly defended positions south of the River Somme became even more vulnerable to attack. When XVII Corps reallocated defensive sectors, all the regiments of the remaining three divisions were forced to assume responsibility for greatly increased frontages. Infantry Regiment 61, for example, which took over the line previously held by Bavarian Infantry Regiment 16 south of Chaulnes, had no choice but to place all of its three battalions in the front line, leaving it with no reserves at all.[40]

Once a *Schwerpunkt* was defined it was axiomatic that considerable risks would be taken elsewhere so as to give it appropriate priority. That said, virtually to denude the Santerre of infantry and artillery in the certain knowledge that an attack was imminent shows what a desperate situation faced General von Below at the end of June. There appear to be two main reasons why this calculated risk was nevertheless accepted. The official appreciation had always been that French commitments at Verdun might not completely prevent French involvement in a Somme offensive but that the size and scope of any contribution would necessarily be limited. As the weeks went by, with French reinforcements arriving, XVII Corps determined with complete accuracy where the southern limit of the assault was going to fall and so was able to make the necessary judgement.

Thus once the scope of the attack was clear geographical considerations came to the fore. Allied thoughts of forcing crossings over the Somme were always fanciful unless, with large scale French participation, operations could have been extended a long way south. It is only necessary to examine the map showing the bend of the Somme in this area to see that an attempt to carry out an opposed assault river crossing to the south of Péronne would have meant having to cross swamps, marshland and numerous water channels. There would have been no prospect at all of success. It is of course the case that German engineers had achieved what was widely regarded as a triumph of construction when earlier they managed to bridge the entire series of linked obstacles at Éterpigny, but that took days of effort and was achieved out of contact with the enemy. As a result, it was obvious that, regardless of any French advance eastwards south of the Somme, sooner or later they would have come up against an obstacle that was effectively impassable. This is more or less how matters developed. Within a relatively short time after battle was joined the pace of events in the south was reduced markedly, whilst elsewhere the French army made increasingly strenuous efforts to outflank Péronne from the north. General der Artillerie Max von Gallwitz, transferred from Verdun in mid July to command of the new Second Army as well as Army Group Gallwitz, commented, 'Because from the end of July to the end of August the Allied thrusts were directed primarily at First Army, my duties as a commander were somewhat limited.'[41]

North of the river, the XIV Reserve Corps' tactical *Schwerpunkt* was the 26th Reserve Division's sector. The importance for the overall integrity of the defence of the high ground running from Serre to Ovillers had long since been recognised and huge efforts continued for almost two years from October 1914 to make its ridges and spurs as near impregnable as possible. Furthermore, when each division was stripped of a complete brigade headquarters in 1915 so as to furnish command headquarters for new formations, 26th Reserve Division, probably uniquely, was permitted to remain a four regiment division and to retain both 51 and 52 Reserve Brigades, commanded by the experienced Generalleutnants von Wundt and von Auwärter respectively. Ideally, the division would have preferred to have been very substantially reinforced but, despite the importance of its sector, it had to make the best of what it had. Writing in the history of 52 Reserve Infantry Brigade, Landwehr Leutnant Gerster, a former member of Reserve Infantry Regiment 119, described how this was done.

"Initially the only response our commanders could make to the obvious offensive intentions of the enemy, which increased day by day, was to review organisational countermeasures. This clarified complicated command relationships and reduced over large defensive sectors. Gradually reinforcements arrived. These, although relatively weak, nevertheless significantly raised our defensive strength. To this end, Machine Gun Detachment Fasbender was subordinated to 52 Reserve Brigade on the 10th May and was initially deployed in the second line. On the 25th May, six Belgian machine guns were allocated for use in the front line. Unfortunately, there was only limited ammunition for the Belgian guns. On the 12th May, 3rd Battalion Reserve Field Artillery Regiment 26 was reinforced by two light gun batteries and two old heavy 150 millimetre batteries. By the 6th June, the enemy, who had not missed the arrival of the new batteries, engaged them with large calibre guns. Following the sub-division of Sector Beaumont on the12th May, on the 22nd May Infantry Regiment 180 was relieved around Serre by Reserve Infantry Regiment 121. This was accompanied by a complete shift in divisional and company boundaries and a reorganisation of the entire front line.

"The Army Command calculated that the most probable enemy course of action was an attack north of the Ancre and therefore inserted 2nd Guards Reserve Division, which had been in reserve, to the right of 52nd Infantry Division around Gommecourt. As a result, all the divisions shifted sideways. Reserve Infantry Regiment 121 only took over part of the old position of Infantry Regiment 180. Reserve Infantry Regiment 119 handed over the former sectors B 1–3 to Reserve Infantry Regiment 121, holding on only to the line south of the road Beaumont-Auchonvillers as far as the Ancre, which was divided into Beaumont-North and Beaumont-South. Thiepval was also reorganised and was divided into Thiepval -North, -Centre and -South. Each battalion was responsible for the defence of one sector. Forces were deployed in depth. In each case three companies were deployed in the front line and one company was in battalion reserve in the second and third trenches, which were further developed vigorously. One battalion was in reserve and at rest. On the 23rd May, the Division also moved the 26th Division Recruit Depot forward into the divisional area in order to have a further reserve readily available and to be able to occupy the Second Position.

"Because it was intended that Infantry Regiment 180 would relieve Reserve Infantry Regiment 109, which was occupying Ovillers, to the south of Reserve Infantry Regiment 99, on the 24th May, Sector Beaumont was allocated to 51 Reserve Infantry Brigade and Reserve Infantry Regiment 119 left the Brigade for the second time. For a while 52 Reserve Infantry Brigade only had the Thiepval sector to defend. This was occupied by Reserve Infantry Regiment 99, whose 4th Battalion had returned to it on the17th May. The relief in Ovillers began during the night of the 7th/8th

June and was completed on the 9th June. Infantry Regiment 180 discovered that its new position was a well constructed system of trenches with deep, spacious, mined dugouts in which they could face the coming attack with confidence.

"The extension to the south of the Brigade front necessitated a regrouping of the artillery. Reserve Field Artillery Regiment 27, which was newly trained, was allocated to 52 Reserve Infantry Brigade. Whereas Ovillers offered accommodation for 2,500 men in the first position, Thiepval, which was stronger and better developed, had space for 3,900 men. There were few dugouts in the Intermediate and Second Positions. Mouquet Farm only had space for a hundred men and in the second position, across the entire width, there were only 200 places in each regimental area. That was not much. A high price was paid further south in July for this deficiency. Further reinforcements and reserves arrived on the 13th June: a battalion of Bavarian Reserve Infantry Regiment 8, 3rd Company Foot Artillery Battalion 51, a company of the Bavarian Reinforcement Battalion 5 and Bavarian Engineer Company 20, which, however, moved over to 28th Reserve Division on the 18th June."[42]

There was, however, one significant avenue available to Second Army. Profiting from the fact that the *Schwerpunkt* division was non-Prussian, decisive steps were taken to strengthen and reorganise its supporting artillery in early summer 1916. That it was able to do this in the face of the refusal of *OHL* to make available additional gunner units, points up one of the peculiarities of the German formations deployed north of the Somme. Contrary to what is generally believed, an 'Imperial German Army' never existed. The navy was certainly imperial, but the army was not; rather, it comprised several contingents. It is true that it was dominated by Prussia, but there were also substantial contributions from the kingdoms of Bavaria, Württemberg and Saxony, with smaller groupings from other parts of the *Reich*. These included, for example, the Grand Duchy of Baden, which furnished 28th Reserve Division, responsible for holding the line from La Boisselle to Mametz on 1 July.

This meant that the different contingents enjoyed a degree of independence from Prussia. Though in time of war all of these, even Bavaria, gave their allegiance to the Kaiser, in many other ways, including the provision of manpower and adjustments to the order of battle, each contingent behaved autonomously. As a result Generalleutnant Freiherr von Soden, commanding 26th Reserve Division, did not have to rely on the willingness of the Prussians to assist. Instead, acting on his own initiative and pursuing the matter up the Württemberg chain of command, he was able quite legitimately to send a request directly to the Ministry of War in Stuttgart for the raising of a new artillery regiment. Responding positively, the authorities there directed, at the end of May, the formation of Reserve Field Artillery Regiment 27.

The plan, which was paralleled within 28th Reserve Division, which also raised a new regiment at this time, was to create the new formation in the field by drawing on existing regiments, mainly Field Artillery Regiments 29 and 65 and Reserve Field Artillery Regiment 26. Additional reinforcements were drawn from the *Ersatz* battalions of the two active regiments. 3rd Battalion Reserve Field Artillery Regiment 26 (light field howitzers), under their commander Hauptmann Jäckh, moved across complete to form the new 2nd Battalion. Most of 1st Battalion, under Hauptmann Wiedtemann of Field Artillery Regiment 65, formed up with its batteries, completing the transition in Pys, Le Sars and St Leger on 6 and 7 June but, because some of its reinforcements – including its light ammunition column – had to be transported from bases back in Germany, it was not finalised in all respects until 29 June.

However, with few exceptions, the entire task took less than two weeks and the two battalion artillery regiment was well equipped with modern weapons and ready to play a full part in the forthcoming battle. As early as 8 June the new commander, Major Reiniger, formerly of Field Artillery Regiment 29, was able to report to General von Stein at Headquarters XIV Reserve Corps that all the batteries would be moved into their actual firing positions within three days. The response was, 'It is good that the regiment is available. We are expecting an enemy attack in a few days' time and, given the lack of artillery, the deployment of your regiment is urgently required.'[43]

It will be recalled that at the beginning of 1916 virtually all the modern heavy guns and howitzers were moved to support the *OHL Schwerpunkt* at Verdun. This policy also affected fire support for 26th Reserve Division. When 8th Battery Reserve Foot Artillery Regiment 10, armed with 150 mm guns, was transferred south on 10 March, its loss was viewed with dismay, the battery having fired in support of the division from the earliest days of the war in the Vosges mountains. It was replaced by a battery operating inferior captured Russian equipment. Reserve Field Artillery Regiment 26 went so far as to remark that, 'From the point of view of the artillery, gradually the entire *Entente* was represented within the divisional sector'.[44]

There may have been deficiencies on the equipment side; nevertheless, the raising of a second regiment meant that a new artillery formation, 26th Reserve Field Artillery Brigade, could be created. To command it, Soden requested the services of a first class gunner, namely Generalmajor Heinrich Maur, for the purpose. Maur had begun the war as a regimental commander; but at the time he was posted to the Somme he was serving on the Eastern Front as Artillery

Commander 79th Reserve Division. Once the requirement was agreed he was rushed west, reporting for duty at his new headquarters in Grévillers on 12 June, where he took command of not only his organic batteries but also a further twelve field batteries (Bavarian Field Artillery Regiment 20, complete with three howitzer batteries; 1st Battalion Reserve Field Artillery Regiment 12; and 1st Battalion Field Artillery Regiment 104 from 52nd Infantry Division).[45] To these were added additional heavy batteries.

On paper, therefore, 26th Reserve Division in the tactical *Schwerpunkt* was supported by twenty eight and a half field and ten and a half heavy batteries; in other words by a total of 154 guns and howitzers.[46] This sounds to be reasonably impressive until it is remembered that not only was Maur's command vastly outnumbered by the British artillery, but it was also equipped with a strange assortment of obsolescent and even obsolete items. These included captured Belgian guns (57, 87 and 120 mm), French guns (75 and 120 mm), Russian heavy field howitzers and a super heavy howitzer. Some batteries had no horses and there were also 90 cm guns and ancient *Ringkanonen* with no recoil mechanisms. Describing the situation, Reserve Field Artillery Regiment 26 stated, 'On the whole the foreign barrels obeyed German orders well. Only the Russian super-heavy howitzer did not always want to toe the line. Sometime it just blasted a huge smoke cloud skywards, reared up reluctantly and fell back down, groaning like a real Russian bear.'[47]

The fact that Maur was able from this unpromising selection of weaponry, which must have caused immense problems for the logisticians, swiftly to create and direct centralised control of his fire power and deploy two major concentrations: Group Miraumont under Oberst Erlenbusch and Group Pys, commanded by Major Reiniger (with a total of five sub-groups beneath them), to powerful effect was a defensive triumph and, as will be seen, essential for the protection of the divisional *Schwerpunkt*. In order to extract the best results from his guns, Maur introduced several innovations. For example, the defensive fire zones forward of the First Position were redefined, reduced in width and were linked to particular fire units. Even more important, however, was his superimposition of a system of squares on the map. The sub-sectors on the divisional front were already preceded by a system of letters: S = Serre; H = Heidenkopf; B = Beaumont; C = Courcelette; O = Ovillers; and P = Pozières. The artillery squares were then given numbers. This simplified both reporting and response to calls for fire. To bring down fire on a particular place, for example, an artillery liaison officer would have to do no more than order, 'Target: Square C7. Battery, five rounds, fire for effect.' and twenty shells would be fired in response.

That said, Maur would have had a far easier task when battle was joined if he had had modern 210mm howitzers (*Grobe Gottliebs*) available to him.

Unfortunately, these outstanding weapons, which spent the war being rushed up and down the Western Front like a fire brigade wherever they were most needed, had of course almost all been transferred south to fire in support of the *OHL* strategic *Schwerpunkt* at Verdun. Further to the south, between La Boisselle and Mametz, 28th Reserve Division had also received artillery reinforcements, though not to the same extent as the Württembergers. By the middle of June, its artillery commander controlled the fire of forty field guns, twenty light and twenty heavy howitzers of various kinds. To these were added sixteen obsolescent field guns and twelve captured heavy guns.[48]

As far as infantry fire power was concerned (altogether, spread along the eleven kilometre sector, there were ninety heavy machine guns, including captured weapons and thirty of the new light machine guns [Danish Madsens with a four man crew and known as *Musketen*]), its placement underlines yet again that the divisional *Schwerpunkt* lay with Reserve Infantry Regiment 99 in the Thiepval sector and that within that the *Schwerpunkt* of *Schwerpunkts* was the Schwaben Redoubt, located on dominating high ground north of Thiepval village. Small wonder, therefore, that it was reinforced by a company from Bavarian Reserve Infantry Regiment 8 before the battle ever began and that counter-attack plans were issued in advance. Small wonder, either, that its loss to the dash of the men of the 36th (Ulster) Division on the morning of 1 July caused such utter consternation in the German chain of command and, as will be described, set in train the most vigorous counter measures to restore the situation. It is quite clear that, within the limits of the available manpower and matériel, at the tactical level everything possible had been done by 24 June to prepare for the battle to come. The greater concern was at the operational level, where the near total lack of reserves held well forward seriously affected the ability of the commanders at corps and army level to respond appropriately and promptly when the blow fell.

Aware of the trial to which Second Army was being subjected as the bombardment began, knowing too how dangerously weak and off balance it was, Sixth Army made every effort, even at this late stage, to provide it with much needed support. Two diary entries by Generalleutnan von Kuhl show how aware he was of the need for action and adjustments to allocations of guns.

"25 Jun 16. Conversation with Tappen [Chief Operations Branch *OHL*]. Me 'We do not need all the artillery which *OHL* has stationed behind us. *OHL* can remove it. We are withdrawing [guns] to form a new army artillery reserve.'
26 Jun 16 Considerable artillery fire throughout the night and numerous raids. However, the corps all take this for deception!! Heavy gun fire against Second Army from Gommecourt to the Somme. It appears that the main attack is intended to be astride the Somme ... Evening situation: The

enemy artillery is in action all along the front. This is creating an impression of a demonstration. By firing from many different positions, the enemy are trying to imply considerable reinforcement of their artillery."[49]

Meanwhile the bombardment ground on. On the 26th Reserve Division front, at its height 10,000 shells per day were landing around Thiepval on the Reserve Infantry Regiment 99 sector alone. Nevertheless, it was generally more or less ineffective in terms of the number of casualties it caused, though the strain on all concerned was undeniable. Altogether during the full seven day period its thirteen battalions suffered fewer than 900 killed, wounded and missing;[50] but elsewhere, especially between Mametz and Montauban and south of the river, where the more effective French artillery was in action, in places it took a huge toll of the defenders' morale and ability to resist. It is small wonder, therefore, that it was precisely on that sector of the front that best progress was made on 1 July. The Second Army report to *OHL* on 28 June makes clear in particular how lack of artillery due to the demands of Verdun and an unwillingness to redeploy guns from other parts of the front was compromising its chances of conducting a robust defence.

"Enemy activity opposite XIV Reserve Corps (North of the Somme) and XVII Army Corps (South of the Somme) resembles, ever more closely, tactics of wearing down and attrition. It must be assumed that the bombardment, which has now lasted for five days, and which from time to time increases to drumfire, before reducing to calmer, observed fire by the heaviest calibre weapons on different parts of our positions, will continue for some time. The enemy's gas tactics, which are being aided by the prevailing west winds, of releasing constantly repeated small clouds of gas, is aimed also at gradual attrition. Because of technical mistakes, the enemy has so far achieved little through the use [of gas]. It is a different matter with the artillery. The enormous enemy superiority in heavy and long-range batteries, which the Army has so far been unable to counter, is proving very painful. Our artillery would have been adequate to respond to an assault launched after a one-day heavy bombardment of our trenches. Because of the procedure which he has adopted, the enemy is in a position to flatten our positions and smash our dugouts through the application of days of fire with 280 and 300 millimetre guns. This means that our infantry is suffering heavy losses day after day, whilst the enemy is able to preserve his manpower. His main forces, which outnumber our infantry many times over, are for the time being probably outside the beaten area of our guns, or protected by overhead cover, which our heavy field howitzers cannot penetrate; whilst the few 210 millimetre heavy howitzers are nowhere near sufficient to cover a forty five to fifty kilometre frontage."[51]

Towards the end of the bombardment Generalleutnant von Soden issued an Order of the Day to all ranks of 26th Reserve Division.

> "All the care and work which has been invested in the development of our positions will be put to a test of strength during the coming days. Now it is a matter of holding fast, courageously sticking it out, each of us doing our duty, not shrinking from sacrifice and strenuous effort, so that, victorious, we shall throw back the enemy. Each one of us must realise that the ground for which we fought bloody battles must without fail be held. No British or French soldiers may push their way unpunished into our lines. I know that in this conviction I share the view of all ranks of the division and I face the coming events with complete confidence. Our battle cry shall be, 'With God for King and Fatherland!'"[52]

Soden was right about what the defence was up against and the only way it could hope to prevail. All he could do now was to encourage his men but, inwardly, faced with odds of between eight and ten to one in favour of the British army, he, like many others in positions of responsibility, was deeply concerned about his overall weakness. 'The only divisional reserve', he wrote, 'was Bavarian Reserve Infantry Regiment 8 (Oberstleutnant Bram) of 10th Bavarian Division Burkhardt';[53] and initially after its arrival he was unable to call on it directly, because it was a XIV Reserve Corps asset. Pressing for further support, he was allocated a company of *Musketen* [Madsen light machine gun] teams and these were quickly distributed along the divisional front. The problem was simply that, although both were acutely aware of what was required, neither General von Below or General von Stein had anything available to deploy. By now Falkenhayn's obstinacy and his refusal to countenance significant reinforcement of the Somme front amounted almost to professional negligence, which could well have had catastrophic consequences.

It is true that Clausewitz, writing in 'Principles of War' (published in 1812; not to be confused with his later *On War*), gave as one of his general principles that,

> "The second rule is to concentrate our power as much as possible against that sector where the chief blows are to be delivered and to incur disadvantages elsewhere, so that our chances of success may increase at the decisive point. This will compensate for all other disadvantages."[54]

However, Clausewitz was a practical soldier and pragmatist as well as a philosopher and thinker, so he assuredly did not intend his words to mean that an offensive, which had patently failed to achieve its intended aim within weeks of its opening, was to be pursued obsessively to the point of absurdity, or until elsewhere a changing situation made the risk of fundamental setback or defeat a distinct possibility. On 2 July Generalleutnant von Kuhl made a remarkably restrained diary entry.

> "I believe that *OHL* has allocated its reserves too late to Second Army. Tappen and Falkenhayn still believed that we were also to be attacked, despite the fact that I repeatedly assured [them] that this was not likely, that we had no need for further reserves, especially not the *OHL* artillery reserves to our rear ... The *OHL* ought to have released its reserves sooner."[55]

Of course von Kuhl was referring to what might have been done at the last minute; but it was self-evident to all senior commanders less, apparently, Falkenhayn, that as soon as it became clear what was planned by the Allies and the dimensions of the offensive were known, operations at Verdun should have been suspended once and for all. Then, based on the earlier calculations about the size of forces which would have been required to conduct, say, *Hubertus*, at least twenty divisions and some hundreds of additional artillery batteries, together with all available aircraft, should have been transferred to the threatened front. Then and only then might major German counter-attacks have been launched to break up the Allied thrusts and wreck their plans. Then and only then could serious counter-battery fire have been attempted. Then and only then could the unfortunate *Feldgrauen* in their shell holes have been spared two months of intense fighting, plagued directly by ground attack aircraft and indirectly by the work of artillery observers who controlled the fire of the guns.

One well respected commentator, Generalleutnant Otto von Moser, who commanded 27th Infantry Division with great distinction during the August battles for Guillemont, summed up what Falkenhayn's folly had meant to him.

> "If the German Chief of the General Staff and the Prussian Minister of War [General Adolf Wild von Hohenborn] actually believed from their perspective that they had done everything possible and necessary to equip the German army, then the first few weeks of battle on the Somme shattered this belief completely. This was certainly the way every man who commanded either a higher formation or a junior unit remembered it. They were all truly horrified at the appalling German inferiority and serious lack of combat supplies with which their troops had to struggle and from which they suffered."[56]

Notes

1. Kriegsarchiv Munich AOK 6 Nr. 3 *Kriegstagebuch 1916* p. 414.
2. Kabisch *Somme 1916* p. 41.
3. Nollau History Infantry Regiment 51 p. 84.
4. Sheldon *The German Army on Vimy Ridge* pp. 135–141.
5. Rupprecht *In Treue Fest* p. 422.
6. Falkenhayn *General Headquarters* p. 223.
7. Kriegsarchiv Munich AOK 6 Nr. 3 *Kriegstagebuch 1916* p. 441.
8. BA/MA RH61/50652 *Kriegstagebuch von Kuhl* pp. 6–7.
9. Kabisch *op. cit.*p 37.
10. GOH p. 273.
11. GOH p. 280.
12. Rupprecht *op. cit.* p. 436.
13. *ibid.*pp 443–444.
14. Kriegsarchiv Munich AOK 6 Nr. 3 *Kriegstagebuch 1916* p. 321.
15. *ibid.* p. 326.
16. *ibid.* p. 337.
17. GOH p. 304.
18. Kabisch *op. cit.* p. 41.
19. GOH p. 312.
20. Grote *Somme* p. 15.
21. Falkenhayn *General Headquarters* p. 262.
22. *ibid.* p. 250.
23. GOH p. 315.
24. *ibid.* p. 238.
25. Grote *op. cit.* p. 25.
26. GOH p. 318.
27. Original emphasis.
28. BA/MA RH61/50652 *Kriegstagebuch von Kuhl* pp. 14–15.
29. *ibid.* p. 16.
30. Rupprecht *op. cit.* p. 482.
31. Möller *General von Below* p. 49.
32. Rupprecht *op. cit.* p. 482.
33. Kabisch *op. cit.* p. 42.
34. *ibid.* p. 42.
35. BA/MA RH61/50652 *Kriegstagebuch von Kuhl* pp15–16.
36. Original emphasis.
37. Kriegsarchiv Munich AOK 6 Nr. 3 *Kriegstagebuch 1916* p. 425.
38. GOH p. 317.
39. *Kriegsarchiv Munich* BRIR8 Bd 3. *I. Nr. 28 Regimentsbefehl 24.6.1916.*
40. Keiser History Infantry Regiment 61 p. 158.
41. Gallwitz *Erleben im Westen* p. 93.
42. Hauptstaatsarchiv Stuttgart M410 Bü 260 *Geschichte der 52 (K.W.) Reserve-Infanterie-Brigade.*
43. Moos History Reserve Field Artillery Regiment 27 pp. 1–2.
44. Klaus History Reserve Field Artillery Regiment 26 p. 45.
45. Soden History 26th Reserve Division pp. 101–102.
46. *ibid.* p. 96.
47. Klaus *op. cit.* p. 45.

48. Schwarte *Der Weltkrieg um Ehre und Recht* p. 551.
49. BA/MA RH61/50652 *Kriegstagebuch von Kuhl* pp15–16.
50. Soden History 26th Reserve Division p. 107.
51. Grote *op. cit.* pp. 32–33.
52. Soden *op. cit.* p. 108.
53. *ibid.* p. 107.
54. Clausewitz *Principles of War*
55. BA/MA RH61/50652 *Kriegstagebuch von Kuhl* p. 17.
56. Moser *Ernsthafte Plaudereien* p. 159.

DEPLOYMENT 26TH RESERVE DIVISION 30 JUNE

CHAPTER 3

1st July 1916: The Battle for the Schwerpunkt

T he terrain and position defended by 26th Reserve Division on 1 July 1916 had been studied, selected and then prepared over a period of twenty months. It had been developed in depth and comprised two major positions, each split into two or three defence lines that were separately wired and linked with communication trenches. There were various strongpoints in the First Position: the *Heidenkopf*, near Serre; the village of Beaumont; The *Biberkolonie* [Beaver Colony] astride the Ancre;[1] St Pierre Divion; Thiepval village; Hill 141; and Ovillers. In rear of the First Position came the *Zwischenstellung* [Intermediate Position], which linked a series of redoubts constructed to provide all round defence and to dominate the surrounding area of each. By spring 1916, from north to south, these were *Feste Soden* [Soden Redoubt], the *Grallsburg*,[2] *Feste Alt-Württemberg* [Beaucourt Redoubt], *Feste Schwaben* [Schwaben Redoubt], Mouquet Farm and Pozières village.

Between one and two kilometres to the rear was the Second Position, which ran from Puisieux in the north and then south via Grandcourt to the Pozières windmill. Once again this housed several field fortifications: *Alte-Garde Stellung* [Old Guards' Position], *Moulin Ruiné* [Ruined Mill], *Feste Staufen* [Stuff Redoubt] and *Feste Zollern* [Goat Redoubt]. There had been insufficient time and labour to dig a third position, but plans had been made to construct it along the line Achiet le Petit-Irles-Le Sars-Flers, with yet another intermediate position from Puisieux to Courcelette. Each of these positions was linked to others by means of an extensive network of communications trenches and there were sufficient mined dugouts for the entire forward garrison. Initially these had been dug three metres deep but, in the light of experience gained during the 1915 battles in Artois, these were all deepened to seven or more metres. Located in hard chalk, they were extremely robust, which goes a long way to explain why the bombardment in this area was largely ineffective in the days leading up to 1 July.

The entire sector comprised rolling down land rising to about 150 metres above sea level, or about sixty metres higher than the level of the Ancre, which conveniently split the sector into two, each the responsibility of a two regiment brigade. Great care was taken over the placement of command posts. The battalion commanders were located in the second or third trench of the First Position, or possibly in the Intermediate Position, in deep, strongly constructed dugouts with good, deeply buried, telephone links. The sub sector (regimental) commanders were further to the rear and behind them yet again were the brigade commanders, with command posts in the Second Position. Equal care was devoted to the command posts of the artillery commanders and the entire network was serviced by numerous telephone links, light signalling stations, pigeons, message dogs and relays of runners, all of which had been exercised repeatedly in the previous weeks.

All of the various positions and fortifications had an important role to play, but none more so than the Schwaben Redoubt. Historically, there has been much misunderstanding about its design, construction and purpose. It did not sit above a great complex of underground passages and chambers. Rather, it was a triangular shaped field fortification sited to exploit the dominance of the 150 metre ring contour 1,000 metres north of the Thiepval cross roads. Its importance was recognised as soon as the initial fighting for the Thiepval ridge died down in early autumn 1914. From the start it was covered by fire, patrolled constantly and occupied at night and by early 1915 a single trench had been dug and wired around the feature. Initially this was known as the *Teufelsgraben* [Devil's Trench] and then, as the work continued, it was named the *Schwabenschanze* [Schwabian Diggings]. In its final form, it became *Feste Schwaben* [Schwaben Redoubt] and the key element in the line of fortifications along the Intermediate and Second Positions within the 26th Reserve Division sector, which ran from *Feste Soden* [Soden Redoubt] south of Serre to the *Nordwerk* [Northern Work] north of Ovillers.

The main feature of the redoubt was a pair of trenches, separately wired and linked by five communication trenches (three with two separate links into the forward trench), that ran parallel to the second line of the First Position in subsectors C3 and C4 opposite Thiepval Wood. The first trench, the *Kampfgraben* [Battle Trench], featured twenty traverses and nine dugouts, two thirds of which were clustered towards the western tip of the redoubt where it met the Thiepval-St Pierre Divion track. This, coupled with the fact that this point housed two heavy machine guns and two *Musketen* teams, coupled with others located elsewhere in the fortification, indicates that this small, but utterly dominant, point geographically was the *Schwerpunkt* of *Schwerpunkts* for the entire Second Army. Hauptmann Herbert von Wurmb, an officer of Bavarian Reserve Infantry Regiment 8, who received the Knight's Cross of the Military Max Josef Order for his part in its recapture, later underlined this point in the regimental history:

"The Schwaben Redoubt was a point of decisive importance. If the enemy succeeded in establishing himself here on a long term basis, not only would the whole position of the 26th Reserve Division on the southern bank of the

Ancre have been extraordinarily endangered, but also the entire operational viability of the divisional artillery on the northern bank would have been called into question because, from the Redoubt, all the batteries there would have been in full view."[3]

In rear and parallel to the *Kampfgraben* ran the *Wohngraben* [Accommodation Trench], which had twelve traverses and housed a further eight dugouts, including that of the company commander and another for the medical aid post. Running away eastwards and forming the 'hypotenuse' of the triangle was *Schlütergraben* [Splutter Trench], which joined up with *Lachweg*, adjacent to the Thiepval – Grandcourt road. There was also a battalion command post at the junction of *Lachweg* and the so-called *Auwärter-Stellung* [named after the commander of 52 Reserve Infantry Brigade], which ran southeast to Mouquet Farm. That was it; that was all the redoubt comprised, but it sat on ground of such critical importance to the defence that it was the Second Army *Schwerpunkt*, the focus of all resources and priority effort from General von Below downwards.

The defence of this area was primarily the responsibility of 3rd Battalion Reserve Infantry Regiment 99, though on 27 June 1st and 4th Companies Bavarian Reserve Infantry Regiment 8 were ordered forward to subsector C1 (St Pierre Divion) and Schwaben Redoubt respectively so as to reinforce the troops *in situ*.[4] Headquarters 1st Battalion Bavarian Reserve Infantry Regiment 8 was established in Grandcourt, whilst 2nd and 3rd Companies, together with Machine Gun Sharpshooter Detachment 89, commanded by Leutnant Zimmermann, reinforced the Recruit Companies of Infantry Regiment 180 in the Second Position. For the time being, although called forward at night for digging duties, 2nd and 3rd Battalions Bavarian Reserve Infantry Regiment 8 remained based in Irles and Warlencourt. As the bombardment ground on and intelligence accumulated that the 52 Reserve Infantry Brigade front was about to be assaulted, 3rd Battalion, together with its attached Machine Gun Sharp Shooter Detachment 45, was ordered forward to *Feste Zollern* [Goat Redoubt] at 11.30 pm on 28 June, there to link up with *Pionier* [Engineer] Company Schefold and to occupy the Second Position.

Following an accurate engagement of *Feste Zollern* by super-heavy howitzers at noon on 30 June, Headquarters 52 Reserve Infantry Brigade had to move and occupy its alternate command post in Courcelette.[5] There were also occasional minor adjustments to the forces allocated to the defence but, finally, at the moment of the main attack on 1 July, only 2nd Battalion and the regimental staff of the Bavarians, together with one machine gun company, were held back in reserve by 26th Reserve Division. The First Position and Schwaben Redoubt were manned as previously described and the Second Position in this critical area (the 'Grandcourt

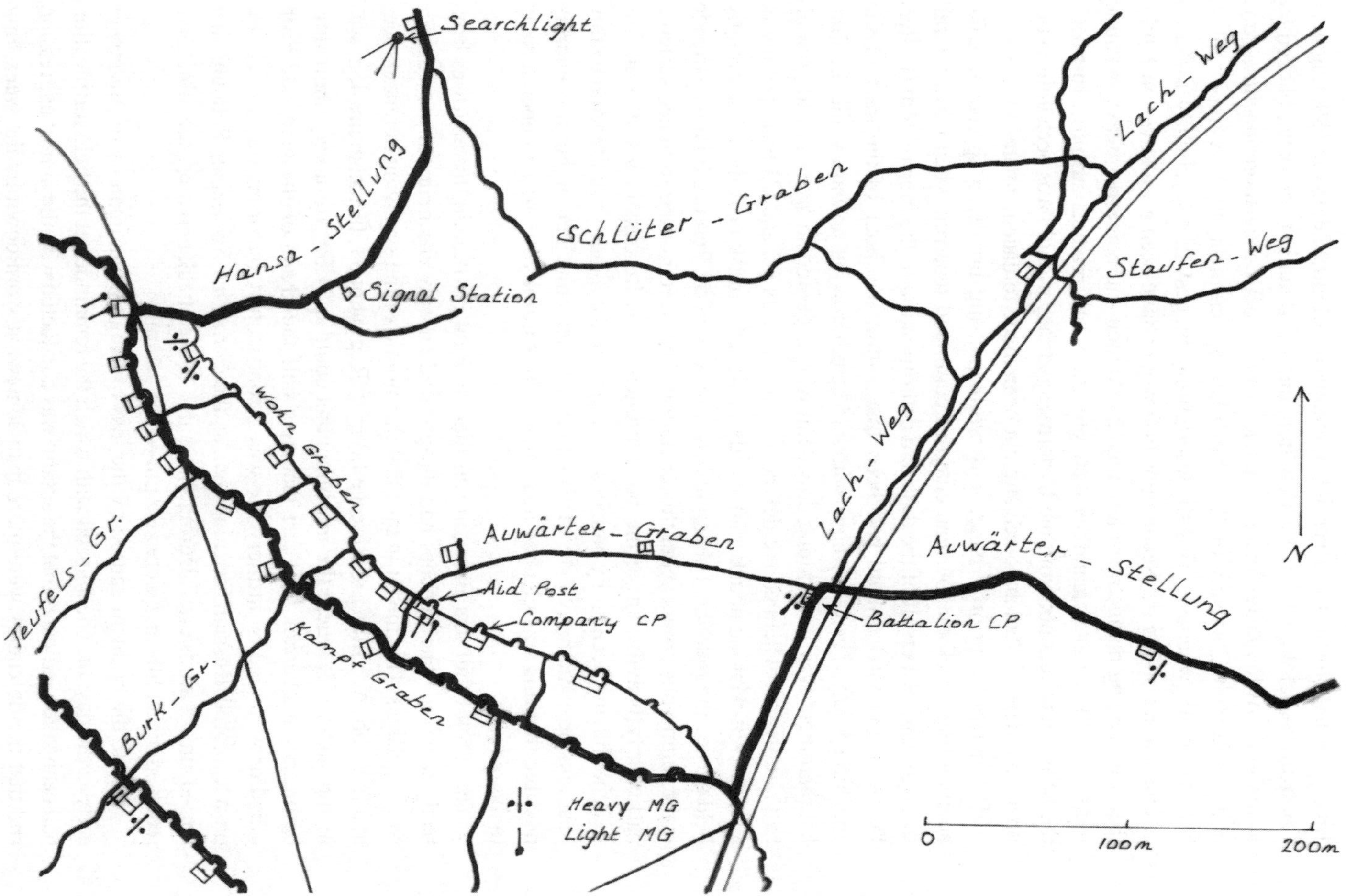

Loos - Weg

Staufen - Weg

Auwärter - Stellung

Loch - Weg

Battalion CP

Schlüter - Graben

Auwärter - Graben

Aid Post

Company CP

Heavy MG

Light MG

Searchlight

Signal Station

Hansa - Stellung

Wohn Graben

Kampf Graben

Bunker Gr.

Teufel - Gr.

N

200m

100m

0

Line') was held by the two Recruit Companies of Infantry Regiment 180, Engineer Company Schefold, half of 1st Battalion and 3rd Battalion complete, backed by a minimum of ten heavy machine guns.[6] To the south were more machine guns and the Recruit Company of Reserve Infantry Regiment 99. It is important to bear in mind, whenever British descriptions suggest that in slightly different circumstances taking the Second Position would have been a walkover on 1 July, that it was being manned by more than 2,000 men and numerous heavy machine guns. As will become clear, they were present in sufficient strength to wrest back the Schwaben Redoubt from the Ulstermen, so they would have been able to put up a stout defence had any such attempt been made to dislodge them.

The defensive priority clear, it is worth pausing briefly to appreciate what an appalling shock the German chain of command received when news filtered through that, as a result of the dash and determination of the men of 36th (Ulster) Division, the vital ground had been lost within one hour of the start of the attack on 1 July. The Ulstermen, who had begun moving forward while the final bombardment was still coming down and who exploited an area of dead ground, had rapidly overwhelmed the defences in sub-sectors C2 and C3 then, putting in a skilful left flanking attack, had swiftly achieved a break in at the most strongly held part of the redoubt. The unpublished history of 52 Reserve Infantry Brigade makes numerous points about this operation. This sector of the front had suffered particularly heavily during the bombardment, its wire obstacles and front line trenches having been hit by both heavy mortars and enfilade shell fire from battery positions near Auchonvillers.[7] This may have been coincidental, but it is entirely possible that this was planned and carried out carefully in order to open a route to the redoubt.

The result of all this attention was that the First Position in this area was been badly wrecked. The trenches had disappeared entirely and many of the dugouts were smashed. This meant in turn that the morale of the surviving defenders was at a low ebb. According to Reserve Infantry Regiment 99, the main break in was in sub sector C3, where the machine guns could only fire for a very short time before being overrun. The fact that over half the crews of the guns had been killed or wounded by artillery fire was a contributory factor, as was a direct hit on a captured Russian machine gun at the corner of Schwaben Redoubt that buried almost all its crew. During the course of the attack two more machine guns received direct hits and were also put of action.[8]

Despite the problem caused by the loss of a significant quantity of fire power early in the day, the sheer speed with which the remainder of the field fortification had been taken indicates that the assault was conducted with the utmost aggression and that the defenders were more than somewhat worn down by the week long bombardment. In fact, the whole redoubt fell so quickly that it suggests that at least some of the defenders were caught down in their dugouts, there to be killed by grenades or satchel charges or forced to surrender. This setback was the stuff of nightmares for the German commanders, who needed no reminding about the crucial importance of the Pozières – Serre high ground and the Schwaben Redoubt within it. As far as they were concerned, the British were now occupying the highest part of the Thiepval Plateau, able to observe far into the rear areas and to overlook all the approach routes and battery positions, especially those north of the Ancre. Immediate counter-action was essential.

They were acutely aware that Thiepval itself could now be threatened with assault from the rear, that St Pierre Divion could also fall and that subsequently Beaumont Hamel itself could become untenable, because it could then be threatened from the rear and fired on from three sides. Luckily – and to the amazement of the Germans subsequently – the orders to 36th (Ulster) Division were not to expand the break in left and right, but to push on forward towards the German Second Position south of Grandcourt. At the time none of that was known. However, it was clear that the defence faced a critical situation, though it was only one of many such problems in the Second Army sector that morning. It is instructive, therefore, to consider the way that priority was given to the defence of the designated *Schwerpunkt* on 1 July 1916, when there were many other urgent demands on manpower and resources elsewhere on the battlefield.

Once the attacks began the exact situation north of Thiepval was unclear. Telephone cables, even those buried two metres deep, had been broken in many places, so it took a while before the situation was reported accurately. One initial message to Headquarters 26th Reserve Division, for example, read, 'Our own troops are attacking in the direction of Authuille'.[9] In fact what had been seen were German prisoners being despatched rearwards by the Ulstermen. Quite soon, however, a Reserve Infantry Regiment 119 post in *Feste Alt-Württemberg* [Grandcourt Redoubt], north of the Ancre, saw that the Schwaben Redoubt had been captured.[10]

Information concerning the break in having been passed directly to Generalleutnant von Soden, he immediately gave orders for the organisation of a full scale counterattack. Then, at 9.55 am, he directed that 2nd Battalion Bavarian Reserve Infantry Regiment 8 and its attachments was to march forward from Irles and to come under command of 52 Reserve Infantry Brigade on arrival. The actual operation was to be directed by the Bavarian regimental commander, Oberstleutnant Bram.[11] Although it was relatively straightforward on the morning of 1 July to pass orders to brigades, static regiments and the artillery command centres, there were then problems with further distribution. There were, for example, no working links forward from divisional headquarters in Biefvillers or back from the temporary command post of 52 Reserve Brigade in Courcelette to Pys and Irles, where reserve elements of Bavarian Reserve Infantry Regiment 8 were located. However, Reserve Leutnant Trainé of the Württemberg Reserve Dragoons was available at Divisional Headquarters for such an eventuality and he rode forward, taking the orders in person.[12] The detailed order to Major Roesch, commanding officer 2nd Battalion, read:

'Enemy has forced his way into the Schwaben Redoubt. 2nd Battalion Bavarian Reserve Infantry Regiment 8, with 1st Machine Gun Company and one platoon of the *Musketen* Company is subordinated to 52 Reserve Infantry Brigade. The Battalion is to move immediately, dealing with any enemy encountered, to the Ancre Valley and is to advance to the Second Position via *Stallmulde* [Boom Ravine]. Sector South I to South III is to be occupied and held, with main effort on the right flank. 52 Reserve Infantry Brigade will be kept informed from here. Signed: Freiherr von Soden.'[13]

While all this staff work and redeployment was taking place, on the ground as early as 8.00 am Leutnant Arnold, 1st Recruit Company Infantry Regiment 180, had already spotted what was happening.

"From dawn on 1 July," he later reported, "I was observing in the direction of Schwaben Redoubt from Sector South II. I was immediately to the south of the Thiepval-Grandcourt road. At about 8.00 am I saw the enemy in about two company strength advancing from Schwaben Redoubt along *Schlütergraben* [Splutter Trench] and *Serbenweg* [Serbian Way]. Our timely rifle and machine gun fire (from Ilion's platoon, which was subordinated to us) meant that only isolated enemy soldiers got into *Staufenweg* [Stuff Trench]."[14]

2nd Recruit Company also began firing at leading elements of 36th (Ulster) Division from its trenches in the Second Position near Grandcourt a little later. 'At 9.00 am, the company manned their positions and fired at advancing British detachments, and others who were digging in. They pulled back towards the *Hansastellung* [Hanseatic Position] and Schwaben Redoubt at 11.00 am.'[15] Unfortunately, there was no telephone link available, so the chance of organising an immediate counter-attack went begging. However, more or less simultaneously, gunners in 26th Reserve Artillery Brigade had also observed the advance towards *Artillerie Mulde* [Battery Valley] and took immediate action in defence of the *Schwerpunkt*. British accounts often state that the stalling of the advance on the Grandcourt Line was caused by the Ulstermen running into concentrations of British fire. It is entirely feasible in the confused situation that this happened but, much more significantly, their movement was observed by Oberst Erlenbusch, commander Reserve Field Artillery Regiment 26, himself.

Erlenbusch, commanding Artillery Group Miraumont (sub groups Adolf and Beauregard) had almost a bird's eye view of proceedings from his headquarters on Hill 131, south of Miraumont. He immediately directed the fire of the heavy howitzers of 1st Battery Field Artillery Regiment 20 to engage the incursion and to maintain fire on it until further notice. There being problems with the telephone links, he then sent Gefreiter Schmid on a bicycle to sub groups Berta and Adolf bearing a simple message 'Destroy the enemy in *Artillerie Mulde*'. Dodging his way through hails of fire and shells, Schmid did precisely that, though even before his arrival the alert commander of 3rd Battery Reserve Field Artillery Regiment 26 had also seen what was happening and, on his own initiative, had his guns hauled out of their pits and turned towards the enemy break in. Once this was done and together with 2nd Battery Reserve Field Artillery Regiment 27, he began sending salvo after salvo at the Ulstermen from his location just to the north, near *Moulin Ruiné*.[16]

Given that some of the guns of the latter regiment were only 400 metres from the *Artillerie Mulde*,[17] it is small wonder that the German reports speak only of 'enemy patrols' moving forward and then digging in near the former Battery Position 723 on the western slope of the *Mulde* to obtain a degree of protection from the lacerating fire. In fact, reports from troops on the ground were even more dismissive. At 2.58 pm, for example. Reserve Infantry Regiment 99 received a situation report from Thiepval North, which had had to be relayed through Headquarters 52 Reserve Infantry Brigade. The somewhat delayed news provided its commander, Major von Fabeck, with important background information that later led him to despatch an important two-section patrol towards the Schwaben Redoubt. Almost laconically, certainly devoid of any sense of urgency, it stated, 'C1 is firmly under our control. Front line trench in C2 is in British hands. In C3 the British have broken through as far as the Schwaben Redoubt. Isolated small groups have pushed forward to the area of the *Artillerie Mulde*, Grandcourt. Apparently this is an enemy assault group which has broken through and, somewhat helplessly, is digging in on the western slope of the Artillery Hollow...'[18] In view of the fact that some of the nearby four gun batteries fired over 3,000 shells that day, the artillery effectively held the line while the counter-attack was prepared.

In addition, Generalmajor Maur, commanding 26th Reserve Artillery Brigade, was soon fully aware of the threat to the *Schwerpunkt* and the integrity of the divisional position. Under his direction, the massed fire of his guns was concentrated on the Thiepval area, almost to the exclusion of other parts of the divisional sector. When, for example, 3rd Battalion Reserve Infantry Regiment 119, defending the Beaumont Hamel area, complained to the regimental commander,

Oberstleutnant Freiherr von Ziegesar, that almost no artillery defensive fire was coming down to its front and that troops from the British 29th Division were massing once more to attack, the reply came, 'Destroy them with machine gun fire'.[19] The sheer number of machine guns and huge quantities of ammunition available to the division made this entirely feasible; and not just around Beaumont Hamel. Maur's guns maintained heavy harassing fire all day long in and around Thiepval village and wood, but his efforts were also supplemented by machine gun crews firing at everything that moved between Thiepval Wood and Schwaben Redoubt. No fewer than five guns were able to fire in enfilade forward of sub sectors C2 and C3 and one of them, Gun 9 in the so-called Brewery Position near Thiepval crossroads, fired 18,000 rounds that day.[20] Small wonder that it proved to be effectively impossible to reinforce or resupply the men who had captured the redoubt.

At 10.35 am, already about ninety minutes after the Ulstermen had secured Schwaben Redoubt, 26th Reserve Division had formally ordered 52 Reserve Infantry Brigade to plan, organise and conduct a counter-attack to regain the redoubt. It was the responsibility of Generalleutnant von Auwärter, commanding the brigade, to produce and distribute the tactical orders. The possibility of such a dangerous development had, nevertheless, been foreseen and Auwärter had received a warning order on 27 June: 'At 12.00 midday today', noted the brigade log, 'the Brigade received Operation Order No. 2453 from Division that Sector Thiepval North is to be reinforced as necessary. If the enemy gets established there, he is to be ejected at once. Further elements of 1st Battalion Bavarian Reserve Infantry Regiment 8 can be made available to replace troops moved forward out of the Intermediate or Second Position for this purpose...'[21]

This order was passed down at 2.56 pm that day by Reserve Infantry Regiment 99 to companies, complete with detailed administrative instructions for the reception, guiding and accommodation of the Bavarian company in Schwaben Redoubt.[22] Contingency plans had been laid earlier and the intention now was to counter-attack with three tactical groups, each commanded by a battalion commander of Bavarian Reserve Infantry Regiment 8, with the regimental commander, Oberstleutnant Bram, in overall command. Roesch and his men of 3rd Battalion, who had been on full alert since 5.30 am, marched off at once but, such was the weight of artillery directed against the rear areas, his advance via *Stallmulde* [Boom Ravine] was interrupted so frequently that it was not until 3.00 pm that it even neared Grandcourt and not until then did he receive his actual orders for the attack.

It was not only Roesch and his men who suffered from the friction of war. Despite the hot weather, the ground all around the Second Position was described as 'unbelievably muddy'.[23] It slowed down all movement and made even the shortest move very slow and extraordinarily strenuous for the troops involved. It was impossible to coordinate a preliminary bombardment, because not even Headquarters 26th Reserve Division could hazard a guess as to when the start time might be and, to confuse matters even more, a halt was called to the battle procedure at one point because a false report reached Group 1 stating that the British had evacuated Schwaben Redoubt. Meanwhile time passed, whilst constant artillery fire and machine gunning by British aircraft further complicated matters. Even Oberstleutnant Bram himself had his problems. The only way he could get forward was on foot, it being impossible to move any other way that morning. He had received his orders from Division at 11.20 am, at which time he was still in Pys. He then had to link up with Generalleutnant von Auwärter in Courcelette for a short briefing. This he managed at 12.15 pm but, moving at best speed, it was still 2.00 pm before he and his adjutant, Oberleutnant Grabinger, reached *Feste Staufen* and he could begin to pull the threads of the attack together.

General von Auwärter planned to tackle the operation as follows:

Group 1, commanded by Major Prager, commanding officer 1st Battalion Bavarian Reserve Infantry Regiment 8, and comprising 1st Battalion staff, 2nd Company Bavarian Reserve Infantry Regiment 8, 1st and 2nd Recruit Companies Infantry Regiment 180, Engineer Company Schefold and 1st Machine Gun Company Reserve Infantry Regiment 119, was to assault Schwaben Redoubt from the right [northern] sector of the Second Position.

Group 2, commanded by Major Beyerkohler, commanding officer 3rd Battalion Bavarian Reserve Infantry Regiment 8, and comprising 3rd Battalion staff, 3rd, 11th and 12th Companies Bavarian Reserve Infantry Regiment 8 and Machine Gun Sharpshooter Detachment 89 was to assault Schwaben Redoubt from Point 153.

Group 3, commanded by Major Roesch and comprising 3rd Battalion Bavarian Reserve Infantry Regiment 8 complete, was to attack Schwaben Redoubt via *Feste Staufen*.[24]

The plan was soon to be overtaken by events. It was not long before the bad news reached Headquarters XIV Reserve Corps. Generalleutnant von Stein immediately directed that the attack be expedited and, at 10.45 am, an amended divisional operation order was being digested and forwarded by 52 Reserve Infantry Brigade: 'The Corps Commander has ordered that Schwaben Redoubt is to be recaptured at all costs. To that end the arrival of 2nd Battalion Bavarian Reserve Infantry Regiment 8 is not to be awaited. Rather the attack is to be launched with forces from the Second Position.'[25] Five minutes later, Generalleutnant von Auwärter issued his own amended orders to Bavarian Reserve Infantry Regiment 8.

'The British have forced their way into the Hanseatic Position and Schwaben Redoubt. Major Prager, with Companies Schmeißer, Schnürlen, Hudelmeier and Engineer Company Schofeld, together with 1st Machine Gun Company of Reserve Infantry Regiment 119 and Sharp Shooter Troop 89, is to conduct this attack from the right flank of the Second Position. Major Beyerköhler will advance on Schwaben Redoubt from Hill 153 with three companies.'[26]

Formulating the orders was the simple part of the proceedings. Distributing them was another matter altogether. Runners had to be employed, which cost a significant amount of time. Even worse, there was no communication between the different assault groups and more time was then lost as the troops moved with great difficulty towards their start lines. As has been mentioned, it took Oberstleutnant Bram three hours to reach *Feste Staufen*, but that hardly mattered because by 2.00 pm none of the assault groups were in position. All this time brigade and divisional headquarters were in complete ignorance of what was happening and the hours went by in an atmosphere of terrible nervous tension. To make matters worse, repeated attacks were launched against Reserve Infantry Regiment 99. Ammunition, especially grenades, was running short, casualties were mounting and Major Fabeck sent repeated requests for support or positive action against his open northern flank.

Struggling forward, 2nd Battalion Bavarian Reserve Infantry Regiment 8 suffered severe casualties in *Stallmulde* and became scattered. So confused was the situation that 8th Company found itself split off and arrived at Headquarters 51 Reserve Infantry Brigade. From there Generalleutnant von Wundt despatched it, together with forty engineers, to reinforce St Pierre Divion. Established at last in *Feste Staufen*, Oberstleutnant Bram's attempts to grip the situation were made harder due to battlefield obscuration; but urgings from on high, reports arriving and his own observations, made the overriding need for speed clear. He decided that there would be more chance of success if he launched the attack with the forces on hand rather than waiting for all to arrive; and so he directed that the counter-attack was to begin at 4.00 pm. Fortunately he was able to speak personally to Major Beyerkohler, commanding Group 2, and also Hauptmann Graf Preysing, from Reserve Field Artillery Regiment 26, who had the unenviable task of coordinating the artillery support for the counter-attack.[27] However, Major Roesch did not receive his orders until 3.00 pm and those for Major Prager were delayed until 3.45 pm. The net result was that a series of sequential attacks eventually went in but that the hoped for synergy was not achieved.[28]

Gradually, despite all the delays, counter action began to gather momentum. Preysing called for a major concentration of shell fire just after 3.00 pm against the Ulstermen in *Artillerie Mulde*. This, supplemented by the fire of the guns of 1st Machine Gun Company Reserve Infantry Regiment 119 under Hauptmann Mehl and rifle fire from the Recruit Companies south of Grandcourt, finally proved too much. The scattered elements of 36th (Ulster) Division pulled back in disorder towards Schwaben Redoubt, but very few made it through the hail of fire. Major Prager, commanding Group 1, had also been observing developments and decided to take the initiative. He issued an order at 3.15 pm to 2nd Recruit Company Infantry Regiment 180 to attack the *Hansa Stellung* [Hanseatic Position], running north from the Schwaben Redoubt, at 3.40pm. This duly happened and the recruits set off in two waves to clear it. Originally 1st Recruit Company was also to have participated. 'The company had been ordered to join in the assault on the *Hansastellung* but, at about 3.13 pm, a counter order arrived cancelling this. The company moved to occupy its previous position; that is to say with its left flank on *Staufenweg* [Stuff Trench].'[29] To the south Hauptmann Wurmb, commanding 3rd Company and part of Major Beyerkohler's Group 2, observed what was happening and ordered his own men to advance. He was followed by 11th and 12th Companies under Reserve Leutnants Schiller and Klug respectively.

Unfortunately, yet another false report was received stating that Schwaben Redoubt had already been recaptured. This prejudiced effective artillery support, as did the advanced start time. A heavy price was paid, especially by 2nd Recruit Company, which came under sustained machine gun and mortar fire from the Ulstermen as they crossed open ground on the way towards the *Hansa Stellung*. In his subsequent report its company commander, Leutnant Scheurlen, wrote:

"After the first wave had crossed the Artillery Hollow, Grandcourt, the second wave left the trenches. Although the right half of the first wave succeeded in forcing a way into the *Hansa Stellung*, the left half had to wait until the support of the second wave enabled it to get further forward. Despite heavy rifle and machine gun fire, this part of the company also succeeded in working its way forward to within one hundred metres of the *Hansa Stellung*, albeit at the cost of heavy casualties (twenty three killed and a hundred wounded). In so doing, Offizierstellvertreter Rädle (who was severely wounded in the upper arm by a shell splinter), together with his platoon, took twenty prisoners and two Lewis guns. Simultaneously, Unteroffizier Stumpf and four men (Gessmann, Reng Georg, Bregizer and Dötlinger) launched an assault on about twenty British soldiers who were attempting to hold out in shell holes in front of the Hanseatic Position. He captured one officer and two men. The remainder were killed."[30]

In other words, despite losses amounting to sixty percent of the troops engaged, this attack achieved very little, though a few prisoners were taken and two Lewis guns were also captured and delivered to divisional headquarters later. The advance of Group 2 south of the Grandcourt – Thiepval road and astride *Staufen Graben* [Stuff Trench] was also soon in difficulty. Under machine gun and mortar fire, losses began to mount. Reserve Leutnant Englehardt was killed within the first few metres by a shell splinter and a few minutes later both Leutnants Klug and Schiller also fell, the latter together with all three of his platoon commanders and twenty other ranks. Slowly and painfully the survivors pushed forward but, despite numerous acts of heroism and severe losses, progress was slow and was soon threatening to grind to a standstill. Held up by the fire of a mortar and a machine gun, Unteroffizier Haas, 3rd Company, in the first of a series of extraordinarily gallant acts that day, led his section in a skilful minor action which knocked out both weapons and opened the route forward as far as the junction between *Staufen Graben* and *Lachweg*.[31] In a separate action, Siegmann's section of 3rd Company pushed forward half right, was joined by Reserve Vizefeldwebel Stolz and succeeded in capturing Captain Craig, 11th Battalion Royal Irish Rifles, who was a British MP, together with a sergeant.[32] There, however, for the moment the attack stalled, under small arms fire from various different directions. Generalleutnant von Soden, himself under pressure, then despatched an order demanding fresh impetus be given to the attack.[33] Relayed at 5.02 pm via *Feste Zollern* by 52 Reserve Infantry Brigade, it read,

'The Adjutant [Oberleutnant Grabinger], 3rd Battalion Bavarian Reserve Infantry Regiment 8, is to despatch, immediately, two patrols bearing written orders to Oberstleutnant Bram in Stuff Redoubt, stating that the Division expects and expressly orders Bavarian Reserve Infantry Regiment 8: to recapture the entirety of Schwaben Redoubt, to occupy it and to bring relief to the hard-pressed parts of Reserve Infantry Regiment 99. This is a direct order.'[34]

Although the recapture of the redoubt was uppermost in Soden's mind, it was far from the only issue he had to consider that day. The commitment of virtually all the forces which had been manning the Second Position mean that it was now vulnerable to a renewed attack. Fortunately, one of the first steps taken by Headquarters XIV Reserve Corps that day was to order forward 1st and 2nd Battalions Infantry Regiment 185 and to subordinate them to 26th Reserve Division. Marching to the front via Frémicourt, Beugnâtre and Favreuil to divisional headquarters in Biefvillers, 1st Battalion, commanded by Hauptmann Leonhard, was subsequently directed to continue to Courcelette and to come under command of 52 Reserve Infantry Brigade and thus to provide a welcome reinforcement to that hard pressed formation. Temporarily, the division retained control of 2nd Battalion which, together with Machine Gun Platoons 311 and 559, was despatched to a holding area near Pys.[35]

Forward in *Feste Staufen*, Soden's message left no doubt as to what had to be done and Oberstleutnant Bram, making best use of his resources as reinforcements trickled in, managed to make further progress during the next two hours, though in places the situation was very precarious and the advance was held up repeatedly by the dogged resistance put up by the Ulstermen. As part of the effort to inject more momentum into the counter-attack, Major Beyerkohler moved up behind his assault groups but, in a clash with small British pocket of resistance, he was shot dead and command over this part of the attack devolved on Hauptmann Wurm. By approximately 7.00 pm the group in contact here was sheltering in a series of shell holes left and right of the main trench. 3rd Company, now commanded by Vizefeldwebel Georgi, was reduced to about forty men and there were, in addition, small groups from 11th and 12th Companies, led by Vizefeldwebel Zeißner and Offizierstellvertreter Buckreis respectively. All the rest were pinned down by enemy fire, killed or wounded.[36] The fire of the Ulstermen was intense. Wurm's batman was hit and wounded while standing right next to him then, a few moments later, one of his sentries, lifting his head to look over a bank, was shot straight through the forehead and killed instantly.[37]

At more or less this time a reinforcement of about seventy men of 7th Company arrived, having been sent forward by Oberstleutnant Bram; but initially it too was unable to push forward along *Lachweg* due to the weight of fire being brought down. On arrival Hauptmann Wurmb took them under command, adding them to the remaining forty men of his own company and a handful from 11th and 12th Companies under Offizierstellvertreter Buckreis. Orders also went out at about this time to Major Prager to direct 1st Recruit Company Infantry Regiment 180 to add its weight to the attack. Leutnant Arnold, wounded during the attack, produced a brief report about it subsequently.

"At 7.00 pm, the company received the order to move to the *Hansastellung* Position and from there, together with Company Hudelmeier and the Bavarian troops, to capture Schwaben Redoubt...The company advanced in three waves in the direction of the *Hansastellung*: First wave, Leutnant Arnold; second wave Unteroffizier Seitz; third wave Leutnant Schnürlen. There was one hundred metre spacing between the waves. The first wave crossed the Artillery Hollow, Grandcourt but, as it moved up onto the heights it received such a hail of machine gun and rifle fire that a further advance was out of the question for the time being. As the third wave appeared, heavy enemy artillery fire came down, causing the company very severe casualties. Leutnant Schnürlen was killed so, despite being wounded in the arm, [I] took over the company, rallying the remnants in the *Artillerie Mulde*. Leutnant Arnold then pulled back to Grandcourt, having ordered Unteroffizier Weida to lead the remainder of the company back to their former dugouts once it went dark. At 10.30 pm Leutnant Arnold returned to the company and led them up to the *Hansastellung*."

Once again piecemeal action had failed to achieve the aim of recapturing the redoubt and the situation threatened to become desperate unless the *Schwerpunkt* could be secured that evening. The pressure on the entire chain of command, but especially on Oberstleutnant Bram, was intense. At 7.39 pm an earlier situation report he had written arrived at Headquarters 52 Reserve brigade.

"The enemy is occupying an area astride *Auwärtergraben*, both sides of the road Thiepval-Grandcourt, front facing east. The left wing of our assault force is in the area of *Bulgarengraben* [Bulgarian Trench]. Fresh orders have been sent to Group Prager to attack Schwaben Redoubt from the northeast, but there is still no contact with this group. The whereabouts of the 6th, 7th and 8th Companies Bavarian Reserve Infantry Regiment 8 are unknown, as is that of the staff of the 2nd Battalion. There are no reserves left to assault Schwaben Redoubt. Thirty men of the Recruit Company have been given the mission of establishing contact between the 1st and 3rd Battalions Bavarian Reserve Infantry Regiment 8. Support is requested.'[38]

Very high stakes were involved; but at this time Major Fabeck, commanding Reserve Infantry Regiment 99, intervened and, despite his incomplete knowledge of the situation, his own serious losses and the fact that his men were heavily engaged from 6.00 pm beating off further strong British attacks against Thiepval Centre and South,[39] he despatched a strong fighting patrol in the direction of Schwaben Redoubt. The war diary of 52 Reserve Infantry Brigade describes what happened.

"The attack on Schwaben Redoubt stalls short of the position. A patrol, comprising two sections of 14th Company Reserve Infantry Regiment 99, commanded by Offizierstellvertreter Lunau, has the mission from the regiment to establish how far forward the British have penetrated. Without further orders, Offizierstellvertreter Lunau launches an attack on the British who have captured a section of the right flank of the Intermediate Position approximately 150 metres wide. In so doing he captures an enemy machine gun and clears the trench of enemy. He presses on, ejects the enemy from the *Lachweg* and *Martinspfad* [Martin's Path] and advances to the *Wohngraben* [Accommodation Trench] of Schwaben Redoubt. In so doing he captures a further three machine guns and a machine gun sledge. One of these machine guns had held up several Bavarian companies for a number of hours, preventing them from advancing. The attack of 14th Company Reserve Infantry Regiment 99 cleared the way to Schwaben Redoubt for the Bavarians."[40]

In all, Lunau, aided by Vizefeldwebel Koch and Kriegsfreiwilliger Pfeifer in particular, succeeded in clearing the enemy out of 1,100 metres of trench.[41] Meanwhile Hauptmann Wurmb, following a quick appreciation of the ground to his front, ordered Offizierstellvertreter Buckreis to carry out a flanking movement to divert the attention of the British defenders while he devised a way of pushing on up the trench. The timely arrival of a gun of Machine Gun Sharpshooter Detachment 89, commanded by Unteroffizier Bauer, eased the situation by firing at and destroying a sandbag barrier at almost pointblank range, whilst others present threw grenades. With more machine guns coming into action on the German side, pressure built up on the British guns. Finally, by about 8.45 pm, with a total of three extra guns under Offizierstellvertreter Bernd of the Sharpshooter Detachment also in action, a handful of junior NCOs charged each British machine gun nest and killed or captured their crews. Gefreiters Kerndl and Bollwein of the Sharpshooter Detachment, together with Unteroffiziers Haas and Klein of 3rd Company, all received the Bavarian Gallantry Medal in Gold, the highest award for gallantry for non-commissioned ranks.

While this action was unfolding and remaining in close touch with Hauptmann Graf Preysing, Bram finally settled on a plan to complete the recapture of Schwaben Redoubt. General von Auwärter, linking with the divisional commander and also Generalmajor Maur, finally informed Bram at 9.27 pm that he could expect a one hour bombardment by every battery within range from 10.00 pm.[42] Right on cue, Maur's guns brought down fire for effect on the redoubt and, on the stroke of 11.00 pm, the Bavarian Reserve Regiment 8 survivors, commanded by Hauptmann Wurmb, combining with a group Lunau's party from Reserve Infantry Regiment 99, attacked in the pitch black night. Sending a twenty man party commanded by Leutnant Zimmermann to clear round the redoubt anticlockwise,[43] Wurmb himself took charge of another group and began to work his way round clockwise to complete the circle. It was at this point that he linked up with Lunau.

Even then the numbers of German soldiers were very small, so both Wurmb and Zimmermann had their men fire a great deal and shout loudly to convey the impression that they were in fact much stronger than they really were. It certainly worked. Singing *Die Wacht am Rhein* loudly, the two further depleted groups (Zimmermann was down to five men)[44] linked up at around 11.30 pm, but before then the Ulstermen had had enough. Isolated and under constant fire all day, with ammunition running out and little prospect of reinforcement or replenishment, they retired on a broad front. Having cleared out the perimeter of Schwaben Redoubt and realising what was happening, Wurmb's men poured fire at the remnants of the 36th (Ulster) Division as they pulled back to Thiepval Wood and then went into hasty defence.[45] In retaking the redoubt they captured about one hundred prisoners and numerous machine guns. 'The British corpses of 700 courageous members of the Ulster Division littered the Redoubt, every foot of which was soaked in blood.'[46]

Rigid concentration on the *Schwerpunkt* by all concerned within 26th Reserve Division had enabled them to remain focussed on the need to stabilise the situation, to exploit to the full the limited means of command and control at their disposal and to overcome their numerous communications problems. It had been a desperately hard fight, but they had prevailed. Not to have done so could have spelled disaster for the defence. As it was, a vital position had been retained and time had been gained to permit reinforcements to flow in and be deployed. Both Bram and Wurmb were awarded the Knight's Cross of the Military Max Josef Order for their performance that day.

South of the River

While the crisis at Schwaben Redoubt was being resolved, French success south of the Somme in the XVII Corps sector was causing a major problem of a different kind. Ironically, part of the reason was the designation of the sector north of the Somme as the Second Army *Schwerpunkt*. In order to give it the necessary priority, the forces south of the river, including of course Bavarian Reserve Infantry Regiment 8 as part of 10th Bavarian Infantry Division, had been stripped out and sent north. This made an already thinly manned area even more vulnerable to attack. At 10.00 am, two hours after the British attack against XIV Reserve Corps, 2nd and 9th Colonial Divisions, together with 61st Division of the French Sixth Army, attacked along a frontage stretching from the Somme south to Foucaucourt. The defending formations, which had been severely weakened by the bombardment, could put up little resistance and in less than an hour Frise, Dompierre and Becquincourt had been captured.

The remaining units of 121st Infantry Division fought on desperately, but it was not long before they too faced being outflanked and surrounded. If that had occurred a French breakthrough would have been almost inevitable. Fortunately for the integrity of the defence, at the very last moment the divisional commander, Generalmajor von Ditfurth, was able to assemble the last of his reserves and commit them forward. It was a close run thing and came too late to save the villages in the forward area. Nevertheless, the French were held for the time being between Herbécourt and Assevillers. The latter place was in fact occupied for a time by French troops, but an aggressive counter-attack by 1st Battalion Infantry Regiment 60 and some elements of Reserve Infantry Regiment 7, preceded by a short, but well directed artillery fire plan, succeeded in ejecting the Senegalese troops once more. This was the only successful counter-attack on1 July, but it did enable the defence south of the river to keep a toe hold on the Second Position.

Despite all these most strenuous efforts, the overall position south of the river was very dangerous. The French gains meant that a major threat to the southern flank of XIV Reserve Corps now existed. By the afternoon of 1 July the advance guards of two divisions that had been in reserve had force marched forward and were beginning to arrive in the area. They were ordered to counter-attack in the Estrées – Assevillers sector, but the few units on hand were too exhausted for it to be feasible. Instead – and probably more efficiently – these troops were used to buttress the defensive line and to relieve the hardest pressed. Having carried out an appreciation of the situation, General von Pannewitz, commander XVII Corps, forwarded a plan to Headquarters Second Army on 2 July. He demonstrated that it would be impossible to launch successful counter-action without considerable artillery support and of that there was no early prospect. However, if nothing was done it would soon be impossible for 121st Infantry Division to hold its positions.

His proposal was to withdraw from the area west of Barleux and Biaches, but to hold firmly onto bridgeheads and to defend along the line Belloy – Barleux – Estrées. In his view this would prevent the entire front from collapsing and could also be used later as the start line for a major counter–attack. Pannewitz made it clear that unless a decision was made quickly the rapidly deteriorating situation could spiral out of control. Given that a renewed French thrust against Péronne was underway on a four kilometre front, this was far from alarmist and, had it been expanded on either flank, his warning could have become a reality. Faced with a critical situation and in consultation with Generalmajor Grünert, his chief of staff, General von Below decided to grant permission. At 5.00 pm Headquarters Second Army issued this order. It was extremely controversial and led directly to Grünert's sacking by General von Falkenhayn:

"In view of the report by Headquarters XVII Corps that the Second Position of 121st Infantry Division cannot be held in the long term, this order is issued: The troops currently manning the Second Position are to remain there as long as possible and at least until darkness falls. Fresh troops are not to be sent to this position, rather the available reserves are to be deployed immediately to occupy the bridgeheads to the west of Péronne and Barleux, to link up with 11th Infantry Division and to establish a stop line as far as Barleux. The Army Headquarters objective is to defend this new line at all costs, to exploit the time available while the enemy artillery is being redeployed to move forward infantry and artillery reserves and later to launch a counter-attack from the line Barleux –Estrées."[47]

Discussing this later with the benefit of hindsight, General Herman von Kuhl, then chief of staff Sixth Army, simply remarked,

> "The French attack along the Somme and to the south of it enjoyed considerably more success … The French succeeded in overrunning the German positions just to the north of the Somme as far as Hardecourt and then southwards as far as Fay, that is to say on a fifteen kilometre frontage. Unfortunately, German troops had to be withdrawn south of the Somme in the direction of Péronne. This broad break in made it possible for the French to fire in enfilade from the southern bank of the Somme to the northern side and to create a difficult situation for the German troops located there."[48]

The immediate consequence was that German formations north of the Somme had to extend their position eastwards to Cléry, where they linked up once more with XVII Corps. Of course Pannewitz and Below had had little choice in the matter. They had been starved of manpower and other resources and it was never their intention for the withdrawal to become permanent. However, Falkenhayn, with recent memories of the problems he had faced at Verdun from French forces on the left bank of the Meuse and reluctant to be diverted from the priority he had given to operations there, was incensed. His reaction was instant and furious, though an examination of his memoirs would not lead the reader to that conclusion. He certainly downplayed the potential risks south of the river and shifted the blame squarely onto Below and Second Army.

> "… the whole of the German first line from Fay to south of Hardecourt, north of the Somme was lost. In several places the attack penetrated the second line. Even in this sector there was no question of the intended breakthrough having succeeded. The position became more serious when the local commander allowed himself to be persuaded by the French successes to evacuate the German second line between the Estrées – Foucaucourt road and the Somme, where it was still in our hands, in order to facilitate the withdrawal of the troops in the line Biaches – Barleux – Belloy – Estrées, who, it is true, had suffered severely from the enemy fire, and their relief from the main reserves sent up from *OHL*. This allowed the enemy during

the first few weeks of the battle to take us in the flank on the north bank, which was very serious for the German troops there, who were heavily engaged to their front, and was of great importance for the further advance of the enemy. This uncertainty as to the way to conduct a defensive battle was quickly overcome."[49]

Apart from the operational aspects of his reaction, it is also important to bear in mind Falkenhayn's defensive philosophy. This was stated by the German official historian as, 'The first principle of positional warfare has to be not to yield a single foot of ground and if a foot of ground is lost, to launch an immediate counter-attack with all forces, down to the last man'.[50] Falkenhayn's personal view was that, 'The principle that the line apportioned to troops for defence was to be maintained at all costs, and if lost to be retaken, was [always to be] rigidly preserved'.[51] In a further expansion of this line of reasoning concerning the voluntary giving up of ground, he also wrote, 'If [an individual] is left a possibility of interpreting regulations concerning retirement, then the ordinary mortal is readily inclined in the hell of a modern battle to interpret them in a way that may indeed offer him salvation, but which is ruinous for the whole front. It gives rise to voluntary surrender or premature retirement, which it is also impossible to stop at the main line of resistance.'[52]

So much for the underlying philosophy. Faced with a *fait accompli*, Falkenhayn drove to Headquarters Second Army and, in a brief but stormy meeting, removed Generalmajor Grünert from his post and ordered his replacement by Oberst Loßberg, who had rescued a highly dangerous situation at Third Army in Champagne the previous year. Most of those in senior appointments and qualified to judge took a dim view of these decisions. Crown Prince Rupprecht made his feelings quite clear in a diary entry.

"Quite apart from the fact that it is inappropriate to change a Chief of Staff at a moment of supreme crisis, such a measure also amounts to lack of confidence in the relevant commander, who does in fact bear the ultimate responsibility for any decisions which are taken. This, in turn, diminishes the commander in the eyes of his subordinates. As I have already noted, the blame for what happened lies at the door of *OHL* itself, which did not arrange in time for reinforcements to be allocated to Second Army."[53]

Rupprecht's chief of staff, Generalleutnant von Kuhl, was still more scathing about Falkenhayn, even weeks later, as this private diary entry dated 30 July shows.

"This morning at First Army Headquarters in Bourlon Below was very put out at the sacking of Grünert, whom he valued very much. The measure was of course directed at him. He is completely convinced that the withdrawal of troops south of the Somme was correct. By those means time was gained, because it would have taken the French thirty six hours to redeploy their artillery. That would have enabled us to reorganise and ready ourselves and we could have maintained our positions ever since. North of the Somme everything is still being deployed in bits and pieces and even now newly arriving troops are being rushed to the front in trucks; all of this the consequence of insufficient resources. Falkenhayn has never conceded the point and always countered that Sixth Army could not make that judgement whenever we stated that we were firmly convinced that we were not going to be attacked."[54]

Change of Army Chief of Staff

Irrespective of any reservations among his subordinates, the decision stood, so Loßberg was summoned and drove through the night for a meeting with Falkenhayn at Mézières. He arrived at 1.00 am on 3 July and at once had a meeting with Falkenhayn, who received him from his bed. Loßberg presented him with a long list of requirements, including large scale reinforcements, additional artillery, aircraft and other supplies. He then went on to stress that it was essential for all attacks at Verdun to be stopped immediately. According to Loßberg, once he had pressed the matter, Falkenhayn finally shook hands with him in agreement. However, Loßberg later wrote in his memoirs, 'General von Falkenhayn did not keep to his agreement. Instead he continued the offensive at Verdun right up until he was relieved as Chief of the General Staff of the Field Army on 28 August 1916.'[55]

In this assessment he was quite correct. Although it is true that, in the wake of the German attack towards Fort Souville on 11 July, Falkenhayn ordered Fifth Army to go over to the defensive, in fact this did not happen.[56] News arrived, for example, at Headquarters Army Group Gallwitz on 1 August that another major attack had been carried out at Verdun, that half of the Souville Ravine had been captured and 800 prisoners taken. General der Artillerie Gallwitz commented, 'So the pressure to go on attacking is still there'.[57] As late as 20 August Gallwitz was again noting that at Verdun, where the relationship between the German Crown Prince and his chief of staff, Generalleutnant von Knobelsdorff, had deteriorated so badly that the latter was given the Oakleaf to his Pour le Mérite and moved to command X Corps, the last straw had been continuing insistence by the latter (who was the *de facto* commander of the army) to carry on the attacks between Fleury and Souville.[58] Then, the following day, 21 August, only one week before the end of Falkenhayn's tenure, *OHL* issued a directive stating, 'The overall situation makes it absolutely necessary to maintain the impression on the enemy in the Meuse area that the Germans have not given up on the offensive there and that it is being continued systematically.'[59]

Arriving at St Quentin, Loßberg then threw himself with his usual vigour into mastering the situation and ensuring that his headquarters staff was strengthened and made thoroughly aware of his requirements and working methods.[60] The key man for the remainder of the German defensive effort until the battle died away was now in post. He always demanded and expected much of his subordinates, but he granted all his branch chiefs automatic access to himself day and night,[61] did away with unnecessary, time consuming, staff meetings and briefings and drove nobody harder than himself. He had no sleep during the night 2/3 July other than in the back of the car as he was driven north then, once he arrived at St Quentin, he embarked almost immediately on a full tour of inspection of the front, followed by endless other commitments. General von Below was ill at the time, so Loßberg undertook this tour personally, issuing guidance, instructions and orders wherever he went. It was a full two days later before he lay down to sleep.

'From the morning of 3 July my duties demanded a great deal of work. Following the night drive from Vouziers via Mézières to St Quentin, I next got to bed for three hours during the night of 5/6 July. My nightly rest throughout the entire Battle of the Somme was very seldom much longer. However, I had the ability to snatch naps during any spare moment; I could even catch up on lost sleep during car journeys. My strong constitution enabled me easily to survive all the strain, which lasted for months.'[62]

The 'great deal of work' which kept Loßberg and the higher staffs at full stretch during most of July comprised for the most part in rushing forward as soon as they arrived all and any reinforcements, often at regimental or even battalion level, to plug gaps in the line. There was, however, one very important exception. Having been outflanked, Fricourt, had to be evacuated early on 2 July. In turn this meant that enormous pressure built up on Reserve Infantry Regiment 110, 28th Reserve Division, which was defending La Boisselle. After heavy fighting, this village too was lost a day later. This was a crisis of the first order because, if further ground had been yielded and if what was effectively the southern shoulder of the vital Thiepval – Serre ridge also gave way, there was a real threat to the integrity of the defensive *Schwerpunkt*.

At the tactical level, Generalleutnant von Soden reacted immediately. At 5.10 pm on 2 July, 26th Reserve Division issued an order by telephone to its left forward regiment. 'Reserve Infantry Regiment 110 is pulling back via La Boisselle. Infantry Regiment 180 is to hold Ovillers to the last man.'[63] This was followed by the arrival of a written order at 9.30 pm. 'Infantry Regiment 180 is to defend

Ovillers to the last man. It is not to take a single step backwards from its current positions without a written order from division ...'[64] At Headquarters Second Army there was equal concern about this latest threat to the vital ground and, so as to reinforce the *Schwerpunkt*, Loßberg took a bold decision. Concentrating on this problem and temporarily to the exclusion of other pressing requests for reinforcement, on 3 July he deployed the outstanding 3rd Guards Division in its entirety to the Ovillers – Pozières area. There, during the coming days, the élite Lehr Infantry, Fusilier Guards and Grenadier 9 Regiments suffered a huge number of casualties; but they held on and averted disaster.

The priority thus afforded to the vital ground is in sharp contrast to the position adopted by General Haig, commander of the BEF, as recorded in his diary following a tense meeting with General Joffre during the afternoon of 3 July.

'Joffre pointed out the importance of our getting Thiepval Hill ... I was considering the desirability of pressing my attack on Longueval ... at this General Joffre exploded in a fit of rage. 'He could not approve of it'. He 'ordered me to attack Thiepval and Pozières' ... The truth is the poor man cannot argue, nor can he easily read a map.'[65]

On the contrary, the fact of the matter is that, after two years of directing major battles against the German army, Joffre had developed clear ideas about what was considered important by his enemies. He definitely could 'read a map', could spot a *Schwerpunkt* when he saw one, but the command relationships meant that he did not have the power to *order* General Haig to do anything. The result of this was that for the remainder of the battle the French and British armies effectively conducted independent operations. There were only rare exceptions, one coming on 15 September. For all kinds of reasons even basic coordination was poor so, as a result, the Allies generated very little in the way of synergy. The German defenders, whose greatest fear was a repetition on the Somme of the costly battles of attrition around the Butte de Tahure in Champagne in autumn 1915, had thus been let off the hook by the British. Instead of having continually to find relieving formations to defend the *Schwerpunkt*, Second (later First) Army was able to leave its defence throughout the summer and early autumn to 26th Reserve Division. At a time when elsewhere a division per day was being worn out, 2nd Battalion Infantry Regiment 180, for example, remained in the line at Thiepval for no less than eight and a half weeks.[66]

This decision was arguably the greatest mistake General Haig made during the entire battle. To shift the emphasis to the British right flank simply played into the Germans' hands, especially when much of the fighting took place in a wooded part of the battlefield that neutralised many of the attackers' advantages and favoured the defence. It took the British army three months to fight its way up to Thiepval village from the southeast and, even when that place fell, intense fighting for possession of Schwaben Redoubt continued. In the final battles no fewer than fifty *Musketen* teams were deployed to try to prevent its capture. Joffre knew what he was talking about.

Notes

1. The name of this field fortification was derived from the fact that it was impossible to dig in the swampy ground by the Ancre, so the initial defences were based on the construction of stockades built from hundreds of tree trunks. Prior to the opening of the 1916 battle most of them had been replaced by concrete constructions, of which not a trace remains today.
2. This was located high above Beaumont Hamel village and named after the commander of Reserve Infantry Regiment 99 in 1914, Oberst Grall.
3. *Kriegsarchiv Munich HS 1984.*
4. *Kriegsarchiv Munich* HS 2205 Bram *Anteil des Bayer. Res.Inf.Regts. Nr. 8 an der Somme-Schlacht* p. 4.
5. *Hauptstaatsarchiv Stuttgart* M410 Bü 260 *Geschichte der 52. Reserve-Infanterie-Brigade II. Teil.*
6. *Kriegsarchiv Munich* HS 2205 Bram p. 5.
7. *Hauptstaatsarchiv Stuttgart* M410 Bü 260 *Geschichte der 52. Reserve-Infanterie-Brigade II. Teil.*
8. Müller History Reserve Infantry Regiment 99 pp. 103–104.
9. Wurmb History Bavarian Reserve Infantry Regiment 8 p. 68.
10. Soden Freiherr von *Die 26. (Württembergische) Reserve-Division im Weltkrieg 1914–1918 I. Teil* p. 110.
11. *Kriegsarchiv Munich* HS 2205 Bram p. 9.
12. Klett Fritz History Württ. Reserve Dragoner Regiment im Weltkrieg p. 100.
13. *Hauptstaatsarchiv Stuttgart* M410 Bu 239 *KTB 52. Reserve-Infanterie-Bde.*
14. *Kriegsarchiv Munich* BRIR8 Bd 4 *Bericht über die Tätigkeit der 1. Rekr. Komp. 180 am 1. und 2. Juli 1916.*
15. *ibid.*
16. Klaus History RFAR 26 p. 49.
17. Moos History RFAR 27 p. 4.
18. Hauptstaatsarchiv Stuttgart M410 Bü 239 This is a good example of the extreme difficulty faced by commanders of the period, who frequently had to make important decisions based on incomplete or out of date information.
19. *Hauptstaatsarchiv Stuttgart* M407 Bü 42/103 *III. Reserve Infantry Regiment 119 Gefechtsbericht.*
20. Müller *op. cit.* p. 112.
21. *Hauptstaatsarchiv Stuttgart* M43/19 *RIR 99 Gefechtsbericht für die Zeit vom 24.6–30.6.16.*
22. *ibid.*
23. *Kriegsarchiv Munich* HS 1984 Wurmb *Erinnerungen an die Eroberung der Feste Schwaben.*
24. *Kriegsarchiv Munich* HS 2205 Bram p. 7.
25. *Hauptstaatsarchiv Stuttgart* M410 Bü 239.

26. *ibid.*
27. Wurmb *op. cit.* p. 70.
28. *Hauptstaatsarchiv Stuttgart* M410 Bu 239.
29. *Kriegsarchiv Munich* BRIR8 Bd 4 *Gefechtsericht d. 1. R. Komp. 180 v. 1.7.16.*
30. *Kriegsarchiv Munich* BRIR8 Bd 4 *Bericht über die Tätigkeit der 1. Rekr. Komp. 180 am 1. und 2. Juli 1916.*
31. *Kriegsarchiv Munich* HS 1984 Wurmb.
32. Stosch *Somme-Nord I. Teil* p. 41.
33. Soden Freiherr von *op. cit.* p. 111.
34. *Hauptstaatsarchiv Stuttgart* M410 Bü 239.
35. Mücke History Infantry Regiment 185 p. 26.
36. Stosch *Somme-Nord I. Teil* p. 42.
37. *Kriegsarchiv Munich* HS 1984 Wurmb.
38. Hauptstaatsarchiv Stuttgart M410 Bü 239
39. *Hauptstaatsarchiv Stuttgart* M410 Bü 239.
40. Hauptstaatsarchiv Stuttgart M410 Bü 239
41. Müller: History RIR 99 p. 104
42. *Hauptstaatsarchiv Stuttgart* M410 Bü 239.
43. *Kriegsarchiv Munich* HS 2205 Bram p. 12.
44. *ibid.* p. 12.
45. *Hauptstaatsarchiv Stuttgart* M410 Bü 239.
46. *Hauptstaatsarchiv Stuttgart* M410 Bü 260 *Geschichte der 52. Reserve-Infanterie-Brigade II. Teil.*
47. Grote *Somme* p. 43.
48. Kuhl *Der Weltkrieg 1914–1918 Band I* p. 492.
49. Falkenhayn *General Headquarters* p. 265.
50. GOH p. 355
51. Falkenhayn *op. cit.*p 36.
52. *ibid.*p 37.
53. Rupprecht Kronprinz *In Treue Fest* p. 495.
54. Kuhl BA/MA RH61/50652 *Persönliches Kriegstagebuch* pp. 19–20.
55. Loßberg Fritz von *op. cit.* p. 215.
56. Kabisch *Somme* pp. 54–55.
57. Gallwitz *Erleben im Westen* p. 75.
58. *ibid.* p. 90.
59. Gehre *Die deutsche Kräfteverteiung* p. 31.
60. The headquarters was strengthened by the arrival of one Hauptmann Manstein, amongst others. Obviously Loßberg also had a well developed eye for talent when he requested the services of the future field marshal.
61. Loßberg p. 223.
62. *ibid.* p. 224.
63. Soden Freiherr von *op. cit.* p. 113.
64. Vischer Alfred *Das 10. Württ. Infanterie-Regiment Nr. 180 in der Somme-Schlacht 1916* p. 21.
65. Sheffield and Bourne (Eds) *Douglas Haig War Diaries and Letters 1914–1918* p. 198.
66. *Hauptsataatsarchiv Stuttgart* M99 Bü142 *Gefechtsbericht des 10. Württ. Infanterie-Regiments Nr. 180 über die Kämpfe im Abschnitt Thiepval vom 25.9. Bis 7.10.1916* dated 4.12.1916.

Chapter 4

Haig Lets the Defence off the Hook 1st–15th July

The 1st July had been marked by numerous local, hastily mounted, counter-attacks, or 'counter-strokes' as they were then known to the German army, most notably at Schwaben Redoubt and south of the river, where elements of Infantry Regiment 60 and Reserve Infantry Regiment 7 of 121st Infantry Division succeeded in retaking Assevillers from French colonial troops. However, the first systematically organised counter-attack of the hundreds mounted during the battle by the German army took place on 2 July. It was launched through the depth positions of 12th Infantry Division by elements of 12th Reserve Division, reinforced by Bavarian Infantry Regiment 16, 10th Bavarian Infantry Division, whose sister regiment, Reserve Infantry Regiment 8, had played a prominent role at the Schwaben Redoubt. The plan originally was to reinforce an attack launched by surviving local troops during the evening of 1 July, but not all of the necessary additional forces were close enough and it proved impossible to link up with the 12th Infantry Division formations. Instead, the revised plan was to attack at dawn the following day and restore the line from Hardecourt to Longueval.[1] In the circumstances, this was highly ambitious but proof that, despite all their initial problems, the defenders were not going to be content to just sit tight and absorb punishment. An attempt by the remnants of Bavarian Reserve Infantry Regiment 6 to assault the hastily constructed positions of 16th Battalion, Manchester Regiment, from a start line in *Artillerie Schlucht* [Caterpillar Valley] was in fact launched at 9.30 pm, but was beaten off easily and all was quiet once more by 10.30 pm.

The battalions of Bavarian Infantry Regiment 16, the only uncommitted formation of 10th Bavarian Division on 1 July, were located several kilometres to the rear, with individual companies dispersed from Le Transloy to Barastre and Haplincourt. At 12.15 pm a hauptmann from 28th Reserve Division, which had just assumed responsibility for the whole of the Montauban-Fricourt sector, arrived with orders for the Bavarians to come to immediate readiness; one hour later they were ordered to march forward to Flers, initially to be ready to reinforce wherever the local commander considered the threat to be greatest. The units set off at 1.15 pm, widely spaced because of the threat of shelling and observation from the air, reaching the

Flers area at approximately 4.00 pm. Shortly after their arrival, Generalleutnant von Hahn, commanding 28th Reserve Division, sent a written order stating, 'The position of 28th Reserve Division is to be occupied; from right hand boundary Bazentin le Grand to left hand boundary sugar refinery east of Longueval'.[2] This equated to a 3,000 metre frontage and so was a fairly tall order. Nevertheless, responsibility was split by Oberstleutnant Bedall as follows: '1st Battalion is to occupy the second position along the southern edge of Longueval and from there to the west. 2nd and 3rd Battalions are to take up positions in regimental reserve between Flers and Longueval, front towards the latter."[3] Reinforced by Machine Gun Sharpshooter Troop 87, 1st Battalion moved into position. It was probably just as well that there was no further British attack that day because, when counter-attack orders arrived early on the evening of 1 July for an operation at dawn the following day, the Bavarians were well deployed to take part.

The initial orders to 12th Reserve Division were somewhat different. Held back in reserve in concealed positions in the area of Rancourt, St Pierre Vaast Wood and Bouchavesnes, its regiments were brought to immediate readiness early on 1 July and ordered to move forward to counter the loss of the First Position between Maricourt and Curlu. Exaggerated reports arrived, stating that both Bernafay and Trônes Woods had been captured, so Reserve Infantry Regiment 51 was ordered forward to take up positions, ready to attack between Ginchy and Guillemont. While still on the march that evening, fresh orders arrived at 8.30 pm.

"Trônes Wood is free of enemy. 12th Reserve Division is take possession of Montauban and the Intermediate Position as far as the north west corner of *Bayernwald* [Bois Favier, 1,000 metres west of Hardecourt]. Reserve Infantry Regiment 51's boundaries are northwest edge of Montauban to the *Baligandstützpunkt*[4] ... Boundary between 3rd and 1st Battalions, southeast corner of Montauban ... 2nd Battalion is to move into the German Second Position between Guillemont and the Sugar Refinery."[5]

Meanwhile, at 8.45pm, fresh orders arrived at battalion level from 16th Bavarian Infantry Regiment.

"1. Reserve Infantry Regiment 51, on the right flank of 12th Reserve Division, attacking from the east towards the northeast corner of Montauban, [should have reached] the Ginchy – Hardecourt road between 7.00 and 8.00 pm.
2. 16th Regiment is to participate in the attack of 12th Reserve Division and is to seize the high ground from the *Jamin-Werk* (midway between Mametz and Montauban)[6] to Montauban.

3. 1st Battalion is to sidestep to the right in its current position, so that 2nd Battalion to its left has room to deploy with its left flank [anchored] on the Longueval – Maricourt road, with its right flank 600 metres to the west.

4. 3rd Battalion is immediately to despatch two companies to occupy the [Second Position] by the Longueval sugar refinery.[7] Once 1st and 2nd Battalions are in position, the remaining two companies of 3rd Battalion are to move forward to the sector Longueval – Bazentin le Grand (exclusive).

5. Machine Gun Sharpshooter Troop 87 is subordinated to 1st Battalion; Machine Gun Sharpshooter Troop 44 to 2nd Battalion and Machine Gun Company Bavarian Infantry Regiment 16 remains under command of the regiment but is to be co-located with 3rd Battalion.

6. Reserve Field Artillery Brigade 28 will support the attack by bombarding the village of Montauban and the ridge to the west.

7. The importance of maintaining contact with the right flank of 12th Reserve Division is emphasised.

8. The regimental attack is to conform to progress made by the 12th Reserve Division attack.

9. Regimental command post – Flers

10. Report once all is ready. 3rd Battalion is to observe and report on the progress of the attack.

Signed. Bedall.[8]

So much for the orders process. Translating their requirements into action was a different story. The various units and sub units spent the night stumbling around in unfamiliar territory trying to orientate themselves, move into position and maintain contact with other friendly forces. Small wonder, therefore, that the advancing groups became entangled with one another and other groups. 4th Company Reserve Infantry Regiment 51, for example, tasked with advancing through Trônes Wood, was only able to keep direction by following the more northerly railway line through it from east to west then, having emerged in to the open once more, found itself in amongst a Recruit Company, which had no clear orders, other than to hold firm. They had no idea how far forward the British advance had come, so the attackers forged on west, pushed through Bernafay Wood and, by 4.30 am, were on its western edge.

Once all the companies had arrived, they shook out along the line of a ditch which offered very little in the way of protection. As dawn broke this activity must have been observed by the British because, all of a sudden, a heavy concentration of artillery fire crashed down on the forward edge of the wood and also directly on it, sending splinters and smashed tree branches in all directions. It was not long before the shelling, supplemented by a great weight of small arms fire from the direction of Montauban, sent some survivors rushing back into the cover of the wood and from there all the way back to Trônes Wood, where Major Engel, commanding officer 1st Battalion, rallied them and organised them into a hasty defence of the wood, with strict orders to defend it to the last.

Attempting to attack to the left of Reserve Infantry Regiment 51, 3rd Battalion Reserve Infantry Regiment 38 ran into similar problems. Unable to make contact with Reserve Infantry Regiment 51, its commanding officer decided to attack unsupported at 2.45 am with all four companies in line. Over unfamiliar ground, in the dark, against an enemy of unknown location and strength: this was a recipe for disaster; only the seriousness of the overall situation could possibly have justified it and, given the fact that the battalion came under heavy artillery fire then ran into withering small arms fire and was almost totally destroyed in short order once it stepped off towards Montauban, the decision to act in this way must be regarded as extremely dubious. The survivors were scattered to such an extent that later that morning only the battalion staff and fifteen men met up at the southwest corner of Hardecourt.[9]

From the point of view of 12th Reserve Division, the counter-attack on Montauban was an almost complete fiasco – smashed by fire before it could even launch, though a few isolated groups did manage later to link up tenuously with Bavarians to their west. The picture was very similar for Bavarian Infantry Regiment 16. Moving forward from 1.15 am, its 1st and 2nd Battalions reached the safety of the *Artillerie Schlucht* [Caterpillar Valley] at around 2.30 am. Given the obvious problems of communication with 12th Infantry Division – none of the officer-led patrols despatched to link up returned – the best that could be done was to depend on the previously agreed signal for the start of the attack, namely the firing of a succession of green flares. Unfortunately, the night sky was full of flares, many of which were fired as the battalions were moving into position but, despite the fact that some appeared to be coming from the anticipated direction, no unambiguous message could be derived from them. It transpired the following day that much of the confusion was caused by survivors of 6th and 7th Companies Bavarian Reserve Infantry Regiment 6,[10] located in the quarry 1,000 metres north of Montauban and commanded by the regimental medical officer, illuminating the night sky and firing for all they were worth to beat back British probing patrols.[11]

Even before 1st Battalion could move into open ground it was on the receiving end of a heavy concentration of shell fire and forced to take cover. Despite receipt of the report by an officer's patrol that the crest was occupied by a 'British nest', where troops could be observed digging in, the decision was made to start the attack at once, regardless of 12th Reserve Division.[12] However, repeated attempts shortly afterwards by both battalions to advance from the *Schlucht* to *Staubwassergraben* withered away in a hail of small arms fire as the advancing troops began to climb the surprisingly steep hillside towards it and cross the crest. 1st Battalion later reported, 'During the climb up the northern slopes [we] came under such heavy machine gun and rifle fire that the commanding officer decided – now also under fire from Montauban itself – to press on no further, but instead to defend the *Artillerie Schlucht*.'[13] This account ties in well with that of the Manchesters, recorded in their history.

"At 3.00 am, just as dawn was breaking and the order to 'stand down' was about to be issued, long lines of grey figures in greatcoats and helmets[14] were seen advancing over the ridge, shoulder to shoulder – on they came, wave after wave. The second counter-attack had begun.

"There was no need to issue fire orders. As the Germans topped the ridge our men opened rapid fire with deadly precision, many climbing out on to the parapet to get a better field of fire. The Lewis guns served splendidly. It had been said, 'You can take the village, but can you hold it?' 'We can do it', said the men and they did. The lonely wounded, lying among their dead comrades on the ground behind the village under the starry sky, heard the hellish crash of the artillery preparation and the rattle of the Lewis gun and rifle fire; saw great jets of flame among the trees of the village and the clustering rockets. 'Can they hold on – will the stampede overwhelm us?'

"They (the defenders) were barely 150 strong with 1,000 yards of communication trench to hold. There were no means of communicating with the guns direct – but the attack was broken up solely by rifle fire. Four waves had been dispersed when our artillery came into action and rendered further attacks impossible."[15]

Although the attack of 1st Battalion failed completely, the picture was more mixed – though with the same ultimate outcome – further to the east, where elements of 2nd Battalion attacked the *Kabelgraben* [Montauban Alley], which ran east northeast-west northwest just north of and parallel to Montauban village. Here, at approximately 4.15 am, 8th Company 2nd Battalion, with 5th Company off to its left (east), attacked a 120 metre length of trench. Its commander, Leutnant Schwub, reported subsequently:

"We attacked at dawn (4.15 am). This section of trench opposite the company was defended by approximately one platoon of 16th Battalion, Manchester Regiment, with one machine gun. As we charged, the enemy threw hand grenades at us then disappeared hastily into bushes at the eastern edge of

Montauban. To begin with the machine gun carried on firing but, before we reached the trench, it had been carried away down a short sap which had been driven forward from the edge of the village. Its head was located about thirty metres from the captured trench; some of the defenders continued to throw grenades at us as we jumped into it.

"In the trench itself I came across a wounded British sergeant and lying in the left half of the trench we had assaulted were several dead. The trench itself was deep and wide, front facing northwest. It was equipped with many firing points and at its base were several small shelters. We found about twenty five knapsacks, groundsheets, bullets, hand grenades, rations, together with a large number of weapons, some of which had wire cutting attachments and, above all, ammunition boxes and replacement spare parts for a machine gun. The name of the unit, 16th Manchester Battalion [*sic.*], was found on letters, in an English prayer book and on groundsheets. The enemy wore steel helmets, covered with sacking. Battle continued on the right flank, where the enemy were driven back to where a sunken road crossed the trench.[16] A second machine gun was in action covering sections of trench. It was impossible to progress further and the lack of hand grenades forced the attackers to pull back behind a sandbag block erected to their rear.

"... We improved the trench, front facing southeast and dug out foxholes as protection against artillery fire. The occasional arrival of hand grenades meant that the right flank could be held. It was in fact quiet during the morning, but the intensity of battle grew during the afternoon. What made it worse was the possession by the British of the sunken road, which threatened our rear. We succeeded in withdrawing at 9.30 [pm] because the British were not expecting that. During the afternoon our own heavy artillery pounded the northwestern edge of Montauban. Some shells landed short in our trench, causing quite heavy casualties. The exact address of one British soldier was 16th Service Battalion Manchester Regiment, 13th Company [*sic.* presumably 13 Platoon]."[17]

In the wake of this failed attack, typical of countless others which were to take place during the coming weeks as every British advance was disputed by the defence, Oberstleutnant Bedall requested 28th Reserve Division to allow him to pull back to the Second Position to reorganise his units and so be available for redeployment for tasks which promised a better chance of success. This was approved. The battered Infantry Regiment 23 and Reserve Infantry Regiment 51 were left temporarily facing Montauban, whilst the Bavarians, after a short pause for reorganisation, were moved west; 3rd Battalion to be under the command of

185 Infantry Brigade in Mametz Wood, the remainder to positions in and around Longueval, where they relieved exhausted troops from several different regiments. During the next fortnight of extreme danger for the defence, the German army was forced to employ on a grand scale the same 'puttying up' procedure that the British army had employed at the crisis of the First Battle of Ypres in late 1914. Finding and deploying resources was nerve wracking for commanders and exhausting for the troops involved; whilst the consequent mixing of units created administrative chaos that was overcome only slowly. At corps level, General der Artillerie von Stein, commanding XIV Reserve Corps, remarked,

"Here I experienced in the fullest sense the meaning of the phrases 'weight of decision' and 'dealing with uncertainty'. In order to prevent a breakthrough on the left flank, I had to pull out of the line battalion after battalion which had just beaten off the major attack, transfer them by truck to the left and throw them into battle. When I gave the senior General Staff officer, Major von Löwenfeld, the same order for the last available battalion, he said to me in a deadly serious voice, 'Excellency, that is the last one!' I then replied, 'Never forget this moment all your life. It is essential to able to decide to deploy the very last of your resources, because the enemy may also be at the end of his.' That battalion was just sufficient to prevent a breakthrough until reinforcements from the army command began to arrive."[18]

Down at unit level the mere administration and resupplying of those stationed forward posed immense problems for the support troops. For example, during the first half of July the field kitchens of the Fusilier Guards, 3rd Guards Infantry Division, as well as Infantry Regiment 185, 208th Infantry Division and Reserve Infantry Regiments 15, 77 and 91 from 2nd Guards Reserve Division, all had to be concentrated in one small area north of Courcelette. This meant that resupply teams not only had to try to survive constant British harassing fire, but also were forced to attempt to find space in *Stockachergraben* [Stockacher Trench], the only communication trench connecting with the front line that was still relatively intact. For the carrying parties concerned, picking a way forward in the pitch black night carrying bulky and heavy loads drove men to the limit of physical endurance, especially when they had to cast around to link up with groups of men from their regiments deployed almost at random in the tangled forward positions. Some claimed that it was only a highly developed sense of duty and good humour that helped them through the trial. According to Reserve Infantry Regiment 91, all queries concerning the location of particular sub units would be met by a standard reply, 'I'm afraid I'm a stranger here myself!'[19] Amusing in retrospect as it may be, it could hardly be said to represent the most efficient use of resources.

Haig, having taken the decision, to Joffre's dismay, to abandon for the time being any further attempt to capture the high ground from Pozières to Serre, directed that the emphasis of the British campaign was to gain ground to the south of the Albert – Bapaume road from Fricourt east to Montauban. As a direct result Fourth Army spent the days 2 – 13 July carrying out no fewer than forty six narrow front attacks, which cost 25,000 casualties[20] in preparation for an assault on the German Second Position from Bazentin le Petit to Longueval. Meanwhile the staff at Second Army under its new chief of staff worked flat out to stabilise the situation, introduce a coherent system for the absorption of reinforcements and to develop counter-attack plans. This was much easier said than done. The demands of the contact battle, which continued to lead to minor crises, and the emergency deployment of reserves on arrival at the front to plug gaps in the line, made fundamental changes difficult to achieve.

Nevertheless, Loßberg, with the full approval of General von Below, was able to reorganise the higher levels of command. The corps commands became Groups, named after their commanders. Thus XIV Reserve Corps became Group Stein and assumed responsibility for all forces from the northern boundary of Second Army to the current boundary between XIV Reserve Corps and XVII Corps. Group von Quast (commander IX Corps) took command of 121 Reserve Division, 22nd Reserve Division, Division von Frentz, 11th Infantry Division and 44th Reserve Division. Group von Pannewitz took command of XVII Corps (35th and 36th Infantry Divisions). Further south, also under General der Infanterie von Pannewitz, the Guard Corps formed a group from 1st and 2nd Guards Infantry Divisions and 15th Landwehr Division. Within twenty four hours of the first decision, a further 'Group Goßler', based on the reinforced VI Reserve Corps and comprising 11th and 12th Reserve Divisions and (temporarily) what remained of 12th Infantry Division, was formed and inserted into the line between Groups Stein and Quast. Gradually the Group headquarters provided continuity at the front, with divisions posted in and out as necessary. From time to time these higher headquarters were themselves relieved, but this was a fairly rare occurrence.

If the command framework was beginning to take shape, this made no difference to the 'hand to mouth' way the battle was being fought. The plans to launch one or more major counter-attacks never came to anything. They depended upon sufficient reinforcements of all kinds being made available and they never were. Loßberg raised the subject on several occasions with Falkenhayn, but his responses were always evasive.[21] However, acknowledgement of the new threat astride the Somme did cause *OHL* to scale back operations on the Verdun front. According to the War Diary of Fifth Army, Falkenhayn passed the verbal order, 'Strictly defence [only]' on 11 July.[22] However, that decision did not lead to any significant redeployment of either aircraft or heavy artillery, so the German army had to fight for the next two months sadly lacking the means to conduct a major modern land campaign – and the men in the trenches suffered accordingly.

Meanwhile the battle for Bernafay, Trônes, *Bayernwald* and Mametz Woods continued to rage. It was fought frequently at close quarters and always with high casualties on both sides, largely because whenever either side captured some ground or gained an advantage, the other immediately counter-attacked. South of the river, reinforcement of the defenders meant that slowly their ability to resist increased. Intense fighting around Biaches and La Maisonette not only led to the French being rebuffed, but also was expensive in lives, so much so that the French Colonial Corps had to be given priority for relief. 'Everywhere the German infantry fought with great obstinacy and put up the strongest possible resistance. The German artillery engaged targets around La Maisonette vigorously, causing serious casualties.'[23]

North of the river, in the Second Army sector, further changes to the command structure were introduced with the aim of improving the ability to resist. On 5 July Group Quast assumed responsibility for the area south of the Somme all the way to Vermandovillers. In other words, one headquarters was now responsible for the complete frontage that the French army was attacking. Then, nine days later, the Group Stein area of responsibility was further reduced when IV Corps, commanded by General der Infanterie Sixt von Armin, was inserted between Groups Stein and Goßler. To give an idea about the speed with which Second Army was being reinforced, 11th Reserve Division was deployed to Maurepas, 183rd Infantry Division to Contalmaison, 123rd south of Maurepas, 7th to Martinpuich, 8th to Flers and 24th to Guillemont. South of the river, 18th Infantry Division relieved 44th Reserve Division near Estrées and 17th Infantry Division strengthened the Barleux sector.

All these formations, which had been sourced from Third, Fourth, Sixth and Seventh Armies, were desperately needed and swiftly deployed; but their arrival could not make up for the fact there had not been a timely arrival of vital reserves before battle was joined, so the fighting power of the new arrivals, which had to be deployed piecemeal, was rapidly dissipated. As a result, gradually, despite all efforts by the defence, which was fighting over terrain ideally suited to that purpose, the British Fourth Army captured the ground it would require to form up and then attack the German Second Line. Some idea of the continuing mixing of formations and units during this confusing period may be gained from examination of an order issued on 12 July by 3rd Guards Infantry Division. This formation had been originally deployed with its organic regiments (Fusilier Guards, Lehr Infantry and Grenadier 9) to shore up the crumbling Pozières – Ovillers area but now found itself, with sundry other formations and units under command, responsible for a broad swathe of territory based around the Bazentins.

"SECRET! DIVISIONAL ORDER

1. Newly subordinated to the division are:
   3rd Battalion Reserve Infantry Regiment 91
   Landwehr Brigade Ersatz Battalion 56
   3rd Battalion (Heavy Howitzers) Foot Artillery Regiment 1 (Staff, 6th and 9th Batteries)
   Large scale reinforcements are on the way.
2. The enemy has been shelling our positions throughout the day with heavy artillery. We are still holding the northern edge of Mametz Wood.

   Special orders have been issued, subordinating 1st Battalion Infantry Regiment 190 to Oberstleutnant Kummel, 3rd Battalion Reserve Infantry Regiment 91, to strengthen the right flank. [This unit] is to be inserted between 1st and 2nd Battalions Bavarian Infantry Regiment 16. This reduction in battalion frontages should permit reserves to be extracted for use in counter-strokes and to develop lines to the rear.
3. 183rd Infantry Division has not succeeded in advancing the front line as far as the Pozières – Contalmaison junction point. It appears as though 183rd Infantry Division is still occupying part of Contalmaison. Infantry from 7th Infantry Division will be deployed tonight to the northwest of the western edge of *Klein Bazentin Wald* [le Bois de Bazentin]. They are shortly to go over to the offensive. 12th Reserve Division recaptured most of Trônes Wood during the night.
4. The [Second] Army demands that we hold the Second Position and the northern edge of Mametz Wood. Patrols within Mametz Wood are to be so strengthened that they can offer effective resistance. Not more than one fresh company may be deployed.
5. The regimental commander Infantry Regiment 190 is appointed commandant of the *Riegelstellung* [Major Stop Line] *Foureaux Riegel* [Switch Trench][24] and Third Position [southeast of Flers]. For technical advice he is allocated Hauptmann Paulisch, Pionier Battalion 274 [*sic*.][25]
6. Troops [allocated to commander Infantry Regiment 190] 2nd Battalion Infantry Regiment 190, Machine Gun Company 190, Landwehr Brigade Ersatz Battalion 56 (which is due to arrive at Le Transloy during the afternoon of 12th and may be called forward from 8.00 am 13th to dig). Machine Gun Company 190 is to be deployed permanently in the positions by 8.00 am 13th and the remaining troops from 8.00 pm 13th. Regimental staff Infantry Regiment 190 is to be established in Gueudecourt from 8.00 am and the telephone point is to be manned thereafter.

7. Despite the problems with our positions, the constant artillery bombardment and very limited reliefs, for a further short period, deploying the very last shreds of our strength, we must hold out. The British must not break through! The war is going to be decided here. I express my fullest appreciation to all troops for the courageous way they have held out so far.[26]

While the battles for Bernafay, Trônes and Mametz Woods were being played out, Bavarian Infantry Regiment 16 conducted an extremely vigorous programme of patrolling, primarily to gather intelligence and to maintain accurate situation maps but also to take advantage of any opportunity which presented itself. One such, organised by 7th Company on orders from 2nd Battalion during the night 9th/10th July, succeeded in bringing in a seriously wounded British officer and a slightly wounded British soldier, both of whom provided useful unit identification information. The same night two officer's patrols of 8th Company recovered a pair of grenade launchers from the quarry north of Montauban. In recognition of these feats, the commanding officer published the following in his routine order for 10 July.

"Yesterday evening Patrol Redlhammer 7/16 captured and brought in a seriously wounded British officer and a lightly wounded British soldier. In fullest recognition of this daring and conscientious action by this skilfully led patrol, I grant the participants of this patrol the following cash rewards: Gefreiter Redlhammer, as leader, 10 Marks; Gefreiters Seidl and Grashuber, 5 Marks apiece. The amounts are to be collected from the battalion adjutant against receipts.

"To the men involved in the officer's patrols led by Drechsler and Heindl 8/16, I award 25 litres of beer (to be received from the canteen at the next opportunity!) and I express my happy recognition of you all and especially the two named officers."[27]

It would be interesting to know how many men survived to collect their rewards.

The Attack on the Second Position 15 July

The overall situation was no better on the eve of the major British attack on the Second Position. During the early hours of 14 July, the front from north of Mametz Wood east to Longueval was defended from west to east by, successively, 1st Battalion Infantry Regiment 184, 183rd Infantry Division; 3rd Battalion Infantry Regiment 165, 7th Infantry Division; Reserve Infantry Regiment 91, 2nd Guards

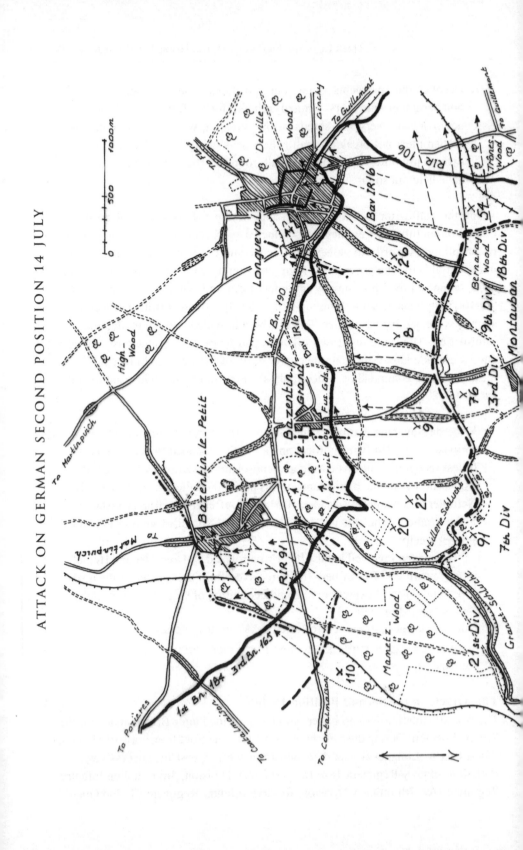

ATTACK ON GERMAN SECOND POSITION 14 JULY

Reserve Division, reinforced by remnants of 3rd Battalion Bavarian Infantry Regiment 16, 10th Bavarian Infantry Division; Elements of 3rd Battalion Infantry Regiment 190, 220th Infantry Division, Recruit Company Fusilier Guards, 3rd Guards Infantry Division and, finally, 1st and 2nd Battalions Bavarian Infantry Regiment 16. Can there ever have been a greater mixing of units and formations at a critical part of a battlefield? How 6 Guards Infantry Brigade and Generalmajor Rauchenberger, commanding Bavarian 20 Infantry Brigade, who were charged with responsibility for this sector, were expected to exercise effective command over this assortment is anybody's guess.[28] To make matters worse, mounting casualties, increasing exhaustion and the strain of maintaining their positions, despite acute shortages of water, rations and ammunition, all combined to cause acute concern up the chain of command. Reserve Leutnant W Steuerwald, one of the company commanders of 1st Battalion Reserve Infantry Regiment 91, originally based at Gommecourt, which had been one of the numerous units moved from north to south by General von Stein a few days earlier, later provided an impression of the difficulties being faced.

"During the morning of 13th July, the artillery fire eased slightly. Hauptmann von Rauchhaupt ordered that the part of 1st Company under Reserve Leutnant Kaufmann, which was still on the northern edge of Bazentin Wood, was to move forward to the position, to extend the line of 4th Company and to attempt to link up the sector of Major von Kriegsheim (3rd Battalion Lehr Infantry Regiment). The move succeeded. Manning our front line now were 1st, 4th and 2nd Companies … Could the position be held until 15th July? Artillery fire came down heavily around 11.00 am. The troops had suffered casualties from the fire during the move forward and the attack which followed. Hour by hour the casualty list grew. How would we fare in the event of an attack which seemed to be ever more likely? It would be extremely difficult to move forward the Reserve Company or other support through the artillery fire. The same applied to trench stores and ammunition. Our men had been rationed for three days, but the shortage of water was already making itself felt. There was still a well in Bazentin, but every time it was cleared out it was hit by fire once more. The 3rd Company had made a huge effort to get water forward, but it was just a drop on a hot stone. The mineral water store in Bazentin, as well as the complete engineer depot, had been destroyed by enemy shelling.

"There was a dressing station for the wounded, but this had almost been wrecked by several direct hits… There was constant telephone contact with the artillery liaison officer, but that was not worth much, because counter battery fire had almost completely accounted for our artillery. The sector commander, Oberstleutnant Kumme of the Lehr Infantry Regiment, was only reachable by telephone from time to time. All other information had to be passed using runners, who often did not reach their destinations. Only one single runner got through from Brigade and he brought – a Divisional order concerning administrative matters in the battle area! The situation was further worsened by the fact that Kriegsheim's men were relieved by two companies of recruits. Towards 1.00 am, the companies demanded material to construct a barbed wire entanglement, signal flares, hand grenades, ammunition and water. 1st Company had forty five to fifty men left and the 4th Company reported around one hundred, some of whom were from 2nd Company. 2nd Company had sixty and the 3rd Company 120 men. The company commanders all felt that a further attack on Mametz Wood had absolutely no prospect of success, but they hoped to be able to hold their positions if they had time to work on them.

"On the 14th July, the French national day, an attack by their British allies was entirely likely. The activity of the enemy artillery made this almost a certainty. Fire increased to extreme intensity and involved all calibres. It was dreadful. 8th Company Reserve Infantry Regiment 77 was reduced to its commander (Reserve Hauptmann Denicke) and his runner. Our artillery had no chance of taking on the enemy batteries. It could not even seriously counter the forward move of the British troops. At around midnight strong patrols were detected moving forward. The position was occupied. No attack took place, but around 3.00 am 2nd Company observed strong infantry forces on the edge of Mametz Wood. The company was stood to, followed shortly afterwards by 4th and 1st Companies. The enemy advanced in strong waves, occasionally even in assault columns. Small arms fire and grenades were directed against the British ranks. Three waves of attackers were beaten off. One machine gun from Sharp Shooter Troop 77, which fired to the last round, caused the enemy heavy casualties.[29]

During the attack itself, at about 8.00 am, the regimental command post of Bavarian Infantry Regiment 16 in Bazentin le Grand was overrun and all the personnel, including Oberstleutnant Bedall, the Adjutant, Hauptmann Freiherr von Lutz, and the medical officer, Stabsarzt Dr Eber, were all captured and transported to Britain as prisoners. Although Bedall and Lutz remained in British hands, Eber, as a doctor, was repatriated as early as 9 October 1916. Whilst in Southampton Bedall wrote a brief report about 14 July which he gave to Eber to deliver on his return to Germany. The latter knew that he would not be allowed to take the original with him when he left Britain, so he committed it to memory and wrote it out once more as soon as he reached the Netherlands. It reads:

"The extremely heavy artillery fire, which had been landing on the Infantry Regiment 16 positions between Longueval and Bazentin since 1 July, increased in strength further during the night 13/14 July. The heaviest calibre guns were in action. During the early hours of 14 July (about 3.00 am) the heavy artillery fire was suddenly lifted to the rear so an [imminent] attack could be assumed. Because all links with the artillery were broken, red flares were fired from our regimental command post in Bazentin le Grand. Because all links with higher headquarters were also cut, I despatched two runners to 6 Guards Infantry Brigade (Flers) with the message that Infantry Regiment 16 was in a critical situation and was in urgent need of support. I cannot say if these reports reached their destination.

"At 5.00 am I could observe from my command post the adjoining sector beyond my right flank (west). This had been manned by 3rd Battalion Lehr Infantry Regiment, but it suffered enormous casualties during the night 13/14 July and had been relieved that same night by a company of the [3rd Guards Division] Recruit Company. I saw men pulling back into the wood southwest of Flers [sic.].[30] As a result, a wide gap through which the British advanced opened up between Bazentin le Grand and Bazentin le Petit. The British were approaching the village of Bazentin le Grand in dense masses at about 5.30 am. At once I ordered the machine guns held back in the village to move into fire positions and engage the lines of British soldiers.

"It was incumbent on me to hold out to the best of my ability, because a divisional order issued the previous day[31] had spoken of the need to hold out to the limit of endurance because reserves were on their way. Furthermore [I did this] in expectation that the requested supports would still arrive and so the situation would be improved. Once most of the machine gun crews had been killed or wounded and the weapons rendered unusable, the British got into the village. We defended our dug out with the last remaining machine gun then, when this also became unusable, we attempted to defend ourselves with hand grenades. Finally, we were forced to surrender.

Signed Bedall"[32]

On the face of it, this reads as a clear criticism of the Guards' recruit company, but it is impossible to know the precise circumstances of the withdrawal nor, if the pressure against that part of the line was intense, is there any guarantee that any other of the hard pressed units in the line could have held on any longer. The men involved had all completed their basic training and were being put through in-theatre training when the emergency demanded their early deployment. Whatever the truth, there can be no doubting the sacrificial courage of these men. Despatched to the area 280 men strong under Hauptmann von Tschirnhaus, Fusilier Guards, when the battle for the Second Position was over it returned with only twenty men, commanded by a single feldwebel.[33]

The net result on the ground was that, threatened from the rear, the remnants of 1st Battalion Reserve Infantry Regiment 91 had no choice but to pull back, fighting from crater to crater, to Bazentin Wood. Reserve Leutnant W Steuerwald once more:

"Fresh masses pressed forward and there was heavy hand to hand fighting. It was possible to hold the left flank of the position until about 4.00 am, but by then strong enemy forces had broken through to the left. They reached Bazentin le Grand, then soon afterwards Bazentin le Petit, where, between 5.00 am and 6.00 am, Oberstleutnant Kumme [commander, Lehr Infantry Regiment] was captured. As a result, 4th and 1st Companies were rolled up from the left and even the rear. 2nd Company managed to hold on and beat off all frontal attacks until 6.00 am, then they ran out of ammunition and hand grenades and, in addition, the enemy was through in the sector of their right hand neighbours. 3rd Company could not withstand the weight of the attack alone. It fought on, holding the northern edge of Bazentin Wood until 8.30 am, then it was surrounded. At 2.00 pm the Battalion staff and that of 3rd Battalion Bavarian Infantry Regiment 16, with which it shared a Headquarters, was captured. The Battalion, which was right up to strength on 9th July, was in ruins. The three company commanders: Kaufmann, Milz and Lohse, were dead; and with them many of the best. Amongst the officers were numbered Leutnants Schnare, Scherrer, Wirtjes and Feldwebelleutnants Boß, Glaenzer and Schweitzer. Only Leutnant Blasberg and Feldwebelleutnant Bartels made it back and both were wounded. Six officers and 200 men went into captivity … At a Divisional Headquarters attempts were made to interrogate us. Again and again we were asked, 'How could it be that when we attacked after hammering the trenches for days on end, there were still battleworthy troops manning them?'"

At the eastern end of the battlefield, namely in and around Longueval, a rather different situation developed. According to the British official historian, at 8.00 am and at 5.00 pm XIII (British) Corps reported that Longueval was firmly in British hands, only to have to amend the reports at 11.52 am and 5.30 pm to admit that only a foothold in the southern part of the village had been captured.[34] The fact that Longueval held out acted as a brake on more ambitious British plans to push further north once the Second Position had been taken and was of considerable significance for the way the battle subsequently progressed, so it is worth examining briefly what happened. Covering the gap between Bazentin le Grand and the road junction just to the west of Longueval was 1st Battalion Bavarian Infantry Regiment 16, with 2nd Battalion responsible for the village itself. The reinforced 8th Company defended the partially complete central strong point in the built up area itself, whilst its 5th, 6th and 7th Companies, mustering a mere 500 bayonets, was spread thinly along a 1,200 metres frontage south of the village, defending the approaches from Montauban and Bernafay and Trônes Woods.

Given their general weakness and in an effort to avoid being surprised, strong listening posts were pushed forward during the night 13/14 July onto high ground south of the village and a high state of alert was maintained, especially as dawn approached. In overnight patrol activity, clashes led to the capture by 8th Company of a sergeant and a signaller from a British patrol contacted near the quarry north of Montauban. These were brought into the German lines then, at around 3.00 am, 5th Company, operating at the southwest corner of Longueval, spotted the approach of British lines of infantry. Closing swiftly on the defence, the main weight of the attack came in against the southeast and southwest tips of Longueval, where 7th and 5th Companies respectively were soon fighting for their lives against overwhelming odds. Flares fired by Reserve Leutnant Thurnreiter, 5th Company, revealed masses of Scottish soldiers closing up on the barbed wire, with flamethrowers leading.

Showers of stick grenades were thrown and all the defenders opened rapid fire with rifles and machine guns, halting the thrust, but it was not long before enemy elements had pushed through between 1st and 2nd Battalions and were threatening the rear of 5th Company. Closing to within grenade throwing range of the Bavarians, the subsequent battle was hard fought, but did not last long. Out of ammunition, with their numbers continually thinned as grenade splinters and bullets found a mark, the wounded company commander, Reserve Oberleutnant Weber, took the decision to surrender rather than see the remainder of his men killed in a hopeless situation. Elsewhere along the overextended front, 6th Company was also quickly overrun, its survivors sidestepping behind the right [western] flank of 7th Company, which had been bent back to avoid immediate encirclement. Here they deployed to strengthen that sector against a further British advance, while the remainder of 7th Company enjoyed considerable success in holding out against frontal attack. Some idea of the intensity of the battle was recorded later by Major Brennfleck. An extract of his account notes:

"A platoon of 4th Company went into action, blocking a communication trench and temporarily forcing the enemy back across the Bazentin le Grand – Longueval road. Unteroffizier Halsbeck of 4th Company distinguished himself here. Spotting the danger and acting decisively, he gathered together his men and in a daring hand grenade attack pushed the British back, causing heavy casualties and capturing a machine gun. This dampened the attacking ardour of the British for a while. Halsbeck was awarded the Bravery Medal in Silver. Calls for hand grenades by the companies became ever more urgent but, apart from a small stock of twenty, everything the battalion had had already been issued. Without access to this one effective weapon, the battalion's ability to resist would soon have been exhausted. Attempts were made, therefore, to dig out buried grenades and to search the battlefield for them.

"Gefreiter Anton Rauch and Reservist Roscher, both of 1st Company, volunteered to neutralise enemy mortar and machine gun posts to the front. Taking no account of the constant fire, they, supported by their men and the fire of Machine Gun Sharp Shooter Detachment 87, ignoring the peril to themselves and showing extraordinary courage, captured the very youthful, wounded colonel of 12th Battalion West Yorkshire Regiment,[35] a captain, twenty five men and four machine guns. Both received the Bravery Medal in Silver. The grenades of the prisoners represented a valuable addition to the stocks, as did the hand grenades on the persons of the many fallen to our front. Two of the captured machine guns were still serviceable and were immediately deployed to good effect on the left and right flanks of the battalion. The wounded colonel praised the courage of the battalion with words of high recognition – there is no room for insincerity in such circumstances. He was bandaged up in the aid post and given what was left of the supplies of drink – a bottle of white wine ...

"By 3.15 pm the remainder of 3rd and 4th Companies were overrun, messages ceased to arrive from the company commander and soon the final few courageous men could be seen heading off into captivity, having given up the hopeless fight. The ring of defenders around the battalion commander was driven ever tighter. The last five hand grenades were thrown at the enemy and with that the resistance of this little band of men was at an end. It would have been impossible to break through to the rear in daylight, whilst to have continued the battle any longer would have meant total destruction and nothing would have been achieved. The enemy had already closed up to a distance of only fifteen to twenty metres so, at 3.40 pm, the battalion commander and what was left of his faithful soldiers surrendered to the enemy."[36]

Coming on top of two weeks manning the defences in the Bazentin – Longueval sector, the assault of 14 July was the final straw for Bavarian Infantry Regiment 16. Very few of its personnel escaped death or capture and, when it finally rallied in Beaulencourt prior to a further move to Le Mesnil on 15 July, by its own assessment it had been, 'virtually wiped out'. Missing were the regimental staff and the staffs of 1st and 3rd Battalions, almost all the Machine Gun Company and its weapons, Machine Gun Sharp Shooter Detachment 87, which had been subordinated to 1st Battalion, and the regimental signals section. It had actually received reinforcements on arrival at Beaulencourt, but this only brought its strength to: 1st Battalion one officer and 147 other ranks; 2nd Battalion six officers and 365 other ranks; and 3rd Battalion no officers and 111 other ranks. Of the machine gun sub units, the organic company was reduced to twenty one other ranks, whilst Machine Gun Sharp Shooter Detachments 87 and 44 could only muster fourteen other ranks and one officer and thirty other ranks respectively.[37]

Generalmajor von Lindquist, commander 3rd Guards Division, sent the regiment an effusive message of thanks which concluded, 'Our positions are still being held by fresh troops. Counter-attacks are in progress. That this was made possible was in no small measure due to Bavarian Infantry Regiment 16. The Fatherland is duly grateful.'[38] Grateful it may have been but overall losses of the regimental commander, seventy one other officers and 2559 other ranks was an appalling tragedy. Both the other regiments of 10th Bavarian Infantry Division, Bavarian Reserve Infantry Regiments 6 and 8, had also suffered huge losses. Small wonder, therefore, that it took weeks to reconstitute the division; small wonder, either, that it was despatched to the Eastern Front in mid-August to recuperate and retrain well away from the intensity of the Somme.

In the middle of the night 14/15 July reports arrived at Second Army from two different headquarters north of the Somme, both unanimous, that there had been a British breakthrough between Bazentin and Longueval and that they were marching on Flers. What happened next gives a clear insight into how Loßberg coped with emergency situations. He had previously been made aware of the existence of a significant gap in the defences in that area, so he had no reason to doubt the essential correctness of the reports. There was no time to be lost, so at once he telephoned General von Below to provide him with a situation report, then swiftly organised counter action. 5th Infantry Division and 8th Bavarian Reserve Division in army reserve and 8th Infantry Division, part of which was already involved in a relief in the line to the north in the Sixth Army sector, were directed to move forward, assisted by a number of trucks, to converge on the alleged enemy force around Flers and to counter-attack into the flanks of the penetration under command of Group Armin (IV Corps) to the north and Group Goßler (VI Reserve Corps) to the south. Additional reinforcements, including the Saxon 24th Reserve Division, were also allocated. That done, Loßberg then despatched forward two liaison officers in cars, instructing them to scour the areas north and south of Flers to establish the exact situation, then get to a telephone to brief him.

Having taken decisive action, he then telephoned *OHL* and was put through to General Falkenhayn, who was asleep. According to Loßberg[39] the mere mention of a breakthrough made Falkenhayn extremely agitated, but he calmed down once the measures taken had been explained to him. At 11.40 pm [*sic.*; probably this should read 12.40 am] the orderly room of Grenadier Regiment 12, 5th Infantry Division, located in Vermand, west northwest of St Quentin, received a message by telephone, 'The Division is stood to and is to march forward during the night to Rocquigny'. These orders were then amplified at 1.50 am then again at 2.50 am, when they read, 'The British have broken through in a northeasterly direction between Pozières and Longueval. The division, together with 8th Infantry Division and 8th Bavarian Reserve Division, is to conduct a counter-attack and is to advance in two columns.'[40]

Inevitably it took some time to pass the word to the battalions and companies, which were scattered in billets and bivouac sites over a wide area, but by 5.30 am two large columns, with 5th Infantry Division right and 8th Bavarian Reserve Division left, were on the march and heading in the direction of Bapaume. Infantry Regiment 52, 5th Infantry Division, was even further away from the initial assembly area than Grenadier Regiment 12, so it was allocated a number of trucks to assist the movement of its leading battalion. The remainder of the regiment, however, had to undertake an exhausting forced march in order to meet up with the remainder of the division in time.[41]

Despite all efforts, not all units and subunits were present when the columns set off. Reacting to a slightly different message, 'The British have broken through with their right flank at Flers',[42] Bavarian Reserve Infantry Regiments 18, 19 and 22, 8th Bavarian Reserve Division, had struggled to find their assembly areas in the pitch black night. By 2.45 am, the regimental staff and 1st Battalion Bavarian Reserve Infantry Regiment 19 were in position behind Bavarian Reserve Infantry Regiment 18, but of the 2nd and 3rd Battalions and their machine gun companies there was no sign. The 18th had to set off, but 3rd Battalion 19th did not appear until 3.30 am and the arrival of 2nd Battalion was even more delayed. By the time the regiment was finally assembled, the 18th had disappeared into the distance. Eventually, after hard marching with heavy packs, a halt was called at Boucly, still to the east of Péronne; and Bavarian Reserve Infantry Regiment 22 was despatched ahead towards the alleged breakthrough point. It was then discovered that 2nd Battalion Bavarian Reserve Infantry Regiment 19 was still adrift. It was discovered several kilometres to the south and ordered to join up with the main body with all speed.

Setting off once more at 8.20 am, the Bavarians finally reached a holding area between Templeux-la-Fosse and the cross roads to its south at 9.35 am, there to await further orders. While all these movements had been taking place, no firm information was reaching General von Below's headquarters. To state that these were worrying hours for the chain of command is barely to hint at the anxiety at all levels. Loßberg repeatedly telephoned the corps headquarters during the night and in the early morning, but nobody could explain what was happening. In fact, it was not until about 10.00 am on 15 July that matters were clarified. One after the other the liaison officers, who had spent the night quartering the area and questioning local troops, telephoned in quick succession to inform Loßberg that it had all been a false alarm.

It had been discovered that the 'enemy penetration' was in fact a group of 500 prisoners being escorted to the rear. 'A huge weight was lifted off my shoulders', wrote Loßberg, 'as it was also from those of the army commander and General von Falkenhayn, to whom I passed an immediate report.'[43] A furious Loßberg put this down to panicky reporting in a tense and confused situation and he launched an immediate, but unsuccessful, inquiry into how it had happened. He did state subsequently that all involved in major battles had had similar experiences, due to the fact that everyone's nerves were stretched to breaking point and that the usual breakdown of the telephone system following heavy bombardments meant that units and formations were generally isolated from one another and had no effective way of passing information to neighbouring units or higher headquarters. This allowed rumours to spread and he thought it most probable that this particular instance might have been caused by soldiers abandoning their posts and giving exaggerated reports to their commanders.

Nevertheless, he went on to explain that reports of this type had to be treated as true until investigations proved them to be wrong; speed of reaction in crises being of paramount importance. It might be thought, given the highly precarious situation, that the reserves summoned to the scene would have been retained and deployed against further possible British action, but this is not what happened. As will be seen, the orders to 8th Division stood but, once Loßberg established – and it did not take him long to find out – that the front had settled down along the line Pozières, northern edge of Longueval, western edge of Guillemont to the eastern edge of Hardecourt and that the gap would be plugged during the course of the day, he considered that the immediate crisis was over and, at 10.30 am, he released 5th Infantry Division and 8th Bavarian Reserve Division for deployment elsewhere. In response the already weary troops, many of whom had already covered more than thirty five kilometres that day, marched off through the heat of the day to new holding areas, not reaching them in many cases until 5.00 pm. Meanwhile, Loßberg's attention was already moving onto other pressing matters, especially because it was quite apparent that the British army, playing into the hands of the defence yet again, was now thrusting at ninety degrees to the original axis of advance and was thus drifting even further away from its French allies.

The situation for 8th Infantry Division (which had begun the process of conducting a relief in the Sixth Army area) to the north, was rather different. Although the front had stabilised to some extent, there was a distinct gap, or at least a sector of major weakness, to be dealt with. So, just after midnight of the night 14/15 July, it was directed to march at once to the Gueudecourt area. Its orders read,

> "1. The British are apparently in possession of High Wood. It seems that there is a gap in the German defensive positions between Bazentin le Petit and High Wood. The situation between High Wood and Longueval is unclear. Infantry Regiment 165 on the left flank of 7th Infantry Division is holding the northwest corner of Bazentin le Petit. On the right flank of 3rd Guards Infantry Division, Infantry Regiment 26 is apparently holding the *Foureaux Riegel* [Switch Trench, running east-west through High Wood].
> 2. 8th Infantry Division is to close the gap between 7th Infantry Division and 3rd Guards Infantry Division and is to occupy the line Bazentin le Petit – Longueval.
> 3. 16 Infantry Brigade is to attack the enemy in High Wood and recapture the old German positions between Bazentin and Longueval."[44]

The brigade commander then appointed troops to tasks and ordered, 'The attack will be mounted by Infantry Regiment 93, right flank eastern edge Martinpuich – northwest corner Bazentin le Petit, left flank western tip High Wood – Church Tower [*sic*.] Bazentin le Grand and Infantry Regiment 72, right flank linking with Infantry Regiment 93, left flank in the direction of the northwest corner of Longueval.'[45] Putting these orders into practice was far from straightforward. It was, for example, already light by the time the troops had closed up to the *Foureaux Riegel* so, with the exception of probing patrols, the attack across extremely open ground had to be postponed until evening. At 9.30 pm, elements of Infantry Regiments 72, 93 and 165, having worked their way into position, moved forward as one. The only opposition came from British listening posts forward in No Man's Land, all of which withdrew in the face of an attack in some considerable strength.

When the attackers halted and dug in, their advance had more or less reached the line northern tip of Bazentin le Petit – High Wood. In the process a number of British soldiers was captured, together with some Lewis guns. Nevertheless, the attackers did not have it all their own way; Infantry Regiment 93 reported that its casualties were, 'quite considerable, mainly from 3rd Battalion'.[46] Over the next few days the men of 8th Infantry Division were subject to constant artillery fire and minor probing attacks. Their casualties mounted, but they succeeded in maintaining their positions. It took weeks of hard fighting for the British army to make significant progress east and north of Delville Wood; Loßberg had been quite correct in his decision not to get mesmerised by the loss of part of his Second Position and to withdraw 5th Infantry Division and 8th Bavarian Reserve Division back into reserve, but it was a severe test of confidence in his own judgement.

Notes
1. Lutz History Bavarian Infantry Regiment 16 pp. 40–41.
2. Kriegsarchiv Munich 16. Inf. Regt. (WK) 3 *1. Bataillon Gefechtsbericht für die Zeit von 1 – 5. Juli 1916* dated 11.8.16.
3. Kriegsarchiv Munich 16. Inf. Regt. (WK) 3 *2. Bataillon Gefechtsbericht für die Zeit vom 1.7. Mittags bis 3.7. Mittags.*
4. The *Baligandstützpunkt* was a field fortification located at highest point of the Plaine du Moulin Choquet, 750 metres south of Montauban and on the road to Maricourt.
5. Schiedt History Reserve Infantry Regiment 51 p. 157
6. The *Jamin-Werk* was a strong point located on the summit of Hill 132 on the modern D 64.
7. This was actually located adjacent to the Longueval – Guillemont road, two kilometres southeast of Longueval. This deployment was obviously intended to secure the assembly area for 3rd Battalion Reserve Infantry Regiment 51, though the order does not make that explicit.
8. Kriegsarchiv Munich 16. Inf. Regt. (WK) 3 *2. Bataillon Gefechtsbericht.*
9. Hasselbach History Reserve Infantry Regiment 38 p. 120.
10. Kriegsarchiv Munich 6 RIR Bd 2 Map *Verteilung der Reste des RIR6 1.VII.16.*
11. Kriegsarchiv Munich 16. Inf. Regt. (WK) 3 *2. Bataillon Gefechtsbericht.*
12. *ibid.*
13. Kriegsarchiv Munich 16. Inf. Regt. (WK) 3 *1. Bataillon Gefechtsbericht.*
14. This must refer to *Pickelhauben*. Initial issues of steel helmets to reinforcing units did not begin until the first week of August.
15. *Sixteenth: Seventeenth: Eighteenth: Nineteenth Battalions, The Manchester Regiment – A Record 1914–1918* p. 26 quoted Maddocks *Montauban* pp. 106–107.
16. This refers to a small track leading northwest from Montauban to the eastern tip of Caterpillar Valley.
17. Kriegsarchiv Munich 16. Inf. Regt. (WK) 3 *2. Bataillon Gefechtsbericht.*
18. Stein *Erlebnisse* p. 80.
19. Kümmel: History Reserve Infantry Regiment 91 p. 227
20. Prior and Wilson *The Somme* p. 127.
21. Loßberg *Meine Tätigkeit* pp. 222–223.
22. Quoted by Foerster *Graf Schlieffen und der Weltkrieg* p. 215.
23. French Colonial Corps, quoted Kabisch *Somme* p. 53.
24. The *Foureaux Riegel*, known to the British as the Switch Trench, ran east – west, clipping the northern point of High Wood.
25. This may be an error because there does not appear ever to have been an engineer unit with that number.
26. Kriegsarchiv Munich 16. Inf.Regt. (WK) 3 *3. Garde-Infanterie-Division I Geheim* dated 12 Jul 16.

27. Kriegsarchiv Munich 16. Inf.Regt. (WK) *24 Bataillon Befehl vom 10.7.16 Beilage Nr. 29.*

28. Kriegsarchiv Munich Infanterie-Divisionen (WK) 4131 *GenKdo XIV .R.K. I a No. 1196 geh.* Dated 3 July 1916.

29. Kümmel: History RIR 91 pp. 216 – 217

30. This must be a reference to High Wood, which cannot be seen from Bazentin le Grand. Either there was an error in what Eber recalled, or Bedall must have meant that the recruits were pulling back in that general direction.

31. In fact the order had been issued on 12 July.

32. Kriegsarchiv Munich 16. Inf. Regt. (WK) 3 *Bericht über den Gefechtstag Bayr. 16.Inf.R. am 14.7.1916* dated 22.11.16.

33. Schulenburg-Wolfsburg History Fusilier Guards pp140–141.

34. BOH 2 p. 83.

35. This reference is a mystery. The circumstances of the wounding and death of the officer concerned do not match the German account in any particular. However, a temporary capture in the confused battle situation of some members of this battalion is quite feasible and in any case it would be most unusual for a German account accurately to name the unit involved on this part of the battlefield unless there was some basis of fact in what was reported.

36. Kriegsarchiv Munich HS 2293 *Der Heldenkampf des I. bataillons 16. Infanterie Regiments – der 14. Juli 1916.*

37. Kriegsarchiv Munich 16. Inf. Regt. (WK) 3 *16. Bayer. Infanterie. Regiment. An K.B.10.I.Div. Beaulencourt 15.7.1916 9,15 pm.*

38. Lutz *op. cit.* p. 47.

39. Loßberg *op. cit.* p. 229.

40. Schönfeldt History Grenadier Regiment 12 p. 95.

41. Reymann History Infantry Regiment 52 p. 115.

42. Jaud History Bavarian Reserve Infantry Regiment 19 p. 74.

43. Loßberg *op. cit.* p. 229.

44. Gruson History Infantry Regiment 72 p. 235.

45. *ibid.*p 235.

46. Falkenstein History Infantry Regiment 93 p. 114.

CHAPTER 5

Army Group Gallwitz: A Failed Experiment

Trouble at the Top

The risk of the German front on the Somme collapsing in the face of renewed Allied pressure was such that, reluctantly or not, *OHL* had no choice in early July but to feed reinforcements to Second Army. As more and more divisions poured into the rail heads behind the line it quickly became impossible for one headquarters to handle them all. Loßberg had requested and secured the services of two additional General Staff officers and other individual reinforcements, but the burden was simply too great; by mid-July Second Army was attempting to command over twenty divisions and the span of command was impossible.[1] The obvious course of action was to divide command responsibility between two armies; the problem was to locate a suitable commander and to build a headquarters.

In search of a solution, Falkenhayn looked towards the Verdun front. There, ever since March, General der Artillerie Max von Gallwitz had been in overall command of all German operations on the west bank of the Meuse, where the battles for control of Mort Homme and Cote 304 had been raging. Gallwitz was highly experienced. He had commanded Twelfth Army in 1915 with success against the Russians, pushing them back across the River Narew as far as the Berezina. He then followed this with command of the Eleventh Army, which played a significant part in the destruction of the Serbian army later that same year. The first indication that something of the sort was under consideration was a visit to Gallwitz's headquarters by the chief of staff Fifth Army, when the matter was discussed. This was followed by a conversation with the German Crown Prince on 16 July. Falkenhayn had decided, stated Crown Prince Wilhelm, to move Gallwitz and his entire headquarters north to the Somme area, there to take charge of operations south of the river, but temporarily under command of General Fritz von Below who, though junior to him, was fully conversant with the local situation. This would have been in complete accordance with the policy, later given full force when the German army began to employ *Eingreif* procedures more generally, of all and any reinforcements being deployed, at least initially, in support of and subordinate to the local commander.

Although fine in theory this took no account of the personalities involved. As soon as the matter was raised Gallwitz immediately demurred. He had no confidence in Below's ability or suitability for senior command and made it quite clear that he was unwilling to be redeployed to a battle in crisis unless he was granted the necessary power of command. If this was unacceptable to Falkenhayn then a less senior general should be sent the Somme, leaving Gallwitz to continue in his present appointment. Falkenhayn quickly decided that in the circumstances he had to stick with his plan to move Gallwitz and by that same evening he had made a decision. Ignoring any possible objections that Below might have raised, he directed that the previous Second Army was to be divided into two. First Army, commanded by General von Below, with Oberst Loßberg as chief of staff, was to take charge of all troops and operations north of the Somme, while Second Army, under General von Gallwitz, (chief of staff Oberst Bronsart von Schellenberg), was to operate south of the river. Gallwitz was placed in overall command of the newly formed 'Army Group Gallwitz' and granted operational control of both armies. In order to provide continuity, especially for the new Second Army, the heads of the operations branch of the two armies swapped appointments and numerous other staff officers were also posted between the two headquarters. Gallwitz and his staff took over the existing headquarters facilities in St Quentin, whilst First Army set up in Bourlon.

Falkenhayn may have been content with this arrangement, but almost all officers holding senior commands in the west viewed the appointment of General von Gallwitz as both commander of Second Army and in overall charge of both armies engaged on the Somme as a fundamental error, regarding it as a further example of Falkenhayn's dubious decision making. Choosing his words carefully, Generalleutnant von Kuhl, chief of staff to Crown Prince Rupprecht, wrote later that it was, 'just as unprofitable as the subordination at the beginning of the war of Kluck's First Army to Generaloberst von Bülow, commander Second Army'.[2] Below's biographer remarked mildly that, 'Naturally General von Below could not view the ruling as in any way satisfactory, in that it appeared to contradict entirely the previous appreciation of his command ability … he considered requesting to be relieved'.[3] For his part, Crown Prince Rupprecht made a robust entry in his diary on 17 July and increased his already extensive manoeuvring against Falkenhayn.

"General von Below is justifiably sickened by this slight. The guilt for the reverses his army has suffered lies with *OHL* and not with him. They ignored his reports and took no account of his requests for reserves. When, at long last, reserves did arrive, it was too late. They arrived in dribs and drabs and had to be deployed immediately to plug gaps. As a result, there has been such a mixing of formations that nobody knows what is happening."[4]

Given that all military logic dictates that the only way to have ensured that the two headquarters astride the Somme worked harmoniously and in unison from the start would have been to have created an independent army group headquarters – something that was later to happen under the command of Crown Prince Rupprecht – it is hard to escape the conclusion that Falkenhayn did indeed intend the arrangement to shift any possible blame from himself and to represent a form of rebuke to Below; it certainly ensured that the seeds of controversy and dispute were sown from the very beginning of this short-lived and unlamented command arrangement. Naturally, it is hardly surprising that the root of the subsequent disagreements related to shortage of manpower and its deployment. From the very first the ability of the German army to conduct effective operations was dogged by the fact that insufficient resources had been made available before battle was joined and that high loss rates and Allied pressure meant that forces on arrival were being used primarily to meet local crises.

It was not as though Below and Gallwitz were unaware of the need to attempt to take a more proactive stance on the Somme. Right at the beginning of the month, Below had suggested the mounting of a large scale counter-attack, but the idea was rejected. Then, on arriving at *OHL* for a preliminary appointment with Falkenhayn on 17 July, Gallwitz had presented a proposal for a major counter-attack into the right flank of the French army. He took the view that a vigorous thrust aimed at the French army between Barleux and Soyécourt could create great problems and probably succeed in cutting off the French troops located to the west of Péronne as a result of the alteration of its main focus to offensive operations north of the Somme.

Having listened, Falkenhayn, all too aware of the manpower and equipment shortages facing the German army and reluctant to scale back his Verdun offensive in any fundamental way, immediately turned down the scheme and is said to have dismissed Gallwitz with the words, 'Hold on, hold on – that is the only thing that matters!'[5] Once the reorganisation was complete, command of the Somme battlefield was divided so that initially each army had three subordinate corps. For First Army these were: Group Stein (XIV Reserve Corps), northern army boundary to the Ancre; Group Armin (IV Corps), Thiepval to Guillemont via Ginchy; and Group Goßler (VI Reserve Corps), south to the Somme then east to Cléry. Second Army commanded Group Quast (IX Corps), from the Somme south to a point near Vermandovillers; Group Pannewitz (XVII Corps) south to Soyencourt, north of Balâtre; and, finally, Group Plettenberg (Guard Corps), extending down to the army boundary south of Noyon.

Inevitably, it did not take long for misunderstandings and disputes to build up and within days there was a full scale row between the army commanders concerning tactical control of the battle and deployment of reserves. One early incident was summarised by Oberstleutnant Loßberg thus:

> "A very carefully planned counter-attack on Pozières to be conducted by 18th Reserve Division was scheduled for 25 July, but due to heavy British superiority it did not achieve its objectives. This caused General von Gallwitz, whose own Second Army also failed in an attack near Estrées, to issue an order to First Army that in future only places of tactical importance were to be recaptured. This order, not without reason, irritated General von Below. At least he said to me in conversation that General von Gallwitz had not properly estimated the great importance of the possession of Pozières."[6]

One glance at the geography of the area and the importance of Pozières as a blocking position defending the operational *Schwerpunkt* stretching away northwest towards Thiepval and on to Serre, immediately underlines why the loss of the village was regarded with such concern by First Army so, when the 1st Australian Division succeeded in wresting almost all of it out of German hands on 23 July, the situation was regarded as critical. Immediate steps were taken to try to restore the situation, though with no success that day. A great many of the counter-actions by the German army on the Somme were effectively hasty counter-attacks, launched with troops and resources immediately to hand. However, carefully planned and prepared deliberate counter-attacks were also mounted at times. The operation against Pozières was intended as one such; in fact, it finally fell between two stools and failed. Nevertheless, the processes involved and the tense and pressurised situation within which the chain of command had to operate are of considerable interest.

7th Infantry Division, which had been pushed out of the village, was in any case due for routine relief on 25 July by 18th Reserve Division as soon as it had completed its redeployment south from the Sallaumines area. Instead, the latter found itself pitched straight into a battlefield crisis. Its commander, Generalleutnant Wellmann, noted in his diary on 25 July,

> "[In the] morning there was a major conference at divisional headquarters [in Haplincourt]. In attendance were Army Commander von Below, together with his chief of staff Oberst von Loßberg and General der Infanterie Sixt von Armin from Headquarters IV Corps. Representing our own IX Reserve Corps was its chief of staff, Oberst von der Heyde. Present also was General der Infanterie z.D. Kunze from 117th Infantry Division, Foot Artillery General Struve and others. I was given the mission of recapturing Pozières ... "[7]

SITUATION POZIÈRES 24–25 JULY

Writing later, Wellman added,

> "The whole thing came as a complete and utter surprise to me and the officers of my staff. It is possible that the staff of 7th Division [with which Headquarters 18th Reserve Division was temporarily sharing accommodation] were aware of this high level visit but, if so, nobody had informed me; I was completely in the dark. Oberst von der Heyde was the first to appear, then one by one the remainder appeared in my operations room. I simply had no idea why they were there or what I was supposed to do ... There was much discussion which I did not understand fully, because I was still in the process of orientation. It finally became clear that Pozières was to be recaptured and my corps commander, General von Boehn, stated formally, 'General Wellmann is given the mission of recapturing Pozières'. I took this as proof of the trust my corps commander had in me, but it would have been better had one of the commanders of 7th or 117th Infantry Divisions, Generals Riedel or Kunze, been given the task because they were fully familiar with the situation."[8]

Making the best of the matter, once the meeting broke up Wellmann and his General Staff captain went into a side room with the corps commander and his chief of staff and discussed the attack in detail. Wellmann, having noted that counter-attacks at first light tended to fail in this area, proposed instead a start time the following afternoon and this was agreed. It was further decided to attack on a two regiment frontage, using Infantry Regiment 157, the left flank regiment of 117th Infantry Division, and Reserve Infantry Regiment 86 from Wellmann's division. Discovering that General Kunze had driven back to his headquarters and leaving General Struve to develop the artillery plan, Wellmann followed him, only to discover that Infantry Regiment 157 was very worn down and not in a good condition to launch an attack. Despite this, for the sake of speed, Welllmann decided not to replace the 157th but to carry on as planned, admitting later that this had been a mistake.

It also transpired that the regimental command post was under such heavy fire that it would be impractical to arrange a face to face meeting between commanders. Instead, Kunze passed details by runner to the 157th and arranged for a liaison officer to be sent to Wellman's headquarters to receive detailed orders. Heavy shelling meant that hours were lost whilst this took place and little time was left for preparation. Much the same delays occurred when Wellmann attempted to pass orders to Reserve Infantry Regiment 86 and he had to content himself with leaving instructions for Generalleutnant Freiherr von Ende, commanding 35 Reserve Brigade, to inform Oberstleutnant Burmeister, commander Reserve

Infantry Regiment 86, about the outline plan and subsequently to pass on more detailed orders, which were received as follows:

"Reserve Infantry Regiment 86 and Infantry Regiment 157 have been subordinated to 18th Reserve Division for the recapture of Pozières. The time of the attack has not yet been fixed. During the night 24/25 July, Reserve Infantry Regiment 86 is to take over the position at the northern extremity of Pozières from the Pozières – Courcelette track to a point 500 metres southeast of the Albert-Bapaume road. (linking with the former forward position of 1st Battalion Infantry Regiment 27). 35 Reserve Infantry Brigade is to arrange the relief in consultation with 14 Infantry Brigade and in accordance with instructions issued by 7th Infantry Division. 2nd Battalion Reserve Infantry Regiment 86 is available for deployment. The 3rd Battalion is to be called forward to Eaucourt l'Abbaye. Reserve Infantry Regiment 84 is responsible for maintaining contact in the front line."[9]

Already the friction of war was causing problems to mount and Wellmann's mood did not improve when he discovered that General Struve's fire plan included no specific concentrations of fire on particular points, but comprised a more or less random process of general harassing fire. Challenged by Wellmann, Struve explained that he was up against several problems. In the first place Allied air superiority meant that there was absolutely no German air reconnaissance over the Pozières battlefield, so he had no idea where the enemy positions lay and there was no chance of aerial correction of fire either. Add in the fact that the village was now in dead ground behind the windmill to the northeast of the village, with the result that there could be no observed fire by forward observation officers, and it is easy to see why it subsequently failed.

Nevertheless, preparations continued and the men of Reserve Infantry Regiment 86 began to move into position. Unfortunately for them they were not left undisturbed to complete their preparations. Some Australian troops were moved forward to reinforce their front line positions at about dawn on 25 July. This was misinterpreted on the German side as a pre-emptive attack and units of Reserve Infantry Regiment 86 were rushed forward piecemeal to counter it. This was a disastrous mistake, because the advancing battalions were caught in heavy fire and, one after the other, suffered such heavy casualties that they were unable to participate fully in the main planned assault or press it home. Trying to impose some order on the escalating chaos, General Wellmann decided to appoint a brigade headquarters to take close control of the attack. 81 Infantry Brigade from 17th Reserve Division was available, because its formations, Infantry Regiments 162 and 163, had not yet deployed, so it was tasked with the job.

Once again this was less than ideal. A brigade headquarters was now attempting to coordinate an attack by elements of two other divisions. It would be over unfamiliar ground and against an enemy of unknown locations and strength. To compound the problems further, as the time for the attack drew closer, Oberst von Beczwarzowsky, commanding 81 Infantry Brigade, reported that commander Infantry Regiment 157 was refusing to attack because his preparations were not complete. Furious and in total disagreement with him, Wellmann passed a message to the brigade, stating that if Infantry Regiment 157 did not attack as ordered he would have its commander court martialled. Despite mounting problems and the fact that the attack was already splintering, the heavy artillery bombardment began at 1.30 pm, four hours prior to the start time.

This certainly caused difficulties and some casualties to the defending Australians but, for all the efforts of the gunners, their work was to come to nothing. Much of the strength of Reserve Infantry Regiment 86 had been frittered away throughout the day and Infantry Regiment 157 did not attack as ordered. When the state of Infantry Regiment 157 after seven days of intense fighting in and around Pozières is taken into consideration, it is small wonder that it was unable to respond to the attack order, but both then and at other stages in the battle; there is clear evidence that the chain of command was unwilling to make any allowance for high casualties or general exhaustion. All the time that a formation was in the line, it was expected to play a full part in any and all operations which came its way; this despite the fact in this case that already by 23 July, for example, 2nd Battalion Infantry Regiment 157, which had deployed five days earlier to Pozières 700 strong, was down to 175 all ranks.

Two of its five remaining machine guns were out of action and several crew members of the other three had become casualties. There was a critical shortage of ammunition and hand grenades, no hot food had been delivered forward, only tinned rations and bread, whilst lack of water and other drinks meant that everyone was plagued by thirst. Evacuation of casualties was a nightmare. On 23 July, with casualties arriving at the aid posts constantly, some seriously wounded men had already been waiting for almost forty eight hours to be carried to the rear.[10] Despite these problems, which were paralleled in the other two battalions, the regiment held a heavy Australian attack during the night 23/24 July and launched several limited counter-attacks during 24 July, which caused the casualty list to rise alarmingly. In a confused situation, misdirected friendly fire also took a heavy toll and did nothing to improve morale. During the afternoon of 24 July, Reserve Leutnant Roske, commanding 3rd Company on the edge of Pozières, reported bitterly, 'Our own artillery has shot up my position so that it is ripe for attack. They are not reacting to green flares [increase the range]. If any enemy attack occurs I shall be unable to defend my position because it is the target of the defensive fire of our heavy artillery.'[11]

Although, as has been noted, the official view was that Major Hengstenberg either refused to attack or at least failed to do so, the regiment recorded subsequently that the mission was simply beyond its capability. It had been subject to heavy artillery fire, followed by a night attack that began at 11.00 pm and continued through into the following day. As a result, when preparations should have been underway to participate in the attack, the entire regiment was under heavy artillery fire and the forward companies spent the whole day fighting for their lives at close quarters; none more so than the gallant Leutnant Roske's 3rd Company, which was attacked frontally, from a flank and the rear. Roske died in hand to hand fighting and there were few survivors. Unteroffizier Wabnik, a junior NCO of 6th Company, left a brief account of the battle from his perspective.

"During the afternoon the British [sic.] succeeded in outflanking us. We were then fighting on two fronts. Ceaselessly we threw a succession of hand grenades. Constantly we fired one round after another from our rifles until the barrels glowed red hot. Our morale sagged in the face of the enemy superiority. Reserve Leutnant Neugebauer, however, rallied us, shouting loudly to hold on and throwing grenade after grenade at the British. Our losses were heavy; comrade after comrade fell back into the trench, shot through the head. The little band of fighters continued to shrink. One or two men, seized with trench fury, launched themselves at the enemy armed with spades, but they were felled by the enemy with their rifle butts. To our front and rear the bodies of dead comrades and dead enemy piled up. This went on until dusk, when the enemy pulled back and we could take a breather."[12]

To make the fiasco even worse, a German air reconnaissance report shortly after the attack began reported, wrongly, that German troops had been seen advancing down into Pozières. It is possible that there had been a mix up with actions around Martinpuich, but no sooner had the correct picture of failure been transmitted upwards than recriminations and a blame game began. IX Reserve Corps accused Reserve Infantry Regiment 86 and 81 Infantry Brigade of sending and re-transmitting false reports. General Wellmann received a written reprimand, accusing him of failing in his duties by not making contact with 117th Infantry Division or properly preparing the two regiments involved for their missions. He was able later to rebut both charges, but the entire episode left a bad taste in the mouths of all involved.

Generalleutnant Wellman summed up the operation in a diary entry late on 25 July. 'Infantry Regiment 157 failed completely to attack. The Reserve Infantry

Regiment 86 assault fell apart in the enemy defensive fire. The brigade commander, Oberst Beczwarzowsky, commanding the two regiments, wanted to renew the attack after a fresh artillery bombardment at 9.30 pm, but this went against the wishes of corps headquarters.'[13] Although nobody on the German side emerges with much credit for this affair, it is obvious in hindsight that the pressure being exerted on an over-extended German army was the root cause of the problem. As a result, circumstances meant that the way it was being forced to fight the battle was hardly conducive to a smooth and harmonious conduct of the defence. As has been mentioned, this setback caused General von Gallwitz's refusal to permit a renewal of the attack on Pozières and also to issue a secret directive concerning the conduct of counter-attacks.

As the army group commander he had every right to do so; but the manner of it, with First Army merely an addressee on the distribution list, together with the Second Army subordinate headquarters, was certainly tactless. As for its tone and contents, it is not hard to see why Below took such sharp exception to it; it reads as a check list for those who did not know their business, an implied accusation hard to accept by a headquarters or its commander, who by then had been at the focus of intense defensive fighting for four weeks. Furthermore, several of the points made were simply beyond the capability of the German army at that stage in the battle. This was especially the case for the artillery, which lacked the aerial reconnaissance assets necessary for accurate target acquisition and was in any case far too weak to take on the Allied artillery on even terms. As a gunner this was something which Gallwitz ought to have appreciated, but apparently did not. The main part of the document reads as follows:

"Unsuccessful attacks in recent days against villages and sections of trench captured by the enemy, cause me to stress the following points once more:

1. If the enemy forces his way into parts of our position, the best chance of success comes from an immediate decision by a subordinate commander to launch a counter-stroke. To this end, all subordinate commanders must be schooled to hold reserves close by.
2. If, for whatever reason, the immediate counter-stroke is unsuccessful, then only a counter-attack, carefully planned in fullest detail, will achieve success. Plans and preparations must be checked by higher headquarters and changes made if necessary.

In this context, attention must be paid to the following points, which also apply to other planned attacks:

a. Precise reconnaissance of the placement and strength of the enemy infantry positions (patrols, observation at ground level and from the air).

b. Selection of a start line as close to ninety degrees to the axis of the attack as possible.

c. Exact definition of boundaries and deployment in depth (of follow-up waves).

   i. Incorporation of storm troops, including engineers armed with flamethrowers, amongst the waves of infantry and tasked to break through to the objective.

      No extended assault lines in woods and built up areas. Small storm columns to be employed instead.

   ii. Carrying parties (trench stores to develop the enemy positions; resupply of ammunition).

   iii. Mopping up parties to clear dugouts and trenches; prisoner escorts.

   iv. Personnel to secure the start line.

d. Precise definition of the objectives. Each subordinate commander and every individual must understand his task.

e. Calculation of the quantity of artillery ammunition required to support the firing period.

f. Allocation of fire[14] on the basis of precise reconnaissance (aerial photographs). Destruction of obstacles and enemy lines, especially the first one. Total destruction or neutralisation of enemy artillery, mortars and flanking machine gun positions. Neutralisation of adjoining lines, including during the assault. Harassing fire on approach routes used by enemy reserves. Pauses in the fire plan to deceive the enemy about the precise moment of the assault.

g. Precise control of timings. Synchronisation of watches. Lifting of artillery fire and simultaneous infantry break in to the enemy position. Advance of the infantry under a protective umbrella of fire. Reporting, communications equipment. Reserve on call.

h. Reorganisation of the artillery after a successful assault. New defensive fire zones must be prepared.

The Commander in Chief von
Gallwitz General der Artillerie"[15]

Of course this did not put an end to the matter. First Army in particular continued to be subject to heavy attack and the situation in and around Pozières and Martinpuich was a constant source of anxiety for the defence. Forced to go through Headquarters Second Army to obtain support and reinforcement, Loßberg, who was well known for making explicit his demands for what he considered to be his army's essential requirements, passed in early August a series of requests to his opposite number in which he sought reassurance and specific undertakings about the number of formations Second Army could make available to him to meet immediate and anticipated needs. Bronsart gained the impression that Loßberg was effectively accusing him of not dealing fairly with First Army and tensions began to mount once more.

It was not long before the dispute reached army commander level again. In response to Allied attacks, First Army launched a number of counter-attacks between 6 and 8 August, generally with success, though ground was lost in the south of the Group Kirchbach sector, where 23rd (Saxon) Reserve Division, subject to heavy flanking fire from south of the Somme, was forced back around Monacu Farm to the west of Cléry. Despite the fact casualties in this division were so severe that its composite formations had to be withdrawn almost at once, this was not the source of friction. That arose yet again because of further German operations directed at Pozières. The Allies had kept up the pressure on this sector of the front following the major clashes towards the end of July, so there was considerable concern – shared by both Group Böhn and First Army – that the worn out formations of 18th Reserve Division would be unable to hold a fresh thrust and that a pre-emptive counter-attack would be completely beyond their powers. The trigger was the capture of Hill 160 [Pozières Windmill] by the Australians on 4 August and their partial break in to the forward trenches of Reserve Infantry Regiment 84, 18th Reserve Division, astride the Roman road. Immediate hasty counter attacks were mounted by, amongst others, the neighbouring 11th Company, Reserve Infantry Regiment 31, but although the line was just held and further close quarter battles continued to be fought during 6 August by sub units of that regiment, aided by reinforcements from Reserve Infantry Regiment 75, the overall situation remained critical.[16]

First Army decided that an attempt must be made to retake this dominating point but, in yet another example of the unrelenting pressure to which the German army was being subject, the best that Loßberg could do was to make use of the Silesian Infantry Regiment 163, 17th Reserve Division, which had been released a few days earlier from First Army reserve to Group Böhn to assist in the construction of depth defensive lines. As a preliminary step, its 2nd and 3rd Battalions were placed under command of 35 Reserve Brigade, 18th Reserve Division, and moved into counter-penetration positions, whilst 1st Battalion and the machine gun companies, initially despatched to be under the command of 81 Infantry Brigade, 17th Reserve Division, were instead directed to move into Army Group Reserve.

Deciding that a counter-attack on a two battalion frontage was essential, Loßberg requested the release of 1st Battalion Infantry Regiment 163 and also of 1st Battalion Infantry Regiment 63, then also in Army Group Gallwitz reserve back at Villers au Flos. With some reluctance, but persuaded by the urgency of the situation to concur, permission was granted. Both units began their march forward, drawing steel helmets for the first time, and were placed under the command of Reserve Infantry Regiment 84, whose commander, Oberst Balthazar, was in overall command of the operation. This was a tall order for Infantry Regiment 63, 12th Infantry Division, in particular. It had been so badly mauled near Montauban by the pre-battle bombardment during the last week of June that it had had to be withdrawn out of the line. Although its relief by Bavarian Reserve Infantry Regiment 6 during the night 30 June – 1 July spared it the fate of the near-destroyed Bavarians on 1 July, one month was little time to restore it to full fighting ability.

Already it can be seen that the hasty improvisation of an attacking force with no previous knowledge of the terrain or experience of working either with each other or within the 18th Reserve Division chain of command was a high risk policy. Nevertheless, the best had to be made of the situation. The plan was to assault through the forward positions of the exhausted Reserve Infantry Regiment 31; 1st Battalion Infantry Regiment 63 right, 1st Battalion Infantry Regiment 163 left. Moving forward during the night 5/6 August, the battalion commanding officers and their company commander assembled at the command post of Hauptmann Becker, the Reserve Infantry Regiment 84 sub-sector commander, to await orders. On arrival the attack orders had not arrived, so the two battalion commanders decided between themselves how to tackle the task. They agreed to advance in platoon waves with flame throwers on the left of the leading elements and engineers dispersed among the various attacking waves. Warning orders were issued and the troops stumbled around in the dark to try to get into position.

Eventually, at 12.15 am, the divisional orders arrived. Fortunately, they were more or less identical with those already issued, so no changes were made, other than to add three machine guns of Machine Gun Sharp Shooter Troop 127 to the fourth wave. Even so, there were problems before the operation even began. At 3.30 am, orders arrived for Hauptmann Weede, commanding 1st Battalion Infantry Regiment 163, directing him to despatch two companies to the Infantry Regiment 63 sector, because its subunits had not arrived in time. Weede did as he was told; but he passed word to Oberst Balthazar that he now required reinforcement and that, in any case, there could be no attack before 4.30 am at the earliest. With great difficulty Weede's 1st and 3rd Companies were redeployed but no sooner had they arrived than the first two companies of Infantry Regiment 63 turned up, so the Infantry Regiment 163 men were released back to their own battalion.

Deploying for the assault was a prolonged nightmare in the dark. The entire battlefield was covered in shell holes, tree stumps, tangled wire and innumerable other obstacles to movement. Despite the exhausting nature of moving at all in such circumstances, start lines were reached in time for a start time of 4.30 am and although the German heavy artillery was wrongly pounding targets in depth, rather than the enemy front line, the battalions set off. Confused by the light of a store of signal cartridges exploding and taking them for a flamethrower in action, the left hand company of Infantry Regiment 163 stumbled into a Reserve Infantry Regiment 31 position. In the event this worked in their favour because, swinging off to the right, subsequently this company actually took an Australian outpost from an unexpected flank, rolled it up and took two prisoners.[17] Meanwhile the remaining companies were able to storm forward and gain a lodgement in the forward enemy trenches. That was about as good as it got. To the right the Infantry Regiment 63 companies could not get forward, so there was an immediate threat to the Infantry Regiment 163 flank. Part of the problem was that none of the flamethrowers worked. In some cases they would simply not light; in others the equipment was hit and blew up, with dire consequences for the operators.

Leutnant Zinnemann, whose brother had been killed four weeks previously and who was severely wounded during the operation, commanded 1st Company Infantry Regiment 63. He later wrote an extremely lengthy and vivid description of the attack from his perspective. An extract provides a flavour of the intensity and swift failure of the attack.

"We only carried rations, ammunition, weapons and digging equipment – in other words we were in assault order. Warlencourt was to our rear and we were approaching a notorious place. I ran up to the commanding officer, 'Herr Major I urgently suggest that we move away from the road. We took casualties here three days ago when the enemy tried to hit the ammunition columns.' 'Yes, you are right. Move left and advance well spread out in the open by column of platoons.' Off we deployed, with the commanders leading and we then advanced, leaning forward and with the chin straps of our protective helmets firmly fixed beneath our chins.[18] Shells roared over our heads, landing in the buildings of Ligny-Tillois [sic. Thilloy], Warlencourt, Pys and Martinpuich [and crashing down] all around us, bursting with flashes and sending pillars of earth up into the air. The noise was appalling and sometimes we got too close to our own fire, because the German artillery was firing, sending over greetings and preparing the attack...

"We run the next one hundred metres as illuminating rockets cast a ghostly glare over the countryside. There, a sunken road – jump in! ... We launch forward towards the first positions, about one hundred metres away. 'Go! On your feet! Double march!' Everyone leaps forward, their bodies bent nearly double. Then a flare and another! Take cover! Lie still. To our front the very earth is ploughed up. It is all a mass of craters, piles of earth – and small arms fire. Bullets whizz close by, cracking and whirring. 'Go on! Leap up then take cover!' Another few bounds and we are in the remains of a newly dug trench. Arounds us vague shapes can be made out. Are they corpses? Living soldiers? Machine gun fire rips overhead. How it hammers. They have seen us, heard us. Flares are going up all along the front. They are all nervous That's bad! It's not going to work! An assault has got to have surprise …

"The German artillery fire lifts towards the enemy, flares go up – we launch forward. The same instant our hand grenades fly in wide arcs at the enemy. There is a rapid series of explosions, screams, the flash of bayonets – more flares – 'On your feet! Double march!' Piercing, animal shouts of *Hurra!* … then more grenades at the enemy. These knock men off their feet or tear them apart … we shall soon close with the enemy … Suddenly we find ourselves in an appalling situation. Ghostly forms are pulling back to our front, but from right and left come torrents of fire – bullets spraying everywhere with a British [*sic.*] machine gun chattering away. In the harsh light of numerous flares, Germans can be seen collapsing … my neighbour on my right makes as to throw – suddenly there is a loud thud, a scream and he collapses in amongst us, a bullet has smashed through his arm. My batman grabs the grenade which falls from his cramped hand and hurls it away. We hit the ground as one and it immediately explodes. It could have finished us all off!

"The assault has only gained twenty metres. We are pinned down in shell holes. Machine gun fire cuts the air above us and the enemy artillery is landing shells to our rear. They cannot get us here where we are within throwing range of the enemy. The arm is bound up. August has sacrificed his trouser belt. The man's morale is in tatters. He wants to go to the rear, but that is impossible. Anyone who lifts his head even one centimetre is shot at. We scrabble away, sweating. Death lurks in the night and what of the morning, in daylight? We are stuck where we are, our spades our only salvation. Soon we have dug a shallow scrape and lie in it one behind the other. To our fronts it is somewhat deeper and our upper bodies disappear under the protective earth, but our legs are still sticking up in the air. Each man digs under the legs of the man to his front. Carefully, we dig in deeper and deeper while bullets crack around us and shells roar overhead. Splinters fly everywhere, but they cannot hit us now. By dawn we are down sufficiently deep to crawl around … "[19]

Even on the Infantry Regiment 163 front, where the attack had gained a foothold in the Australian positions, the situation was extremely precarious. The trenches themselves were barely recognisable, there was effectively no overhead cover whatsoever and, although the troops dug in frenziedly, their protection was utterly inadequate once it became light and the Allied artillery began systematically to pound the few captured trenches. Casualties mounted rapidly; then when the shelling had been going on for several hours and was followed by a counter-attack at about 5.00 pm, the few men still on their feet were left with no choice but to pull back to the so-called *Pozières Riegel*. There their troubles did not end, because the shelling and infantry attacks continued until the attackers were back either in their starting positions or even further to the rear. Infantry Regiment 163 did not list their casualties from this operation specifically but, when it was finally withdrawn a couple of days later, its losses for this tour of duty amounted to fourteen officers and 269 other ranks killed in action, with a further fifty one officers and 1,364 other ranks wounded and 199 missing.[20] In the case of Infantry Regiment 63, Zinnemann's 1st Company had begun the battle on 24 June down near Cléry at full strength. By the time it was relieved (though it had received a number of battle casualty replacements) it had suffered casualties of a staggering three officers, three vizefeldwebels and 197 other ranks killed, wounded or missing. Of these one officer (Zinnemann), one vizefeldwebel, thirteen unteroffiziers and fifty seven other ranks had been incurred attempting to capture Hill 160.

In summary, gallant though the attack may have been, any initial success could not be exploited or even maintained. Such was the weight of fire directed against the attackers that they were forced to withdraw once more to reduce the mounting toll of casualties. Gallwitz, given his attitude to Pozières, saw the entire affair as a pointless loss of life and, in a tense telephone conversation, 'advised' Below to put a stop to such operations before they were ever launched. Below, who enjoyed a good working relationship with Loßberg, despite being frustrated at the earlier exemplary sacking of his previous chief of staff, Grünert, by Falkenhayn in early July, took this as an insult and unwarranted interference with his area of responsibility. It took a lengthy conversation between the two commanders to calm the situation down.[21] The Gallwitz version of events was;

> "I found it painful that the attack on Pozières during the evening of the 6th was followed by yielding that which had been gained. So much blood had been spilt for nothing. In a telephone conversation with Below I made the point that I wanted to exercise a moderating influence over decisions of this type. Below took this as an insult and came to speak to me at length. Because we agreed in principle about counter-attacks, the disagreement was satisfactorily resolved."[22]

The truce so created, if such it was, was short lived. Because of the predominance of Allied thrusts in the northern sector of the battlefield, over the next few days it is no surprise that First Army gradually assumed command of additional Groups as senior headquarters were relieved and frontages reduced. Although these reinforcements were essential, nevertheless all the negotiation and the pressure exerted by First Army led to further increased tension between Below and Gallwitz. Commenting rather peevishly years later, Gallwitz referred obliquely to the matter in his memoirs.

"Loßberg had cast his eyes on the one battle ready reserve formation behind Second Army, namely 1st Guards Division. In my dual role as commander of both the army group and Second Army I was frequently confronted by competing interests. I was never unsympathetic, but had scrupulously to balance my decisions to serve the higher purpose. My chief of staff, however, was unhappy at the continuous prodding and prying into our affairs, all the more so because Loßberg had forbidden his staff officers to provide information to the Army Group without his say so."[23]

Within days the increased tension had come to a head once more; ironically, 1st Guards Infantry Division was involved. It all happened in the wake of serious fighting between Maurepas and Cléry that had caused heavy losses to 1st Bavarian Reserve Division. General von Below arranged for its relief on 13 August by 1st Guards Infantry Division, then still in reserve to Army Group Gallwitz, and this was completed four days later. Gallwitz subsequently summed up the situation with which he was faced during the evening of 12 August in this way:

"Towards midnight I was reading official correspondence when Bronsart [chief of staff Second Army] brought me bad news. Group Fasbender [I Bavarian Reserve Corps] was being attacked heavily. The French had broken into Maurepas a second time. Colonial troops had also apparently seized ground in the Bavarian Reserve Infantry Regiment 1 sector and driven forward to the Second Position. In order to assist a little, I ordered the leading battalion of Footguard Regiment 1, then located near St Quentin, to move in rear of this part of the front. At 12.30 am Bronsart announced that a major assault was underway along the entire First Army front. Loßberg's morning report on 13th stated that it seemed that, essentially, the line had been held, but that the situation around Cléry on the bank of the Somme was problematic. Apparently, all the German strong points and trenches had been overrun up to one kilometre in depth between Hardecourt and the Somme [and I Reserve Bavarian Corps had suffered serious casualties]. I

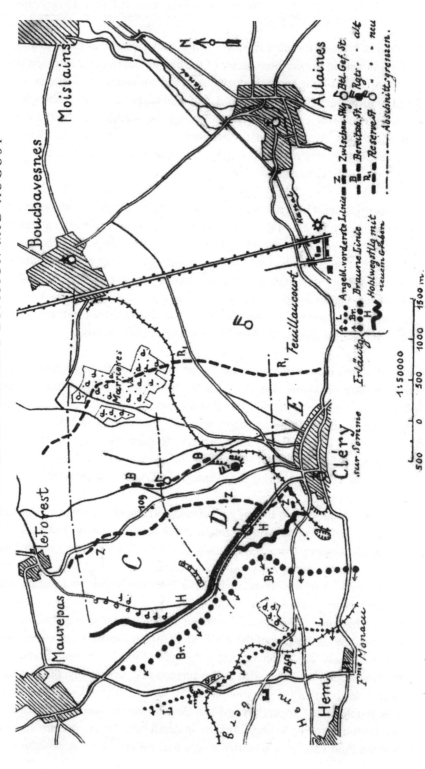

SITUATION 1st BAVARIAN RESERVE DIVISION MID-AUGUST

erhard von Scharnhorst.

Karl von Clausewitz.

Moltke the Elder.

Alfred Graf von Schlieffen.

Moltke the Younger.

Falkenhayn.

The Kaiser flanked by Hindenburg and Ludendorff at *OHL* Pleß.

General Max von Gallwitz.

General Fritz von Below.

Oberst Fritz von Loßberg.

Crown Prince Rupprecht.

General Hermann von Kuhl.

General Freiherr von Soden.

General Max von Boehn.

General Freiherr von Marschall.

German front line in the Santerre: July.

Smashed forward position Ovillers: July.

A well constructed communications trench with overhead cover.

Biaches in ruins July.

Martinpuich under bombardment and ablaze late July.

Entrance to a mined dugout.

A field gun being manhandled into position.

A supply column loaded and ready to set out for the front.

A Guards Reserve Regiment 2 trench, complete with protection from shrapnel at Mouquet Farm: August.

A smashed battery position near Maurepas: August.

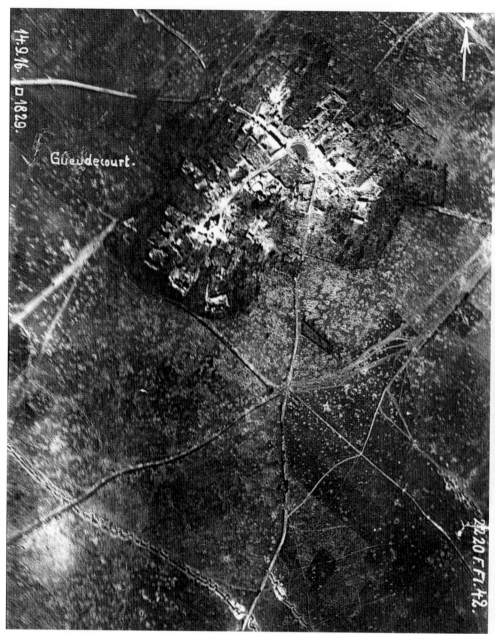

Gueudecourt: September. Note the line of the *Gallwitz Riegel* running diagonally across the foot of the photograph.

A desolate Somme landscape: September.

A 210 mm *Grobe Gottlieb* heavy howitzer.

Position being dug in the dried bed of the Canal du Nord near Allaines: August.

The Kaiser and Crown Prince Rupprecht at a march past near Maretz by recently relieved troops: September.

A final cigarette before a counter attack: September.

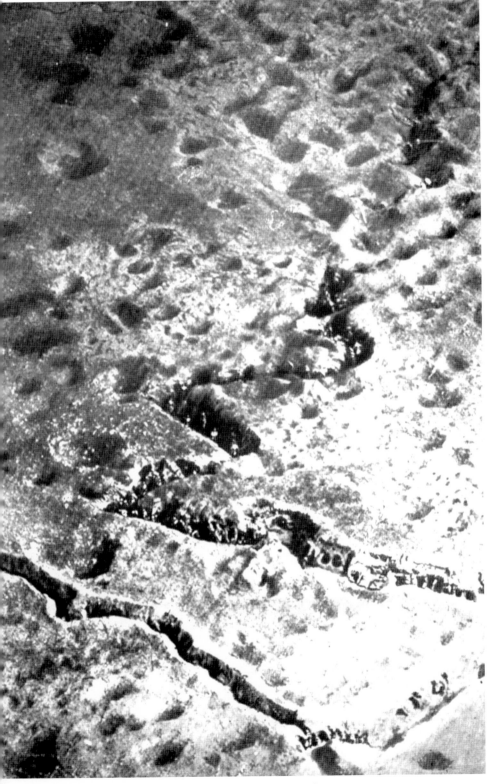

Fighting in a crater field position Vermandovillers: mid September.

A field gun of Field Artillery Regiment 3 dug in and screened against aerial observation north of Péronne: October.

The pitiless effect of random shell fire on men and horses.

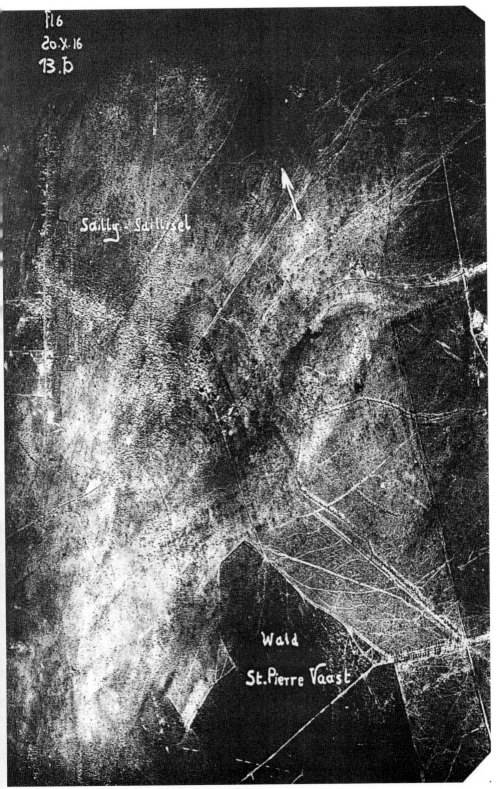

Lunar landscape around Sailly Sailissel: October.

Western tip of St Pierre Vaast Wood: late October.

Butte de Warlencourt: November.

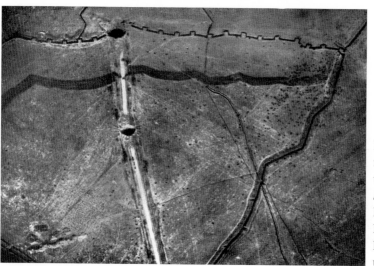

Road demolitions north of Roye during the retreat to the *Siegfried Stellung*/ Hindenburg Line: March 1917. Note the French convoy held up by a major crater.

directed that the whole of 1st Guards Infantry Division was to advance that day to the areas of Templeux, Aizecourt and Allaines and, from there, to relieve the Bavarians the following evening."[24]

It was not long before Gallwitz was having second thoughts about his action. It is naturally possible that the brevity of this tour of duty by the Bavarians east of Monacu Farm was what raised eyebrows at Gallwitz's headquarters. However, their relief of the Saxon 23rd Reserve Division had been marked by a further fierce outbreak of fighting. The French army, unable to progress further south of the Somme, had some time earlier turned its attention to operations north of the river in an attempt to turn Péronne and so gain its operational objective of seizing, or at least interdicting, the railway running from Bapaume to Ham that was critical for the logistical support of the German defence.

It is, therefore, no surprise that a maximum effort was devoted to forcing a way towards Cléry and on to Bouchavesnes. Heavy artillery was massed in support and in consequence the defenders were subject to an appalling ordeal by fire. During the nights 10/11 and 11/12 August the regiments of 1st Bavarian Reserve Division moved in to relieve the Saxons, with Bavarian Reserve Infantry Regiment 1 taking over responsibility from worn down elements of Reserve Infantry Regiments 100 and 103 for the *Braune Linie* [Brown Line]. This line, which was smashed flat and under constant artillery and machine gun fire, ran from the river at a point roughly equidistant from Monacu Farm and Cléry north to the Cléry – Maurepas road, then northwest just to the west of Maurepas itself. Bavarian Reserve Infantry Regiment 2 simultaneously moved primarily into what was known as the *Hohlwegstellung* [Sunken Road Position], which made use of the natural cover provided by the road for a large part of its length, though it also pushed outposts further forward.

Such was the weight of artillery fire and constant probing French attacks, however, that the *Braune Linie* and, to some extent, the *Hohlwegstellung* were soon evacuated. The lack of suitable dugouts or other overhead cover along the *Braune Linie* was a particular problem for the defence. Leaving only scattered skeleton outposts in position by day and slightly larger numbers of troops during the hours of darkness, most of the companies were engaged in the largely fruitless task of trying to repair the battered depth positions, incurring very substantial casualties from the endless shelling. An attempt by Bavarian Reserve Infantry Regiment 2, taking advantage of foggy conditions during the night 11/12 August, to push forward an aggressive fighting patrol west of the *Braune Linie* so as to establish the precise forward enemy locations, clashed with a larger French force and was beaten back. Its commander, Leutnant Schellhase, was severely wounded; the handful of survivors carried him back.[25]

French pressure continued to mount and from 11.00 am on 12 August several hours of drumfire directed primarily at the *Braune Linie* was followed by an all-out assault. At 5.50 pm reports arrived at the command post of Oberstleutnant Ritter von Füger, commanding Bavarian Reserve Infantry Regiment 1, that all his outposts had been overwhelmed, followed by another (originated earlier than that concerning the *Braune Linie*) that the French were pressing forward parallel to the river from a start line near Monacu Farm. All Füger could do was to order his 7th and 8th Companies to man positions on the western edge of Cléry and hold them at all costs. Fighting continued until 11.00 pm, at which moment the remainder of his 2nd Battalion arrived forward. Dividing his sector into two parts, he placed Major Baumann in command of 5th, 7th and 8th Companies to the north, with 2nd and 6th Companies under Major Dessauer deployed further south.

During the night the very few survivors from 1st and 3rd Companies reported that the whole of the *Braune Linie* was in French hands, but an attempt in the dark to launch a counter-stroke with 6th, 4th and elements of 9th Companies failed entirely. It had been over ambitious, none of the leaders knew the ground and orientation in the dark was a near impossibility. Fighting went on until dawn, however. Casualties were severe and went on mounting alarmingly as the French guns ranged in on the new positons and hammered them incessantly. Despite drumfire lasting all day and the following one, there was no infantry attack by the French; but by now 5th and 8th Companies were also reduced to remnants and had to be replaced by what was left of 10th and 11th Companies; 12th Company had already been fully extended trying to close the gap with Bavarian Reserve Infantry Regiment 2 off to the north. In less than three days in the line and occupying unfavourable, barely defensible, positions, Bavarian Reserve Infantry Regiment 1 had been smashed into ineffectiveness almost entirely by shell fire.[26]

It was a similar story for the neighbouring Bavarian Reserve Infantry Regiment 2 and Bavarian Reserve Infantry Regiment 3 located near to Maurepas. In the case of Bavarian Reserve Infantry Regiment 2, the heavy shell fire on 12 August began slightly later, at about 2.30 pm. There then followed, 'a violent firestorm on our positions. The enemy fired shells of all calibres, increasing the intensity of the fire, which lasted almost four hours, to drumfire beyond all previous experience.'[27] At 6.00 pm the fire lifted and, supported by numerous low flying aircraft that fired at anything still living in the German positions, the French infantry attacked. Despite a vigorous defence by the Bavarian machine guns and close support artillery, a foothold was gained towards the northern end of the *Braune Linie*, where the position had been reduced to one great mass of craters. One and a half platoons had been holding this area originally. Of these a mere eight men survived. Here too fighting went on into the night but, despite giving ground and incurring more heavy losses, tenuous contact was maintained with Bavarian Reserve Infantry Regiment 1 to the south and Bavarian Reserve Infantry Regiment 3 to the north.

Heavy shelling and sporadic infantry assaults marked the following thirty six hours and it was with considerable relief that the arrival of the advance parties of 1st Guards Infantry Division was greeted. Luckily, heavy rain on 15 August hampered French attempts to renew its infantry attacks.[28] The actual handover was complex and it was not until the early hours of 17 August that the final sub units were relieved and able to move back into reserve. Nevertheless, the fact that a division had effectively been fought out in less than a week was a legitimate cause of concern. Most of the high level reinforcement planning was based on the assumption that divisions would be able to remain in the line for a minimum of two weeks. Any less on average and it would become impossible to find and transport the necessary replacement formations.

Nevertheless, it is obvious, as it was to General von Below at the time, that the Bavarians had been reduced to dangerous ineffectiveness, that one more concentrated push by the French might have led to a breakthrough along the line of the Canal du Nord in the direction of Bouchavesnes and Moislains, with catastrophic consequences for the defence. The risk was too great. Relief of the battered formation was essential; and there is no evidence in the literature, including that of 1st Guards Infantry Division, to suggest that the action taken was considered to be anything other than entirely appropriate in the circumstances. Generalmajor Prinz Eitel Friedrich, second son of the Kaiser, who commanded the division and later wrote the history of Footguard Regiment 1, merely observed, 'At the precise time it conducted the relief, [1st Bavarian Reserve] Division had to defend against a heavy French attack and was driven back to the Cléry – Maurepas road. Its losses were so great that after it had only been deployed for a few days it had to be relieved.'[29]

However, following the relief, Gallwitz, who of course had overall control of manpower reserves, despatched a sharply worded and totally unjustified written reprimand to Below, in which he condemned him for deploying the Guards prematurely. Below, almost beside himself with fury, was finally persuaded with difficulty by Loßberg to stay his hand and to avoid laying a formal complaint against Gallwitz while he sought to find a solution. Following a telephone conversation, he went to meet Falkenhayn at his headquarters.[30] Having discussed the matter with Loßberg, Falkenhayn then had a lengthy telephone call with Below and arranged to meet him at a rendezvous near St Quentin to thrash out the whole affair. According to Loßberg[31] this meeting mollified Below and the problem was smoothed over.

True or not, it was an unnecessary waste of the time of the senior commanders when their entire attention should have been devoted to fighting the battle and it did not bode well for future cooperation. Numerous critics looked upon the ensuing poor relationship between the two army commanders as another example of poor judgement by Falkenhayn because he had held back from the establishment of an appropriate and necessary command structure a month previously. It is impossible to know what passed between Below and Falkenhayn, or even any contact the latter may have had with Gallwitz. However, one direct outcome and one which he may have promised either or both generals, was the creation of an army group headquarters, commanded by Crown Prince Rupprecht, with Generalleutnant von Kuhl as chief of staff and headquarters in Cambrai. On 25 August Falkenhayn issued orders that Army Group Gallwitz was to cease to operate and was to be replaced by a new army group that was to take under command Sixth, First and Second Armies. In his summing up of this six week period, Gallwitz remarked:

> "To be in the dual position of neighbour and superior is not comfortable. I do not believe that I interfered improperly with the internal workings of the other army, but do understand that even the appropriate involvement due to the command relationship was not always easily accepted there."[32]

The creation of this new level of command, which was initially designated Army Group Crown Prince of Bavaria and only later Army Group Rupprecht, was virtually the last act in office of Falkenhayn. By this stage of the battle Falkenhayn was rapidly running out of time. He had long since lost the respect of his senior subordinate commanders and at a conference of all army chiefs of staff on 14 August at Mézières he made a 'very painfully embarrassing' impression on his audience, who drew unfavourable comparisons between his current attitude with his 'unjustified optimism' when he outlined his plans for the Verdun offensive the previous February.[33] On top of this, his own staff at *OHL* observed with disquiet how his performance deteriorated throughout the month.

> "Colonel Bauer…in the Operations Section of the General Staff, records how unbearable the last part of Falkenhayn's regime was for the more intelligent and individualistic among his officers. 'From week to week…things became more desperate. Falkenhayn, formerly unruffled and superior, was visibly losing his calm and security…Colonel Tappen, the head of Operations Section, [remained completely detached]…one day a junior officer was deputed by the others to approach me and to declare that it was my duty as next in seniority after Tappen to intervene. After some hesitation, I decided to approach the Minister for War, Wild von Hohenborn…I accordingly called on him, but without result. I next tried my luck with Plessen.

At first Plessen was indignant at this peculiar step and it took some time for me to explain that it was only as a last resort that we had undertaken this unsoldierly measure. Finally, I seemed to have convinced General von Plessen... A few days later we returned to Pleß; the position continued to grow more difficult and we were in despair. On the 27th August, when I was walking in the castle grounds at Pleß[34] with Freiherr von der Bussche of the Operations Section, we came across the Kaiser. He was calm and cheerful and told us that Romania would certainly not declare war...A few minutes later we received news in our office that Romania had already declared war. Next morning I approached General von Plessen once more, represented to him that the only man who could help us was Ludendorff and begged him to assist us. Soon afterwards I was informed that the Kaiser had been persuaded: Hindenburg and Ludendorff were sent for.'"[35]

There is of course no suggestion that it was the action of junior members of Falkenhayn's staff which led to his sacking. He had made many enemies during the years he had been in command and several well placed individuals had been plotting against him for many months. The diary of Crown Prince Rupprecht is instructive in this respect.

5th July[36]
"...The dissatisfaction with Falkenhayn's performance is increasing everywhere. I myself have merely written a letter to Graf Lerchenfeld,[37] requesting him to inform the Imperial Chancellor [Bethmann-Hollweg] that matters cannot continue as they are and that we shall be totally ruined through mismanagement if Falkenhayn stays any longer as head of the Army Supreme Command. General von Nagel told me that throughout the entire army, even in Army Supreme Command circles, a strong movement against Falkenhayn is underway... There is also a general view in the Foreign Office that, because of the odium Falkenhayn has drawn down on himself, there is a need for another Chief of the General Staff before peace can be achieved."

7th July[38]
"During the afternoon I had a meeting in Tournai with the Governor General of Belgium, General von Bissing. He had had a discussion with Graf Lerchenfeld, who had briefed him about my reading of the situation and who had put it to him that, because matters could not continue as they were, the Kaiser had to be briefed about Falkenhayn. At more or less the same time and independently of Lerchenfeld, Herr von Lanken, Head of the Political Department in Brussels, had come to him and informed him that, in

the opinion of many in Berlin, especially in the Foreign Office, he was the right man to open the Kaiser's eyes. Generaloberst von Bissing said to me that even though he would not shrink from such a step, a change in Chief of the General Staff at such a time would be seen askance abroad. Furthermore, the Kaiser would regard such a step as an invasion of his prerogative... The only possible successor to Falkenhayn was Generalfeldmarschall von Hindenburg... Now General von Bissing asked me to give him my thoughts about Falkenhayn. I mentioned his disastrous intervention before the Battle of Ypres, his responsibility for last year's defeat at Arras, the crazy offensive at Verdun and the current defeat of the Second Army. As I concluded, Generaloberst von Bissing stated that he had not realised the situation regarding Falkenhayn was so bad; indeed, it could not be allowed to continue.

At that he showed me an encoded telegram from the Imperial Chancellor, who in the meantime had also spoken to Graf Lerchenfeld and who now announced, 'No matter how desirable, because of the seriousness of the situation, a change in the person of Chief of the General Staff would be, if I, as a civilian, represent that to the Kaiser, the opposite of what is wished may happen. It can only be done by a military man, such as Bissing.'"

20th August[39]
"Now that I have waited long enough, perhaps too long, today I composed a letter to the Head of the Military Cabinet, General [der Infanterie Moritz Freiherr] von Lyncker, in which I portrayed the sins of the Army Supreme Command, expressed the view that things could not continue as they were and [stated] that the Army no longer had confidence in General von Falkenhayn. In conclusion I requested General von Lyncker to acquaint the Kaiser with its contents the next time he briefed him."

As mentioned, on 27 August Romania declared war on Austria-Hungary. In the face of increased tension with Romania from early summer, Falkenhayn's staff had been monitoring the situation closely. It was known that Romania was in discussion with the Allies and their borders were closed once more in the wake of the Brussilov Offensive. However, the official calculation was that it would take weeks, or even months, for war stocks to be delivered there via Russia, that the Austrian situation would have to deteriorate markedly for Romania to risk joining the war and that, whatever happened, the harvest would have to have been gathered in first. This would allow time for a pre-emptive strike to be launched, not for several weeks, but certainly soon enough to forestall Romanian plans.[40] Having assured the Kaiser on that basis that there was no immediate prospect of

Romania joining the war, Falkenhayn was now in a very difficult position, as was the Kaiser, who still retained faith in his chief of the general staff and interacted well with him. Reluctantly, but his hand effectively forced, the Kaiser dismissed him and appointed the duumvirate of Hindenburg and Ludendorff in his place. Crown Prince Rupprecht, for one, was exultant. In his diary, he noted on 29th August[41]

"...At 5.15 [pm] a telegram arrived, announcing that Generalfeldmarschall von Hindenburg has been appointed Chief of the General Staff and General Ludendorff as First Quartermaster General! At long last!"

The general presumption was that the Kaiser had finally lost confidence in Falkenhayn and had therefore sacked him. It is impossible to say if the chief of the military cabinet had briefed against him, but in any case Lyncker was not the only individual with *Immediatrecht*, i.e. the privileged right to bypass the chief of the general staff and address the Kaiser directly in private. One such was Generalfeldmarschall von Hindenburg, who clearly felt that in all the circumstances that he had to speak out and press the Kaiser to make changes. Writing in his diary on 30 September, Generalleutnant von Kuhl noted, 'The Crown Prince has heard from a reliable source about the immediate cause of the fall of Falkenhayn. Hindenburg demanded a personal interview with the Kaiser. Falkenhayn refused, but Hindenburg insisted.'[42] In fact this, or something very similar, does seem to have been the trigger. In his memoirs, Hindenburg did write,

"As was well known, it was not the first time that my Kaiser and King had summoned me for a discussion about the military situation and intentions. Therefore, I presumed this time as well that His Majesty wanted to hear my opinion personally and orally about a particular question. Assuming that it would be but a brief stay, I took only essential luggage with me. On 29 August, accompanied by my chief [of staff], I arrived at Pleß, being met at the station by the head of the military cabinet on behalf of the Kaiser. It was from him that I first heard of the appointments of General Ludendorff and myself."[43]

Falkenhayn's version was,

"On 28th August, the Chief of the Military Cabinet, General Freiherr von Lyncker, appeared with a message that the Kaiser had seen fit to summon Field Marshal von Hindenburg to a consultation on the following morning on the military situation that had arisen through Romania's appearance in the ranks of our enemies. To this General von Falkenhayn had to reply that he could only regard this summoning of a subordinate commander, without previous reference to him, for a consultation on a question the solution of which lay in his province alone, as a breach of his authority that he could not accept and as a sign that he no longer possessed the absolute confidence of the Supreme War Lord that was necessary for the continuance of his duties. He therefore begged to be relieved of his appointment.

"As what the Chief of the General Staff regarded as a vital principle was at stake, a conference with him, summoned by His Majesty, could not hope to reconcile the conflicting views. His request to be relieved of his office was granted in the early morning of August 29th.[44]

At this remove and with only partial information available, it is frankly impossible to resolve the question, 'Did he go, or was he pushed?' The important thing at the time was that he was no longer in charge and that the army as a whole drew considerable confidence from the changes at the top. The next few weeks would demonstrate how the new command arrangements would impact on the conduct of the battle. As far as Gallwitz was concerned it had not come about a moment too soon. 'The creation of such [army] groups was long overdue. *OHL* could not oversee and direct everything itself. Had Army Group Rupprecht existed prior to 1 July, at least Péronne would have been better equipped and prepared and would have been better able to beat off the initial break in.'[45]

Notes

1. Möller *Fritz von Below* p. 52.
2. Kuhl *Der Weltkrieg* p. 493.
3. Möller *op.cit.* p. 52.
4. Rupprecht Kronprinz *Mein Kriegstagebuch* p. 503.
5. Gallwitz *Erleben im Westen* p. 60.
6. Loßberg *Meine Tätigkeit* pp. 234–235.
7. Wellmann *Mit der 18. Reserve Division* p. 118.
8. *ibid.* pp. 118–119.
9. Klähn History Reserve Infantry Regiment 86 p. 122.
10. Guhr History Infantry Regiment 157 p. 111.
11. *ibid.* p. 115.
12. *ibid.* pp. 116–117.
13. Wellmann *op.cit.* p. 124.
14. Underlined words and phrases represent original emphasis.
15. *Kriegsarchiv Munich* HGr Rupprecht Bd 216 *HGr Gallwitz Ia Nr 115 Geheim* dated 27 Jul 16.
16. Förster History Reserve Infantry Regiment 31 pp. 88–89.
17. Ritter History Infantry Regiment 163 pp. 154–155.
18. Infantry Regiment 63, one of the first regiments to be equipped with steel helmets, had been issued with them in Warlencourt on 4 August. Kaiser History Infantry Regiment 63 p. 135.

19. Kaiser *op.cit.* pp. 137 – 140.
20. Ritter *op.cit.* p. 163.
21. Kabisch Somme p. 71.
22. Gallwitz *op. cit.* p. 80. It may be a coincidence but, less than three weeks later, Headquarters First Army issued its own directive concerning the conduct of counter-attacks, presumably drafted by Loßberg, but signed by Below. This expands on and nowhere contradicts anything produced by Army Group Gallwitz. See Kriegsarchiv Munich General. Kdo. AK II (WK) *156 Armee-Ober-Kommando 1. 1a. Nr. 489 geh. Armeebefehl für die Durchführung von Gegenangriffen den 23. August 1916.*
23. *ibid.* pp. 77–78.
24. Kabisch *op. cit.*p 71.
25. Helbling History Bavarian Reserve Infantry Regiment 2 pp. 69–70.
26. Schacky History Bavarian Reserve Infantry Regiment 1 pp. 38–40.
27. Helbling *op.cit.* p. 70.
28. Schacky *op.cit.* p. 40.
29. Eitel Friedrich History Footguard Regiment 1 p. 119.
30. Other sources, including Kabisch (Somme 1916 p. 71), suggest that Below did actually complain officially and that General der Kavallerie Freiherr von Marschall, commander of the Guards Reserve Corps, was appointed to adjudicate. Be that as it may, Falkenhayn succeeded somehow in talking Below round and no formal proceedings took place.
31. Loßberg *op.cit.* pp. 240–241.
32. Gallwitz *op. cit.* p. 93.
33. *ibid.* p. 243.
34. A chateau at Pleß in Upper Silesia (modern day Pszczyna in Poland) housed *OHL* from April 1915 – February 1916, then again from August 1916 – January 1917. *OHL* changed location several times during the course of the war. Pleß was selected for its proximity to the Austro-Hungarian Headquarters in Teschen (modern day Cieszyn in Poland).
35. Tschuppik: *Ludendorff* p. 57
36. Rupprecht Kronprinz *op.cit.* p. 497
37. Lerchenfeld, or to give him his full name and title, Hugo Graf [Count] von und zu Lerchenfeld auf Köfering und Schönberg, was a leading Bavarian politician and diplomat who, at the time Rupprecht wrote to him, was responsible for the administration of the *Weichselland* [Kraj Nadwiślański], the westernmost province of the Russian Empire in Poland.
38. *ibid.* pp. 498–499
39. *ibid.* p. 520
40. Falkenhayn *General Headquarters* pp. 255–256.
41. Rupprecht Kronprinz *op.cit.* Bd 2 p. 1
42. Kuhl *Persönliches Kriegstagebuch* 30 Sep 16.
43. Hindenburg *Aus meinem Leben* p. 123.
44. Falkenhayn *op.cit.* pp. 284–285.
45. Gallwitz *op. cit.* p. 94.

CHAPTER 6

Hindenburg and Ludendorff Pick up the Pieces

In a masterpiece of understatement, General von Falkenhayn, the outgoing
Chief of the General Staff noted, 'At the moment when Field Marshal von
Hindenburg took over the conduct of affairs the general situation was serious'.[1]
He also asserted that the situation was 'not desperate'; nevertheless, on handing
over to Hindenburg, according to the latter he shook hands and took his leave with
the words, 'May God help you and our Fatherland!'[2] Bizarrely, when he came to
write his memoirs he also claimed of this period, 'In the Western theatre the force
of the enemy's attack on the Somme, which had attained the utmost concentration
of effort, had been broken'.[3] That statement would have raised hollow laughs
amongst the defenders as September opened and, arguably, as will be discussed
later, the intense fighting in the Morval – Sailly-Sailissel – St Pierre Vaast Wood
area in October were the battles that brought the German army closest to collapse.
   Hindenburg's own assessment painted a very different picture.

"The situation on the Western Front was not lacking in food for thought.
Verdun had not fallen into our hands and the hope that the strength of the
French army would be worn down by the gigantic wall of fire which had
been brought down on the north and northeast fronts of the fortress had not
been realised. The prospect of success for our offensive there had become
ever more hopeless, but the operation had not been halted. On the Somme
the battle had now been raging for almost two months. There we lurched
from one crisis to another. Our lines were permanently under the most
extreme strain."[4]

"... Already by the end of August the Battle of the Somme had taken on
the character of an extraordinarily bitter head on clash of the strength of
the opposing sides. The sole task of *OHL* could only be to make available
to the armies the necessary strength to enable them to endure. We named
this type of battle a *Materialschlacht* [battle of matériel]. From the point of
view of the attackers it could be seen as the application of the tactics of the
battering ram, because their command methodology lacked any overarching
style. The mechanistic and material elements of the battle occupied the
foreground, while imaginative command was pushed all too much into the
background."[5]

For his part, Ludendorff recalled that at their first meeting, 'His Majesty stated that he hoped that the crisis at the front could be overcome ... the situation which had led to the summons of the Field Marshal and I to *OHL* was strained to breaking point. The great defensive war that we had thus far been able to conduct with the best of military means, namely through the offensive, had developed into a simple fight to defend what we held.'[6]

From the very start of their period in charge both Hindenburg and Ludendorff had to maintain a complete overview of the situation on all fronts and juggle their resources to the maximum effect possible. Writing of his first impressions as he began work at Pleß, Ludendorff remarked,

"The situation on the Western front was more tense than I could ever have imagined, but I did not yet have a full sense of how acute matters were. This was just as well, otherwise it would have been too hard to take the difficult decision to withdraw even more divisions from the desperate fighting in the West and despatch them to the East to restore the situation and to land a decisive blow on Romania.

"The Field Marshal and I intended to travel to the West as soon as possible, in order to judge the situation on the spot. It was our task to organise the defence more tightly and to provide assistance. Before that, however, divisions had to be readied for service against Romania and we had to extract from the Kaiser the crucial decision to halt the Verdun offensive. This ought to have been broken off as soon as it turned into a battle of attrition. The gains did not compensate for the losses."[7]

Just over a week after their arrival in Pleß, Hindenburg and Ludendorff managed to find the time to travel west to preside over a most important conference at Crown Prince Rupprecht's army group headquarters in Cambrai on 8 September. The aim of the conference was to produce a clear and accurate picture of the situation and to determine a robust and sustainable way forward. In attendance were both army group commanders and Duke Albrecht of Württemberg, commander Fourth Army in Flanders. In addition, every army group and army chief of staff the full length of the Western Front was present. Each in turn was given the opportunity to brief their situation, to make recommendations and indicate where action or support by *OHL* was needed. The entire proceedings, which opened with a statement by Hindenburg in which he announced the intention to attack Romania and also took the opportunity to express his confidence in all present to continue to prosecute the war successfully, were marked by frankness, open discussions and a positive atmosphere, which impressed all present.[8]

Ludendorff was in the chair for most of the proceedings, calling first on Oberst Loßberg to speak. The latter had of course discussed the line to take with General von Below prior to the conference so, having once given a *tour d'horizon* from the First Army perspective, he stressed two main issues. The first of these was the length of time divisions were being kept in the line; he pointed out that,

> "So far, all German divisions had had to go on fighting to the limit of their endurance. Because this meant in practice casualties of fifty to seventy percent, mostly falling on the bravest of the soldiers, the consequent blood-letting among the divisions was very severe. Even after the arrival of young replacements, such a reduction in fighting power can only be restored very slowly. Maintenance of the fighting power of our infantry is especially important. In this connection I advocated timely relief of the divisions."[9]

Loßberg then went on to the second issue and highlighted deficiencies in artillery, especially the supply of ammunition, and the need for improved aerial observation. He finished by making numerous suggestions for procedural and administrative improvements and then, following the thanks of the chair, handed over to Second Army. Having listened to this briefing, Generalleutnant von Kuhl noted in his diary, 'Bronsart (Second Army) stressed that the divisions vary in the length of time they can be deployed. Those arriving for the second time not so long. The men must be better trained. The French are better trained in close quarter battle. If the men are properly rested and trained they will achieve considerably more. The troops must not be kept in action too long.'[10] Once all armies had briefed, Ludendorff then outlined the broad sweep of the latest changes. Defensive lines against possible landings were to be built in the north of Schleswig Holstein, the right flank of Fourth Army was to be protected along the line of the Dutch border and he announced plans for what were to become the *Siegfriedstellung* [Hindenburg Line], behind Army Group Crown Prince of Bavaria, and the *Michelstellung*, along the line Verdun – Metz in rear of Army Group German Crown Prince.

Contributing to a feeling of confidence that the new leadership would lead to improvements in the situation, both on the Somme and elsewhere, were Ludendorff's assurance that the Verdun offensive had been finally stopped and his announcement of an increase in the availability of reserves. Of eight new divisions, five would be allocated to the Western Front and more were in the process of forming up. Further, although provision of ammunition continued to be problematic, Army Group Crown Prince of Bavaria could expect to receive the following train loads daily: seven for field artillery, four for foot artillery and almost all the available super heavy howitzer ammunition. He also promised additional aircraft, but not immediately. Reassured, the majority of the participants remained behind for a social gathering, but Below and Loßberg had to hurry back to their headquarters in Bourlon, reports having arrived that the Allied artillery had begun the bombardments which were to lead to the final battle for Ginchy on the British front and Bouchavesnes in the case of the French.[11]

Describing the day in his post war memoirs, Ludendorff noted that,

"The requests of the various participants culminated in urgent demands for increases in artillery, ammunition, aircraft and balloons, together with improvements in the system of reliefs, by means of increased and more timely deployment of fresh divisions and other troops. Halting attacks at Verdun made this somewhat easier, but even there we had to reckon on significant wearing down of forces due to local circumstances."[12]

In contrast to the confident atmosphere which prevailed at the end of the day, two of the key participants, Ludendorff and Generalleutnant von Kuhl, both shared a number of concerns which they had been careful not to express publicly. Kuhl's diary entry for 8 September paints a very pessimistic picture.

"I spoke afterwards alone with Ludendorff. We agreed that a great and positive success is no longer possible. All we can do is to hold on and seize a favourable opportunity to make peace. This year we have made too many serious errors. At the very least we should have halted the Verdun offensive as soon as we saw it was not going to work. Lüttwitz (Chief of Staff, Army Group German Crown Prince) had told me that the German Crown Prince hated Schmidt von Knobelsdorf and that the entire army had also hated him ... Ludendorff complained about the difficulties he had inherited ... Ludendorff said to me that he would have wanted to give 'me' (that is to say Crown Prince Rupprecht) overall command of the entire army in the west, but that it would have been problematic to subordinate the German Crown Prince to him."[13]

Following the Cambrai conference there was soon further proof that Ludendorff, in contrast to Falkenhayn, intended to keep a firm grip on the critical situation astride the Somme and to involve himself more or less directly in the conduct of the battle. Only one week later, the first of a constant stream of position papers, directives and instructions was sent out to all major subordinate headquarters. One such, distributed to all army groups and army headquarters on 18 September, is of interest because it indicates the extent to which Ludendorff was willing to influence relatively low level tactical matters. Explaining that, 'Some of the

topics discussed at Cambrai on 8 September still require clarification, explanation
and wide distribution', he addressed expenditure and stocking of ammunition,
replacement of equipment, mine warfare, front line trench garrisons, placement
of reserves, training and subordination of aircraft spotting for the artillery.'[14]
As an illustration of the level of detail he covered, this is what he wrote about
ammunition.

"The serious situation in which First and Second Armies find themselves is
completely recognised, as is the fact that only through the plentiful use of
ammunition is the required effect obtainable. On the other hand, ammunition
must under no circumstances be squandered. Every commander down to
battery and company level must understand that the very outcome of the
war will be put at risk by blazing away pointlessly. The consequent wastage
of guns and increasing lack of ammunition must inevitably lead to serious
crises. A careful watch is to be kept for the following types of inappropriate
types of fire:

a. Harassing[15] shoots fired at particular areas on the basis of guesswork and
without observation. The fact that the occasional enemy battery ceases
to fire as a result is not proof of its effectiveness. All means must be
deployed to ensure [effective] observation.
b. When, upon receipt of the signal 'Defensive fire', a prolonged shoot at
intense rates begins. The outcome (apart from a waste of ammunition) is
inaccurate fire that frequently endangers our own troops and brings about
sharply increased failure rates of numerous guns through premature
detonations and broken recoil mechanisms. These guns are then
unavailable when required in the event of the launch of a real assault.

"Defensive fire, therefore, is most effectively delivered by – and limited
to – distinct concentrations, fired at rapid, but not intense, rates. The
concentrations may be defined by time (for example, three minutes) or by
number of rounds (for example, fifteen shells per gun) or by a combination
of both (fifteen shells in three minutes). These defensive fire shoots are
only to be repeated if the signal 'Defensive fire' is renewed by those at the
front, or if the start of the enemy attack has been observed. It is not a good
idea to wait for a special signal, 'End defensive fire', because sending
it is always likely to be forgotten. It is true that to meet the requests of
the troops an application for such a flare signal has been lodged with the
Ministry of War. A decision on its introduction must await the outcome of
trials at the front."[16]

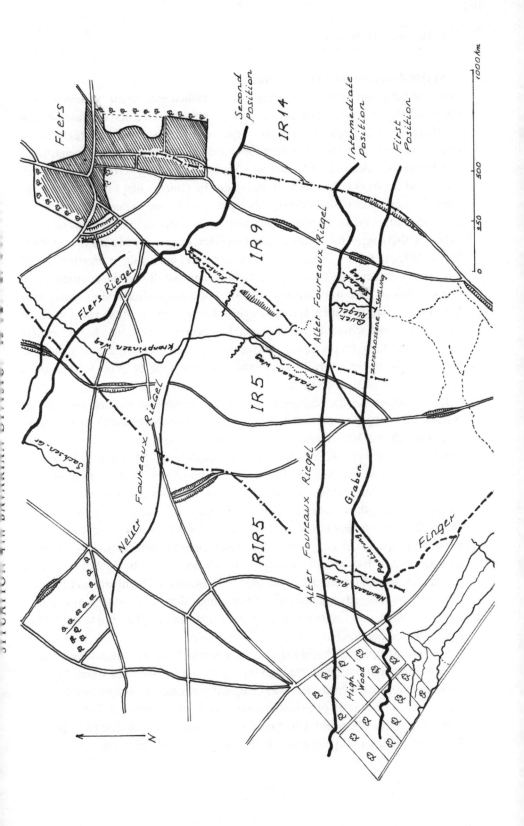

SITUATION 4TH BAVARIAN DIVISION 15 ...

A Major Joint Anglo-French Attack

Whilst these points of principle were being thrashed out, on the battlefield itself desperate fighting continued as the British army battered its way slowly and painfully towards Bapaume and the French army, concentrating largely on its operations north of the Somme, launched repeated thrusts between Bouchavesnes and Morval. Guillemont finally fell on 3 September after an heroic defence which had lasted for weeks, followed six days later by Ginchy, just to the north. Then came the major attack, supported by Mk I tanks, at Flers on 15 September as part of a huge operation on a very wide front. After many attempts to coordinate assaults, at last, on that day, all the Allies attacked together. It represented a maximum effort by the Allies to force a decision on the Somme and the resultant pressure should have posed immense problems to the German defence. It was the culmination of many weeks of 'line straightening' and local operations designed to secure start lines for a serious attempt at breakthrough and destruction of the German forces in the area. In short, it was the heaviest attack delivered since 1 July, but the results were on the whole disappointing, despite the fact it demonstrated once again that, backed by the power of artillery, forward garrisons could be overwhelmed and a certain amount of ground taken.

On 15 September the Martinpuich – Ginchy sector was the responsibility of Bavarian II Corps, commanded by Generalleutnant von Stetten with, from west to east, 3rd, 4th and 5th Bavarian Infantry Divisions under Generalleutnants Ritter von Weninger, Ritter von Schrott and Endres respectively. Blocking the way north to Flers were primarily Bavarian Infantry Regiments 5 and 9 and Bavarian Reserve Infantry Regiment 5 of 4th Bavarian Infantry Division and Bavarian Infantry Regiment 14 of 5th Bavarian Infantry Divisions.[17] All were badly worn down by the preliminary bombardment, so their relief in some cases by formations of III Bavarian Corps had already begun. On 15 September they were heavily engaged, all had more or less serious casualties and all, to survive to fight another day, had to give ground rapidly when the blow fell. During the bombardment Infantry Regiment 14 suffered casualties on 13 September alone of seventeen killed, fifty seven wounded, thirty missing (almost all buried alive by shelling) and a further fifteen, buried but dug out and medically evacuated.[18]

The following day the bombardment increased to drum fire, causing many more casualties and did not let up through the night 14/15 September when, between 1.00 and 6.00 am, the entire area was drenched with gas. The jumping off trenches were manned by masses of British infantry and then, promptly at 7.00 am, wave after wave stormed forward. Leutnant Oeller, commanding 1st Company Infantry Regiment 14, describing the attack of the British 41st Division, reported,

"About 6.45 am the British moved to occupy trenches pushed forward from the edge of Delville Wood astride the Longueval – Flers road. Our machine gun and rifle fire forced them one by one to jump back into the trenches. About 7.00 am the British launched forward out of Delville Wood and along the low ground to the left of the Flers-Longueval road in four or five columns, each eighty men strong and with five to ten paces between columns. The thrust was accompanied by three armoured vehicles, of which one ditched as it attempted to cross the road.[19] When the advance had closed to within two hundred metres, destructive British fire came down and completely smashed the company sector.

"We observed the attack from the moment it left the wood and from then until the break in to our positions we fired a constant stream of flares calling for defensive fire, but nothing came down in response. Because there were only forty five men to defend the 400 metre wide company sector, I withdrew all parts of the company I could contact in good time and took up position on heights to the right of the Flers-Longueval road where I could bring down enfilade fire on the enemy. I also sent word to the Second Position for support. I stayed in position with elements of 12th Company, suffering heavy casualties, until I was deeply outflanked on either side and feared that I might be cut off. At that moment I was wounded in the shoulder and I gave orders to pull back to Flers."[20]

There had been an intention to relieve 4th Infantry Division during the night 15/16 September by 6th Infantry Division. In fact, the process was already underway on the Infantry Regiment 9 frontage, immediately west of that of Infantry Regiment 14, when its 2nd Battalion, which had been in the line the longest, was withdrawn during the afternoon of 14 September. It reached Escaudoeuvres just before midnight; but it was not to be granted much rest once battle was joined. The 15th September was nothing short of catastrophic for this regiment. The attackers who had forced Leutnant Oeller and others back expanded the gap they had created and simply cut off its 1st and 3rd Battalions, most of whom were captured.[21]

By the evening of 15 September its commander, Oberstleutnant Freiherr von Freyberg, was in charge of the shattered remnants of his regiment and two battalions of Infantry Regiment 10 (rushed forward by 6th Infantry Division). It had not proved possible to carry out a successful hasty counter-attack towards Flers, so the Bavarians took up positions north and northwest of the village. Once the regiment was finally withdrawn it proved to be completely impossible to produce a standard after action report because so many of the key personnel had been killed or captured. All that the regiment could do was to interview as many survivors as possible and forward these personal accounts to Headquarters 4th

Infantry Division. This has, however, made available to the modern reader a most unusual and detailed set of low level descriptions of some of the action south of Flers and to the east of the Flers-Longueval road.

Inevitably, the bulk of these were provided by personnel of 1st Battalion and its Machine Gun Company, which had been in reserve; but a very few came from men who had been manning either the First Position in the so-called *Zerschossene Stellung* (= Shot up Position, the eastern extension of *Postierungsgraben*, which bisected High Wood from east to west) or the Intermediate Position, the *Alter Foureaux Riegel* [= Switch Trench]. From them it is at least possible to obtain a flavour of what the defence faced that morning and, it must be said, how swiftly much of it folded. Gefreiter Michel Lutz of 11th Company was manning the front line immediately by a prominent left hand bend in the Longueval – Flers road, 500 metres northeast of the northern tip of Delville Wood.

"At 6.00 am on 15 September very heavy artillery fire started coming down. There were large numbers of gas shells amongst it, so once again we had to mask up. About 7.30 am, five armoured vehicles came driving up. Of these, the second one definitely mounted a gun. The first wagon was brought to a halt by hand grenades thrown from the sap,[22] but the others drove on slowly. Assault troops rushed forward from behind the vehicles and attacked the company. The forward trench was then evacuated and its garrison pulled back to the Second Line, to 1st Battalion."[23]

Infanterist Gregor Löber, also of 11th Company, observed the tanks as well.

"... When the gas had dispersed, about an hour later six armoured vehicles advanced from the British position. They drove in three rows of two, each with 150 metres between them. The second vehicle on the extreme right arrived in front of the centre of 11th Company. It stopped ten metres short of the trench then, when all six vehicles reached the same relative position, assault troops rushed round from behind them. Simultaneously machine guns opened fire from the armoured vehicles and the infantry advanced in line."

When Löber was slightly wounded and withdrew at about 10.00 am, he stated that at that time no British soldier had entered the 11th Company position; but an hour later, he saw them advancing with fixed bayonets along the sunken road to the south of Flers. Infanterist Ries, 9th Company, back in Switch Trench, stated,

"I was with Three Platoon by the battalion command post. Suddenly somebody bawled down into the dugout, 'Get out, the British are coming over the hill!' With a few others, I dashed back about three hundred metres and we occupied a trench together with men from the 5th and 18th Regiments [18th was part of 3rd Infantry Division] ... All of a sudden, I saw masses of British soldiers rushing down the hill at us ... with fixed bayonets. Everyone to the left of us pulled back. Leutnant Wolpert held men back, but he was shot at from the rear and fell dead at once. When I looked around I saw two armoured vehicles to our left rear driving along the *Flersriegel* [= Flers Trench] and firing at us with machine guns. We blocked off to the left and fell back to the right, being constantly pressed and with the vehicles heading towards the 5th Regiment command post ... We then pulled back to the *Gallwitzriegel*."

When the pressure began to build up on the Flers – Martinpuich front and the front line positions were subject to a series of probing attacks, some in quite considerable strength, Infantry Regiment 5 was given the task of developing for forward defence the so-called *Finger Abschnitt* [Finger Sector]. This ran south southeast from just outside the eastern tip of High Wood in the direction of Longueval and here it was that elements of the regiment were attacked early on 15 September. Of course, despite being a new addition to the defences, it was soon spotted by the British and hit just as hard as every other part of the front line by the preliminary bombardment. One unwelcome incident came during the night 13/14 September, just as Reserve Infantry Regiment 5 in High Wood was beating off a grenade attack. A shell landed on a dump by the forward command post and 600 hand grenades and 1,000 signalling cartridges went up in smoke. They were to be missed when the attack began.[24]

During the night 14/15 September the relief of the regiment by Infantry Regiment 18 of 3rd Infantry Division was underway and so when the assault began it hit a mix of sub units from the two regiments. 3rd Battalion Infantry Regiment 18 was in the front line, with the *Foureaux Riegel* further back occupied by companies from both regiments. Relief in the line is always a vulnerable moment, especially so when the men manning the front line have had no time to familiarise themselves with their new surroundings. The initial assault simply overwhelmed the 3rd Battalion, none of whom returned, but then follow up waves launched forward, supported by tanks, at the *Foureaux Riegel*. Here there was bitter close quarter fighting with machine guns and grenades, but it was of short duration. Infantry Regiment 5 was quite specific in describing the shock effect of the tanks at this point. 'The effect of their appearance was shattering, because the infantrymen were powerless against them. They drove along the trench and brought the garrison under machine gun fire. Infantry assault groups then rolled the trench up.' Small wonder that the British attack was soon closing up towards Flers itself. With attacks coming frontally and from a flank, Infantry Regiment 5 commented yet again. 'The arrival of the tanks and our own impotence against them made a visible impression on the men.'[25] Near to panic, despite being led courageously by their surviving junior officers, the remnants of the two regiments soon fell back to the *Gallwitz Riegel*.

The situation for Reserve Infantry Regiment 5, manning positions in and around High Wood, was broadly similar and its forward troops were bundled out of the wood in short order, finishing the day to the north of Flers, like most of the rest of 4th Division. However, its 3rd Battalion had a rather different experience. Badly worn down, it had been withdrawn earlier and was resting at Barastre. Once the extent of the attack became known, it was ordered at 8.30 pm to move back to the front. On the way towards the *Gallwitz Riegel*, it was met by a cyclist bringing orders from 7 Infantry Brigade to move forward and come under command of Infantry Regiment 5. It arrived at its destination about midday, having suffered heavy casualties as it passed through the British artillery fire and, on arrival, it was given an entirely unrealistic task of counter-attacking the *Flers Riegel* with three companies, leaving one behind at the disposal of the brigade commander, Oberst Ludwig Herthies.

Loyally, the commanding officer, Major von Roser, reported that the attack would begin at 12.50 pm, but added that because the total strength of all three battered companies was 150 at the most, there was little prospect of success unless other infantry sub units participated.[26] The attempt was made, but it was doomed from the start and so the battalion spent the remainder of the day participating in several minor operations and, most importantly, assisting in the close defence of the guns located to the north of Flers.

Although the appearance of tanks had come as a total surprise to the Bavarians and they certainly had an effect on the outcome of the battle, it could be argued that one of their greatest contributions was to the morale of the attacking troops, who made maximum use of the physical shelter and fire support they provided at critical moments. However, despite their novelty, some of the defenders reacted to the best of their ability to their appearance on the battlefield. Several members of the Machine Gun Company Infantry Regiment 9 fired at them, though with little success. Gefreiter Ludwig Engelbrecht later reported, 'I immediately fired at the first vehicle, but the bullets had no effect on its armour, so I directed my fire instead to good effect at the advancing infantry'. Schütze Ferdinand Lehnemann, operating in the *Flers Riegel*, just to the southwest of the village at about 8.30 am, stated, 'From the left came a shout, "An armoured vehicle is coming over the hill!". The machine gun was moved about fifty metres to the right to improve its field of fire. It had a stoppage, so a new set of working parts was inserted. I fired at the armoured vehicle and saw a ring fly off it. The soldiers accompanying it all lay dead on the ground.'[27]

Lacking armour piercing SmK ammunition, which soon became standard issue for machine gunners, not much more could be done; but it was a different story when it came to the artillery. Some guns south of Flers were abandoned as their crews rushed to escape the oncoming attackers, but others rather more to the rear in and around the *Gallwitz Riegel* were stoutly manned, despite losses to manpower and equipment. These weapons effectively held any attempt by the British to push on beyond Flers; then when tanks started to probe forward they were easily picked off by gunners firing over open sights. Leutnant Klengel of 1st Battery Field Artillery Regiment 77 described one such engagement.[28]

"Towards 9.00 am the Battery telephone squad returned from the Sunken Road Section, with orders to engage the advancing enemy infantry. The canister rounds were prepared...All non-essential personnel were ordered by the Section Commander to collect grenades and weapons from a cache one hundred metres away and to deploy along the *Gallwitz Riegel*, left and right of the battery position, in order to thicken up the meagre infantry presence there. This could only be carried out fully when the crew of the knocked out left hand gun of the Sunken Road Section arrived... The enemy attack continued... Just before 9.30 am, an enemy armoured vehicle drove in front of the battery position and, with its first shots, set on fire an ammunition wagon, which was parked close behind a forward howitzer position. With its third round, the right hand gun, directed by the Section Commander, hit the armoured vehicle at a range of 925 metres and set it alight.[29] Altogether there were about eight hits, some of them from the left hand gun...The left hand gun continued to fire against the constantly renewed waves of attackers, who drew ever closer.

"In the meantime, another armoured vehicle approached the position of 3rd Battery Field Artillery Regiment 77, which was located a short distance to our right rear. Because it was not engaged for a few moments and was threatening the 'Trench Section', the section commander decided, despite the infantry that was drawing ever closer, to pull his one remaining functioning gun out, with the help of some hastily-summoned Bavarian infantrymen, and to deal with the vehicle. Just as the gunner took aim at it, it was destroyed by a first round direct hit from the 3rd Battery."[30]

As the fighting on 15 September died away, the advance of the British XV Corps had only secured the previously designated Second Objective, with the

Third Objective to the north of Flers out of reach and the Fourth, which enclosed Guedecourt, nothing more than a distant aspiration. That said, even though the Allied assault on 15 September only produced limited gains, the loss of ground, in particular that around Flers, nevertheless worried the normally imperturbable commander of First Army considerably. Loßberg recalled what then happened.

> "General von Below, who temporarily considered withdrawing the left and right wings of the army into positions to the rear, which were partly complete and partly still under construction, decided, *under my influence*,[31] to continue resistance along the current line of battle."[32]

Yet again it was an example of the power of the key General Staff officers. Loßberg had either persuaded Below, or insisted, or both, on this course of action. Reinforcing it, the very next day General Below signed off an order that, from its style, was almost certainly drafted by Loßberg.

> "During the battle on 13 [*sic.*] September, the enemy succeeded in capturing ground in the sectors of Group Marschall [Guards Reserve Corps: Flers] and Kirchbach [XII (Saxon) Reserve Corps: Lesboeufs/Morval]. They have paid a bloody price and it is quite clear that their future attacks will not be as effective.
>
> "The army must – and will – make the enemy fight for every step. Every commander and every soldier, above all the entire artillery, must play a full part in ensuring that this joint exercise of willpower is felt sharply whenever battle is joined."[33]

So much for the exhortation to the greater efforts that the situation demanded and that the army simply had to deliver if it was to continue successfully to prosecute the defensive battle; but First Army also took the opportunity to address issues of reporting, command and control, all of which were a constant concern to Loßberg throughout the battle.

> "Methodical control of the battle by all commanders can only be achieved if they, personally, even in the midst of the most serious fighting, do everything possible to obtain clarity about both our own and the enemy situation. To that end, I request that commanders deploy all means at their disposal, regardless of risk. It is not sufficient to rely on reports received by telephone. Instead, officers from the senior staffs, or the senior commander himself, must gain an overview of the battle by observing it with their own eyes. This is the only way to obtain the correct basis for command and

control. To this end, I recommend that <u>mounted officers of the staffs</u>[34] be despatched well forward and that they be allocated despatch riders who can take their reports for onward transmission to motor vehicles parked further to the rear. In addition, low flying aircraft are to be deployed, in order to obtain swift impressions about the battle situation.

"Further, I warn [you] expressly not to pass on every single item of information, whether good or bad, unless you are totally convinced of its accuracy. If this is not adhered to, it is easy to lead neighbours or superior headquarters to incorrect decision making in battle.

"Every unfavourable situation must be met with iron nerves and a clear and correct decision. Coordination with neighbouring command authorities is to be guaranteed at all times.

"During recent battles insufficient weight has been given to the serious consequences which can arise when gaps appear in the front line positions. Both senior and junior commanders have a duty in these circumstances to ensure that they control strictly the carrying out of the orders they have given. In this connection, too, I recommend the despatch of officers from senior staffs to the front line."[35]

It did prove to be possible, gradually, to improve the situation for the hard pressed defenders. The second part of the battle, for example, was fought with a considerable increase in German aircraft in the skies, coupled with changes to artillery allocations and tactics, but it was perhaps in the area of reliefs and replacements that the biggest difference was achieved in the short to medium term. With receipt of his Prussian field marshal's baton, Crown Prince Rupprecht, appointed army group commander with a coordination role over First, Second and Sixth Armies, had all the authority he needed to allocate manpower and resources to his subordinate commanders, being required only to keep *OHL* informed of his decisions. This led to an immediate improvement in this important area and, given the constant dialogue between the staffs, there were never any unpleasant surprises, especially because it was the declared aim of Ludendorff, despite pressures elsewhere, to put an end to the need for the defenders on the Somme to be 'living from hand to mouth' in this respect.

Meanwhile the battles raged on. On 21 September, Loßberg, to widespread acclaim, was awarded the *Pour le Mérite* for his outstanding service in critical situations. A few days later, on 26 September, Thiepval was finally captured, though the battle for the Schwaben Redoubt itself continued well into October and attempts to continue to press forward elsewhere the following day were generally beaten back. Nevertheless, both sides had suffered heavy casualties and something had to be done quickly. Army Group Crown Prince of Bavaria arranged at once for the relief of three of the hardest hit divisions, namely 50th Reserve, 213th and 214th by 7th Reserve, 15th Infantry and 10th Reserve, but *OHL* also paid a full part. Despite the demands of the Romanian campaign, 6th and 11th Divisions were released from its reserve (in the case of the latter, for a second deployment down in the Santerre) and, demonstrating the value of a complete cessation of offensive operations at Verdun, Ludendorff also ordered the replacement on an exchange basis of six worn down divisions of Army Group Crown Prince of Bavaria by six from Army Group German Crown Prince.[36] Of course this did not mean an end to operations around Verdun. Sufficient forces had to be maintained there, especially when the French army began its counter-offensive in the early autumn but, nevertheless, the switch in emphasis to the Somme was undoubtedly correct. French success in eventually regaining almost all the lost terrain at Verdun may have been good for morale, but it had no strategic importance whatsoever.

It was time for a general stocktaking and although there is no trace of the staff being tasked, it is evident that Ludendorff had called for a full assessment of the situation all along the front and that army groups had passed on the requirement.[37] General von Below signed off the First Army reply on 26 September and General von Kuhl the full army group reply to *OHL* only twenty four hours later, which is an obvious sign that Loßberg had been keeping von Kuhl fully in the picture about what Below's reply was going to contain and probably had also been sending him copies of preliminary drafts. In a detailed report First Army made plain that:

> "During the Battle of the Somme we have had to fight throughout against enemy superiority in matériel and ammunition as well as manpower. In the superior strength of the enemy lies the explanation for the loss of terrain we have suffered, the failure of individual small counter-attacks and the major assault near Bouchavesnes."[38]

The Bouchavesnes debacle

The major assault referred to was a large scale operation directed by Group Ehrenthal [XXVII (Saxon) Reserve Corps] on 20 September. It was clearly still seen, almost a week later, as a stinging setback and a major disappointment. It involved elements of 213th, 214th Infantry Divisions (which only formed up on 8 September 1916) and 54th Reserve Division and was supported by every artillery piece within range, including sixty heavy howitzer and sixteen heavy flat trajectory batteries, firing a combination of 'Green Cross' [phosgene gas] and high explosive shells. For the first time the infantry advanced whilst protected by ground attack aircraft, which engaged the French with machine gun fire and bombs. In other words, everything available had been thrown into the assault in order to ensure success. However, such was the weight of French counter-attacks that by the evening of the same day the German troops had not only been thrown off their objectives but also forced back to their starting points. Fighting continued for a further two days, but no progress was made and the divisions, largely fought out, had to be withdrawn from the defensive line. Because this coincided with the relief of 45th Reserve Division, 5th Bavarian Infantry Division, 4th Guards Division and 185th Division, the manpower situation was placed under considerable strain.[39] Despite the troops and materiel allocated to it, Reserve Infantry Regiment 245 of 54th Reserve Division nevertheless referred to the attack as, 'insufficiently prepared and in insufficient strength'.[40] They could have added that many of the formations involved had already been in the line for well over a week – in the case of 54th Reserve Division over two weeks – before the assault was launched[41] and were therefore already worn down and nearing exhaustion before it even began. It was all further proof of the increasing pressure on the German army as it approached the fourth month of the battle.

Analysis of the setback led to an assessment by First Army that the French had employed a version of infiltration tactics to exploit gaps which appeared in the German positions. As a result, an order was issued and circulated widely on 22 September.

"The British and French, independent of their larger attacks, are employing the following methodology to work their way forward and improve their positions. They first probe forward with patrols. Behind come small detachments of infantry equipped with machine guns, ready to consolidate the small local successes achieved by the patrols. Every gap in our lines is soon discovered by this method and used to create nests [of resistance]. Later come larger detachments that drive further forward and attempt to enlarge the nests sideways. So in this way, at first unnoticed and in any case discounted, British and French nests are established. The seriousness of the situation is generally not recognised until it is too late.

"Experience shows that these nests are then used by the British and French as jumping off places for further local attacks or are exploited as anchor points in order to force a route into our lines during the next major assault."[42]

The First Army report of 26 September went on to make a number of important points, many of which were echoed in the subsequent Army Group one, demonstrating yet again what an influential figure Loßberg, its drafter, had become and how notice was taken at the highest levels of what he had to say. In particular, Loßberg, while calling for increased supply of guns and ammunition in order to be able to offset British and French superiority, homed in on the air battle and returned yet again to his theme of disputing every metre of ground.

"The almost complete air superiority enjoyed until very recently by the enemy has permitted them to exploit to the full the accuracy and quantity of the batteries which oppose us: to wreck our positions and the men within them; to bring down fire on our battery positions; and to impose constant heavy losses on our traffic between the front and rear areas. The enemy further expands on the advantages so gained by the deployment of their superior manpower. This enables them to relieve divisions weakened in assaults before they are totally worn down and, above all, to reinforce their number at those points where the attacks are to be continued ... our attacks almost always butt up against troops deployed in depth and armed with numerous machine guns, whose counter-attacks are supported by vast quantities of artillery fire.

"In the opinion of Army Headquarters, despite all the difficulties associated with holding on, the major decisions during the fighting on the Somme must be based on, and factor in the necessity by means of the most obstinate resistance, the need to make the enemy fight for every bit of ground (*jeden Schritt Boden streitig mach[en]*). Only in this way can enemy battle stocks of matériel, ammunition and manpower be exhausted. Voluntarily to cede large amounts of territory, quite apart from the consequences for morale, which would simply strengthen the will to victory of the enemy, would merely bring in its wake heavy fighting on a wide front under even more unfavourable conditions."[43]

First Army then went on to make a number of specific recommendations concerning the employment of artillery and the allocation of sufficient ammunition. It also addressed the width of divisional frontages with the need either to reinforce ground holding divisions by subordinating additional regiments to them or to deploy three divisions to the front where previously only two had been employed. Although the logic was impeccable, the means were lacking, so the German chain of command had to wrestle constantly with these problems and overdraw on their resources, both human and material, in an effort to overcome their inherent weakness. That said, Generalleutnant von Kuhl, in passing to *OHL* the Army Group response entitled 'The Situation on the Somme', on 27 September, was fully supportive and left Ludendorff in no doubt as to the essential correctness of Loßberg's appreciation.

"The situation in the Battle of the Somme", he wrote, "suffered from the very beginning from the fact that in June, before the offensive began, the former Second Army was not reinforced in a timely manner and because once the attacks began reinforcements only arrived piecemeal. As a result, the enemy was able to start the battle with overwhelming superiority in artillery ammunition and aircraft, which had an amazing effect on the troops newly deployed to the Somme. As a result, the enemy succeeded in breaking in on 1 July in numerous places. This superiority has still not been countered. Numerically, the enemy is constantly superior. Currently, along the front between the Ancre and the Somme, eleven German divisions are facing about nine French and thirteen British ones. In consequence the enemy has succeeded in gaining ground during every major assault. Their divisions are relieved in a timely manner before they are worn right down, then they introduce new ones where they next intend to attack."[44]

Kuhl continued by comparing the availability of replacement divisions to the Allies and the German army, then made the same point concerning holding firm and not yielding ground as Loßberg had. He even used almost identical phraseology:

"It is, therefore, a case of holding on. As long as the current battle lasts it is a matter of making the enemy fight for every bit of ground (*jeden Schritt breit streitig zu machen*)." Then, foreshadowing the general retreat to the Hindenburg Line the following spring, he continued, "Withdrawal into a position to the rear could only be considered after the battle and only then if the consequent shortening of the front and saving of troops was sufficient to compensate for our loss of morale and the increase in enemy self-confidence."[45]

Kuhl went on to endorse everything that Loßberg had written about divisional sectors and troop availability, before describing in detail the challenges and problems facing the German artillery. He then concluded by addressing two matters worthy of full quotation because they encapsulate hard won lessons.

"<u>Command and Control.</u> There are only places in the midst of heavy battles for commanders who have total mastery of the all-arms battle, are possessed of an iron will and are supported by outstandingly competent General Staff officers. Changing the group commander every time a new corps arrives can only be done at the cost of serious damage to command of the battle. The army headquarters must be granted the freedom, depending on the personalities involved, to retain group commanders in charge of their respective sectors even after their corps have been relieved. It must therefore be accepted that individual corps will have to fight or man quiet sectors under commanders from elsewhere. Of course there can be no doubt that it is better if corps go into battle or train so as to improve their battle worthiness under their own commanders.

"Divisions require a second General Staff officer – or another equal to the duties – who, when a new division arrives, transfers to it. This measure has already been introduced in First Army. Of the commanders, especially amongst those *zur Disposition* [inactive and on half pay], who have been recalled to duty, it appears that a number are not equal to the enormous mental and physical strain of the Battle of the Somme. In such cases command of the battle devolves on the chief of staff or the frequently very young General Staff officer. That is not a healthy situation. A remedy is required.

"<u>Construction of Positions and Conduct of the Battle.</u> Currently, only experience gained on the Somme is relevant. Experiences derived from earlier battles must be amended from now on. Positions located on hill tops or forward slopes are generally condemned. Wherever possible, in order to obtain protection from the effect of artillery fire, the position must be placed on a rear slope. In connection with the choice of the infantry positions, the location of artillery observers, who must be placed behind the line is most important.

"The front line of the position is effectively indefensible in the face of overwhelmingly powerful artillery fire. The garrison is either buried alive or captured. The front line trench must therefore be very thinly manned and only equipped with observation and machine gun posts, together with shelters for sentries. It should not have numerous deep dugouts to hold a strong garrison. It is only possible to maintain the front line trench by means of counter-attacks launched by reserves held ready in the support line. That is where the dugouts should be. This second line should not be too far distant, so that timely counter-attacks can be launched. The worse the position, the greater the depth it requires. Reserves can only be moved by day with difficulty, so they must be held close by.

"In the great and decisive Battle of the Somme the side will prevail whose matériel, ammunition and manpower lasts the longest. Any other outcome is barely imaginable. We shall prevent an enemy breakthrough, provided that we relieve [formations] in a timely manner."[46]

It is quite evident that the influence of overwhelming Allied superiority in artillery was causing the German army enormous difficulties. Senior commanders and General Staff officers repeatedly referred to it in their correspondence. At *OHL* one of the most pressing issues was the effect that it was having on the ability of the ground holding formations to defend against break ins and loss of ground. Given the fact that the Allied advance had been so slow during the previous ten weeks, this may seem strange; but it was a very real concern. No sooner had the army group reports reached *OHL* than Ludendorff despatched an immediate reaction that very same day. His *Betrachtung* of 27 September sums up the problem as he saw it.

"All previous enemy offensives have failed more or less quickly in the face of the tenacity of our infantry and the effect of our artillery. For the first time, here on the Somme, unprecedented artillery fire means that our infantry has suffered such bloody losses and its morale has been so badly affected that, without suffering great losses, inferior enemy infantry has been able to force its way into our positions. Our artillery has also suffered heavy losses in equipment and personnel.

"The enemy has achieved this despite the fact that we have increased both weapons and ammunition many times over compared with earlier [practice] and our infantry has almost everywhere performed in a superhuman fashion. It is not reasonable to attribute this lack of success merely to the enemy's numerical superiority in infantry and artillery. The failure seems to lie more in the system itself. We need to examine, therefore, how we can deploy our forces on the Somme more effectively and with fewer casualties."[47]

Ludendorff then continued with a sharp and detailed critique of wasteful aspects of the way defensive fire was being produced, describing it as 'a necessary evil', essential to protect the infantry but a blunt instrument, which consumed vast amounts of precious ammunition. Of course he was correct but, in the days before the ready availability of combat net radio, with calls for help being reduced to flare or light signals, it was next to impossible to change the situation completely, although there was scope for improvement. What is interesting about this paper, however, is the fact that the matter was clearly preying on his mind, because it was issued only two days after an even more comprehensive examination of the question. His document, 'Experiences of the Battle of the Somme', dated 25 September, ranged across a number of key issues: enemy bombardments, counterattacks, use of gas, placement of machine guns, defensive positions and their manning amongst others; but by far the largest section dealt with artillery, including infantry-artillery cooperation. In tackling this question, Ludendorff went into extraordinary detail, underlying once more his determination to translate lessons learned into new procedures and to keep a firm personal grip on the conduct of operations. He began with, and concentrated on, the question of defensive fire.

"Strict control of defensive fire is of decisive importance. The width of a defensive fire zone must not exceed[48] 200 metres for a field gun battery and 250 metres for a field howitzer battery [both comprising four weapons]. The necessary number of batteries must be requested. In certain circumstances this will only be possible by means of ruthlessly weakening fronts which are not under attack. The entire field artillery is to be placed close enough behind the infantry line so as to ensure that its defensive fire will come down at optimal range. The length of defensive fire shoots should not be longer than three minutes. Over-rapid fire damages the equipment and expends ammunition pointlessly. Whether and how frequently defensive fire should be repeated is dependent on an assessment of the battle situation. For the most part this will only be necessary when during an enemy attack renewed defensive fire is called for. Fire is only to be produced if the signals for it are clearly visible or when an attack can be spotted by direct observation.

"The heavy artillery is not to be used to produce defensive fire; i.e. fire brought down close to our own front line and at exactly defined target areas. In cases where it is not already engaged in counter-battery fire, when an enemy attack is anticipated, its fire is to be directed at the enemy trenches as soon as troops can be seen massing there, or at assembly areas and routes leading forward. As far as possible guns should fire high explosive ...

"One of the main tasks of the heavy artillery is and remains the battle against the enemy artillery; far too little importance is attached to this. Despite our inferiority, we must not lose sight of the need to strive to knock out their guns and destroy their associated material. Otherwise we shall be fighting too defensively ... if artillery is used appropriately we can achieve the utterly essential reduction in ammunition expenditure without tactical disadvantage. Continuous defensive fire and participation by the heavy artillery in defensive fire tasks as a matter of principle must be avoided totally. Harassing fire against concealed targets (including enemy artillery) is completely pointless. Only observed fire will produce the required effect by the ammunition available to us.

"Defensive fire may only be called for by infantry commanders (down to platoon commanders) and only then when an actual enemy attack has been detected. Unnecessary defensive fire leads unavoidably to ammunition shortages and therefore to danger to the infantry. Every infantry commander must be clear about this."[49]

In some ways the discussion seemed to be addressing problems of the supply of shells just as much as the need to counter the weight of Allied artillery. If so, Ludendorff still had an important point, one to which Loßberg had alluded earlier when he formally informed Army Group Crown Prince of Bavaria that, 'an increase in the number of howitzers will only be worthwhile if more ammunition is made available'.[50]

Whilst those at the top echelons of the chain of command wrestled with the problems of trying to increase the number of guns and howitzers and improving the supply of ammunition so as to permit the German artillery to compete on more even terms with the British and French gunners, Unteroffizier Johannes Jochimsen from Grenadier Regiment 10, writing about the reality at trench level of Allied artillery superiority, described graphically the appalling risks associated with the simplest movement across the shell swept area between Vermandovillers and Ablaincourt in mid-September.

"Shell fire comes crashing down again on village, chateau park and the position. We strain all our senses ... we need to know where they are aiming. After a quarter of an hour everything suddenly goes quiet. Then the 'blessing' comes down on the Sunken Road. We count the minutes ... ten minutes! Now death swings off to our right. We wait ... Down comes a fifteen minute concentration of fire ... then again ten minutes on the sunken road ... Look out! Right, now's our chance ... We have twenty five minutes to run for our lives. When at long last there is a pause in the banging and crashing around us, we hare off. Correct! The shells are now landing on the *Todeslaufgraben*. Here is the communication trench ...! Some call it the Sunken Road; others insist that it is called *Ludwigsweg*. What do names matter here on the chessboard of death? A shower of shells comes down on our right hand neighbours and a few straggling shells rumble over us and down into the sunken road. The 'Sunken Road', resembles nothing else but a dry stream bed. Only on its northern side runs something which could be described as a bank, into which here and there foxholes have been burrowed out. Perhaps it was here that the reserves who counter-attacked Vermandovillers or Deniécourt crouched and spent the last hours of their lives.

"The way and the former communication trench are half full of spoil dug from the bank ... with discarded rolls of barbed wire ... mortar bomb crates ... with dead men ... and with more dead men ... and yet more dead

men. Now and then we slip in a puddle of blood. We run ... jump ... skid
... climb. Knapsacks ... smashed rifles ... helmets ... muddy letters ...
mess tins ... cartons ... bullets ... sacks – all the empty props of the 'war of
material' are strewn about the communication trench in which, night after
night, men sweat in a race with death. Here much is simply thrown away
as useless ... Forwards ... rearwards ... it is always the same endless road,
littered with the debased means of sustenance. It is as though apathetic but
busy men or uncomprehending children have been randomly ransacking a
dead man's possessions. Dead, empty, irrelevant! This is why our ancestors
let the dead keep their possessions ... take their property with them in the
grave ... that is the only way that makes sense ... its own sense.

"We take everything in, we keep track of every single item, because
everything can bring us ruin or salvation. We are once more hunted, primeval,
beings, seeing magic, bringers of evil or lucky chance everywhere. On ...
on! We have got to make it. Now the skeletons of a team of battery horses
blocks the trench. Over, or under and carry on! Boxes and baskets bear
witness to bitter fighting. On ... on! No, here comes the merry chirping
of an *ent'ract* fired by the guns. 'It's just a filler. Twelve shells every three
minutes ...' On ... on! [The wounded] Grenadier Umlauf collapses. 'Deal
with it! 'Groundsheet, over here!'[51] Two wagons loaded with agricultural
equipment are silhouetted against the sky... Coming from where? Going
where? How come? Harvest time ... harvest time ... but death is roaring
from the edge of the village ... There's nothing for it but to lie flat!!

"Hunted and sweating we push on ... past endless rows of corpses ...
Men dead with their faces to the foe, with their heads turned to home ...
Dead in full battle order, grey-faced pilgrims with white and bloodied
banners ... runners, ration parties ... men going on leave – all rigid, all
plugging the dyke which defends the homeland ... washed up like flotsam
and swept away ... Coming from where?? Going where?? Why?? ... On ...
on! Here lies a ration party ... with their skulls smashed to pulp ... torsos
ripped apart ... cooking pots crushed and food containers smashed. We step
on dead comrades ... twenty paces of nothing but corpses ... a corduroy
road of corpses, decay, staunchness and resurrection. We are fighting bare
chested against the war machinery of the entire world. We have nothing but
men ... **men** with which to defend ourselves.

"But we still have the courage to take on the dull grind, to confront the
soulless madness of this unchained explosive monster. It is just as it was in
days of yore when our forefathers and the Friesians went to sea with their
weapons drawn. War is not an 'adventure' ... nor a 'sport' ... neither is it
mere 'armed conflict' any more. Instead it is an ordeal, a trial of strength, as

once was the battle with primeval animals and primeval forces. The living trample over the dead ... Forgive us you unknown comrades! Yet another salvo forces us into cover. On we go, ghostly figures through the indifferent night, on across the abandoned field tramway ... on down the trench to Ablaincourt. Here at last we can catch our breath."[52]

Despite the efforts being made to improve the fire support available to the defending troops and a slightly amended attitude to trading ground for reduced casualty lists, throughout September and October the battle remained, in Ludendorff's words, 'balanced on a knife edge'.[53] The ground holding divisions had almost universally gone over to crater field defence in depth, causing the Allies, lacking clearly defined trench lines to engage, to waste gigantic quantities of shells in an attempt to suppress them, though there was a price to be paid in terms of problems of resupply, local command and the organisation and coordination of counter-attacks.

The formations of 213th Infantry Division, which only formed up on 8 September and for whom the Battle of the Somme was their first engagement, had strong words to say about crater defence after their deployment to the Sailly Saillisel sector (which was nothing but craters) between 22 and 30 September. Reserve Infantry Regiment 74, an experienced regiment and previously part of 19th Reserve Division, reported:

"Crater positions, despite the advantage that they are difficult for the enemy to spot, must under all circumstances, with all means possible and at the greatest possible speed, be developed into a continuous position by means of wide, shallow communications trenches. Simultaneously, craters to the rear must also be linked in, so as to provide access to the second line."[54]

In restricting itself to the most essential points, the Reserve Infantry Regiment 74 commentary described the methods to be adopted to counter the disadvantages in crater field defence of splintering the defensive line and lack of depth. Its parent division, having analysed the reports of its other regiments, outlined the problems and its favoured solution in the version which was forwarded up the chain of command.

"A crater field position is most useful for advanced posts deployed to protect the main position from surprise and able to call down defensive fire in a timely manner. Against the fact that such a crater field position is hard for the enemy to pinpoint and is thus less vulnerable to shell fire must be set the facts that, because of the lack of communicating links, it is virtually impossible for commanders to exercise leadership; whilst bringing forward and distributing ammunition and matériel is made extraordinarily difficult because of enemy artillery fire and lack of knowledge as to which craters are actually occupied.

"The greatest energy should be devoted to linking up the craters and, if at all possible, to create a second continuous line one hundred metres to the rear. This should be equipped with machine gun nests, which then provide even a severely shot up garrison with the means to guarantee an ability to be able sufficiently to resist an enemy infantry attack. One practical tip is to send working parties forward by night from the rear under the control of a commander who has been given responsibility for the direction of the work. The recommended sequence of work for the construction of rearward positions is dugouts and obstacles, followed by trenches."[55]

As September drew to a close the German army was at full stretch as it attempted to maintain the integrity of the defence and counter the constant Allied pressure. It was still holding on, but the effort of so doing was taking a severe toll on all ranks from highest to lowest. The way this toll manifested itself is the subject of the next chapter.

Notes

1. Falkenhayn *General Headquarters* p. 285.
2. Hindenburg *Aus meinem Leben* p. 120.
3. Falkenhayn *op. cit.* p 285.
4. Hindenburg *op. cit.* p. 124.
5. *ibid.* p 158.
6. Ludendorff *Meine Kriegserinnerungen* p. 187.
7. *ibid.* p. 193.
8. Loßberg *Meine Tätigkeit* p. 249.
9. *ibid.* p 250.
10. BA/MA RH61/50652 *Kriegstagebuch von Kuhl* p. 23.
11. Loßberg *op.cit.* pp. 251–252.
12. Ludendorff *op.cit.* p. 210.
13. Kuhl *op. cit.* pp. 23–24.
14. *Kriegsarchiv Munich* HGr Rupprecht Bd 16. *OHL Ia/II Nr. 35358 op. Geheim* dated 18.9.1916.
15. Original emphasis.
16. *Kriegsarchiv Munich* HGr Rupprecht Bd 16. *OHL Ia/II Nr. 35358 op. Geheim* dated 18.9.1916 pp. 1–2.
17. All the formations involved around Martinpuich and Flers on 15 September were Bavarian, so that prefix will be dropped during the remainder of this description of the fighting that day.
18. History Bavarian Infantry Regiment 14 p. 178.
19. This may have been Tank D7, commanded by Lieutenant AJ Enoch. Pidgeon, *Flers and Guedecourt* p. 74.

20. History Bavarian Infantry Regiment 14 pp. 179–180.

21. Etzel History Bavarian Infantry Regiment 9 p. 89.

22. This sounds to be improbable because the practice of bundling several grenades together as a close range anti-tank measure had not yet been developed. Possibly the vehicle simply broke down.

23. All these personal accounts are contained within *Kriegsarchiv Munich* 9. Inf. Regt. (WK) 7 *Abschrift der Aussagen von Augenzeugen über die Vorgänge am 15.9.16* dated 21.9.1916.

24. Weniger History Bavarian Infantry Regiment 5 p. 71.

25. *ibid.* p 73.

26. *Kriegsarchiv Munich* 5. R. I. R. (WK) 3 III. / R.I.R. 5 Gefechtsbericht des III./ R.I.R. 5 über den 15. u. 16.9.1916.

27. Both these personal accounts are contained within *Kriegsarchiv Munich* 9. Inf. Regt. (WK) 7 *Abschrift der Aussagen von Augenzeugen über die Vorgänge am 15.9.16* dated 21.9.1916.

28. Bolze History Field Artillery Regiment 77 p. 150

29. This may have been Tank D5, commanded by Second Lieutenant Arthur Blowers. See Pidgeon *op. cit.* pp. 89, 90 & 101

30. This may have been Tank D6, commanded by Lieutenant Reginald Legge. See Pidgeon *op. cit.* pp. 89–92

31. Author's emphasis.

32. Loßberg *op. cit.* p. 254.

33. *Kriegsarchiv Munich* 13. Inf. Regt. (WK) 13 *Armee Oberkommando 1 Ia No. 842 geh.* Dated 16.9.1916.

34. Original emphasis.

35. *Kriegsarchiv Munich* 13. Inf. Regt. (WK) 13 *Armee Oberkommando 1 Ia No. 842 geh.* Dated 16.9.1916.

36. Loßberg *op. cit.* pp. 255–257.

37. Referred to as Ia Nr.427 geh. vom 21.9.16 in *Kriegsarchiv Munich* Heeresgruppe Kronprinz Rupprecht Bd. 216 *Armee-Ober-Kommando 1. Ia Nr. 934 geh.* dated 26 September 1916.

38. *ibid.*

39. Loßberg *op. cit.* p. 255.

40. Krämer History Reserve Infantry Regiment 245 p. 65.

41. Reinhardt History Reserve Infantry Regiment 248 p. 86.

42. Bauer History Reserve Infantry Regiment 74 p. 376.

43. *Armee-Ober-Kommando 1. Ia Nr. 934 geh.* dated 26 September 1916.

44. *Kriegsarchiv Munich* HGr Rupprecht Bd. 216 *Heeresgruppe 'Kronprinz v. Bayern' Oberkommando Abt. Ia No. 609 geh.* dated 27.9.1916.

45. *ibid.*

46. *ibid.*

47. *Kriegsarchiv Munich* HGr Rupprecht Bd. 216 *Chef des Generalstabes des Feldheeres II Nr. 200 op. geh.* Betrachtung dated 27.9.1916.

48. Original emphasis.

49. *Kriegsarchiv Munich* Infanterie-Divisionen (WK)13704 *Chef des Generalstabes des Feldheeres Ia/II Nr. 175 gh.op. ERFAHRUNGEN DER SOMME-SCHLACHT.* Dated 25.9.1916.

50. *Kriegsarchiv Munich* Heeresgruppe Kronprinz Rupprecht Bd. 216 *Armee-Ober-Kommando 1. Ia Nr. 934 geh.* dated 26 September 1916.

51. Suspended on a pole and carried by two men, this was the method of evacuating casualties from the front line.
52. Jochimsen *Herz im Feuer* p. 102.
53. Ludendorff *op. cit.* p. 217.
54. *Kriegsarchiv Munich* HGr Rupprecht Bd. 216 *Res. Inf. Regt. 74 13278 Wesentlichste Erfahrungen des Regiments aus den Kämpfen an der Somme* dated 2 October 1916.
55. *Kriegsarchiv Munich* HGr Rupprecht Bd. 216 *213. Inf. – Division I.17.x. geh. Erfahrung in der Somme-Schlacht 22.-30. IX. 16* dated 6.10.16.

CHAPTER 7

Strained Almost to Breaking Point

The creation of Army Group Crown Prince of Bavaria represented a significant step forward, in that an effective and logical chain of command now had control of the Battle of the Somme. However, any hopes that this would reduce the infighting between senior commanders were short lived because the one person the changes did not suit was of course the irascible General Max von Gallwitz. It will be recalled that he had insisted on being given command responsibility for the entire area and this had been granted him by Falkenhayn. Now, two months into a battle of unprecedented dimensions and with no end in sight, he found himself not only removed from army group command, but effectively side lined, because the *Schwerpunkt*, as ever, was clearly located north of the Somme in the First Army sector. Naturally he fought his corner hard, but the real power on the Somme was now vested in three men: Ludendorff, von Kuhl and Loßberg. These three enjoyed close working relationships. At times there was tension but, fundamentally, they were in full agreement about where priorities should lie and how the battle should be fought. As a result of all these factors, it was not long before they began manoeuvring against Second Army.

Post war, by which time much of the heat had dispersed and when memoirs came to be written, the words that actually appeared in print only hint at the tensions that existed at the time, exacerbated by the appalling weight of responsibility these senior commanders and General Staff officers carried. Fortunately, in some cases diaries in which these men gave vent to their feelings have survived. One in particular, that of Generalleutnant Herman von Kuhl, is especially instructive.

"14 Sep 16. It is very hard to work with Second Army. Gallwitz is deeply annoyed that overall command has been taken away from him and he constantly suspects that First Army is receiving preferential treatment (though beyond any doubt the weak point is on the First Army front and there lies the greatest danger). He keeps demanding reserves, criticises every order of the Army Group and always raises objections. Bronsart [chief of staff Second Army] is unsteady, not really sound, despite being able and pro-active. For example, 23rd Division was shortly to be withdrawn: He telephones to say that the division was not yet fought out and it would be unfortunate if it had to go. The following day, when we gave orders that

44th Reserve Division was to move at our disposal behind the right flank of Second Army, he insists that he has no reserves, the 23rd Division is totally worn out. After we agreed to let him keep 44th Reserve Division, he requested today once again to be able to retain 23rd Division; it is in good condition. It is difficult to work with him! Schulenburg (chief of staff Sixth Army) knows him from Verdun and in the same way is sharply critical of him."[1]

"15 Sep 16. Falkenhausen (commander Sixth Army) came here this morning for a discussion about the Sixth Army situation. We agreed that the unfavourable situation was caused by continuing redeployments and adjustments, but the overall situation forces us. Falkenhausen knows Bronsart very well and warned about him (unreliable, lying)."[2]

There is no doubt that von Kuhl had a point. In mid-September, Gallwitz recorded that,

"I sent the army group a situation report, I anticipated further enemy attacks and drew attention to the unequal distribution of forces between the two armies. In First Army, divisional frontages were two and a half kilometres; in Second Army, four and a half kilometres. In order to support individual divisions, I had already sent forward fourth regiments[3] – in the three regiment divisions these were lacking – which complicated reliefs and reduced the usefulness of the divisions held back."[4]

Crown Prince Rupprecht and General von Kuhl frequently visited the various army headquarters. On 19 September, for example, they travelled to St Quentin to meet Gallwitz but, according to Gallwitz, the discussions were not especially constructive and he felt that his ideas and requirements were not being given the consideration that were their due. Having stewed over the matter, two days later Gallwitz placed his thoughts on paper once more. According to von Kuhl's diary,

"21 Sep 16. Today a message arrived from Gallwitz in which he complains that in comparison with First Army, Second Army is not being treated equally. They are just as threatened with a major attack as First Army and are much thinner on the ground. Ever since he ceased to have command of both armies that has been his constant complaint. However, the circumstances are quite different. The main danger is on the First Army front. Here the enemy is trying to break through and has already made rather a lot of progress. Here we no longer have depth to the positions; we have only just begun, with great effort, to produce new defensive positions in rear ... Mutual irritation is developing between the Crown Prince and Gallwitz. When we were last in St Quentin there was nobody from the army headquarters to meet us, not even an orderly, even though we arrived punctually at the appointed time. The Crown Prince had to hang up his own clothes and ask the way to the room where Gallwitz and Bronsart were. The Crown Prince said nothing, but he was displeased. During the discussion he spoke rather sharply to Gallwitz, who replied vigorously. He ought to have taken better care of the Chief."[5]

"23 Sep 16. Our assessment is undoubtedly correct. The *Schwerpunkt* of the offensive, the main weight of the enemy divisions, is directed against First Army. Thus was Gallwitz politely informed, though his message was impolite. (The distribution of forces, as earlier, is extremely unbalanced, although an attack in similar strength is to be expected against Second Army ...). Bronsart requested [us] earnestly not to reply in too hostile a way in order to avoid a row. Gallwitz personally composed the message."[6]

It is apparent that Kuhl then telephoned Ludendorff to brief him on the situation, because Gallwitz made an entry in his diary, which reads, 'Ludendorff doubts Bronsart's returns concerning equipment losses. There is great anger here about him.'[7] That may well have been the case; certainly the army group was increasingly exasperated with Gallwitz, as these next diary entries show.

"27 Sep 16. I have just spoken to Loßberg, on whom superhuman demands had fallen. If we had yielded to Gallwitz, who sent a lengthy message here before the battle (Second Army is disadvantaged, is just as threatened as First Army and must be just as strong), then we should have lost the battle. It is astonishing that Gallwitz can demand in this way. It can hardly be that he lacks insight. Stubborn and exasperated? But he is not a great man. In any case I did not allow myself to be deflected and despatched all reserves to First Army as they rolled in. It was a huge responsibility."[8]

"28 Sep 16. Second Army has now agreed unconditionally that they do not face a major attack. We want to take their artillery to strengthen First Army. Second Army opposed this. The chief stated that Gallwitz would not agree to it. As if we could not order it! Working relationships with Second Army are very difficult. Bronsart is unreliable and constantly changes his mind. Gallwitz is vexatious and stubborn. We cannot obtain a clear view of the situation, so it is difficult to issue orders."[9]

Nevertheless, Second Army conceded in a report that the extension of the French attack to the south was currently improbable and on that basis nine field gun and twelve heavy batteries were transferred north.[10]

> "30 Sep 16 After Second Army was obliged to give some heavy artillery to First Army, suddenly its situation became worse and the possibility arose once more for an attack, even if not in the immediate future. That was the gist of their report today. It is impossible to rely on them. They colour their reports in order to achieve their objectives and make my job difficult. Then there is the obstinacy of Gallwitz … "[11]

The following day, following a discussion at his headquarters in St Quentin with Crown Prince Rupprecht that was supposed to clear the air, Gallwitz noted in his diary, 'He did not pay attention to me and in his lecturing manner passed on 'good lessons', not one of which was new'.[12] This comment did not make it into Gallwitz's memoirs. Instead he highlighted the fact that, 'He [Rupprecht] spoke about the situation. He did not believe that there would be an attack by the enemy on my army. Therefore, I should withdraw even more artillery from the front.'[13] By now all the incessant infighting at high level, coupled with the fearful toll that the extended battle was having on the fighting troops, was beginning to wear down the army group commander himself. Mention of the issue then found its way into von Kuhl's diary,

> "2 Oct 16. The Crown Prince is somewhat dejected. We cannot continue to fight indefinitely on this basis, with all the casualties etc. We ought to pull back into positions in the rear. I sought to prove to him that this is impossible during the battle; it could lead to catastrophe. In addition, work has not even begun on the rearward position *Siegfried* [Hindenburg Line]. It is completely pointless to withdraw to our current Second or Third Positions, because we should be in exactly the same situation within a few days. The whole affair could be traced back to Gebsattel (III B)[14] who was returning from battle and spun him a yarn. It is essential not to give too much credence to those who have just returned from battle; they are still too much under its influence. It does not help at all. We have to stick it out in the hope that the enemy will run out of puff."[15]

Meanwhile the following day Gallwitz was once more pressing his case in writing. 'I reported to the Army Group that it was now essential to believe that Second Army would also come under attack and stressed the lack of artillery or any kind of battle-ready reserves.'[16] Then, on 3 October, during another visit by Crown Prince Rupprecht and von Kuhl, Gallwitz expanded on his theme by criticising the huge amount of paperwork that was being demanded and the way that Ludendorff was curtailing the power of command of subordinate headquarters through personal interventions. 'The conversation led on to me making critical remarks about the peculiar natures of both Falkenhayn and Ludendorff', wrote Gallwitz later. 'Throughout the discussion, which lasted one and a quarter hours, Kuhl stood to one side, serious faced.'[17] Quiet von Kuhl may have been, but he was certainly taking it all in prior to noting down his impressions.

> "4 Oct 16 There is no clarity at Second Army. The reports are coloured, insisting that major battles are in the offing yet nobody accepts the fact ... Gallwitz is irritated and continues to makes difficulties. With all his brains, I never took him for such a petty individual. Bronsart is unsound and Faupel (Ia) [= chief of operations branch] is also a fox. A really unreliable bunch. The great danger is that sometime we shall be wrongly prejudiced and not believe it when a real attack occurs ... The Crown Prince is rather depressed ... but he can always be rallied ... *OHL* is worried, and is always demanding reports ... *OHL* is doing all it can, but it is all very late. If we had taken precautions and preventative measures on the Somme at the right time, none of this would have happened ... In the spring, in Douai, the Crown Prince still did not believe that the British would do anything serious; they would leave everything to the French ... From Mézières [*OHL*] the French were always portrayed as worn down, so we were caught unprepared for the huge offensive. Simultaneously the Austrians failed, then came Romania. All were serious failures by Falkenhayn that could not be rectified.[18]

It was not just at army level that Ludendorff's command style was tending to jar. General von Kuhl always maintained an excellent working relationship with him, but even he found his patience tried at times, especially when the almost intolerable pressure on Ludendorff produced occasional bouts of tetchiness.

> "8 Oct 16 Ludendorff seems to be a bit nervous. [He] keeps demanding exact information about a great many points of detail. Nothing is fast enough for him – very unfriendly telegrams that we should provide information more swiftly. So we have to plague the armies, who are in the middle of a battle, to provide reports etc. There are complaints from all over that the staffs are having to spend their time writing. Ludendorff gets briefed on everything

possible by everyone who has been here, then telegrams arrive demanding to know why this and that has not been done or expedited.[19]

During the following week the increasing annoyance with Second Army finally led to a crisis, according to von Kuhl.

"16 Oct 16. We report our assessment of the situation. This includes an attack on Second Army and its insistence that its front is just as threatened and must be made equally strong ... Bronsart is unreliable. *OHL* is equally very suspicious. The report was sent by signal to *OHL* ... On the basis of our appreciation of the situation, Ludendorff telephoned me. Bronsart will be exchanged for Wild (Armee-Abteilung Stranz).[20]

The actual wording of the signal which brought matters to a head was:

"The overall Army Group appreciation has not changed. The enemy *Schwerpunkt* will continue to be located north of the Somme. Here the enemy is constantly introducing fresh forces; whilst south of the Somme the attacks are being conducted with formations that have been there for some time, supported, nevertheless, by strong artillery and plenty of ammunition. As far back as 22 September the Army Group could not share the assessment of Second Army that enemy attacks would be conducted with the same energy both south and north of the Somme and that this assessment meant the First and Second Armies needed to be allocated equal numbers of forces. Equally it cannot agree with the Headquarters Second Army assessment of 12 October that the Second Army front from its right flank to a point midway between Fouquescourt and Parvillers should be regarded as a main battlefront in the sense defined by *OHL 175 OP* dated 25 September, or that it should be reinforced by a further ten field gun and six light field howitzer batteries ... if Second Army is being allocated somewhat fewer forces than First Army, that is a result of careful consideration of the significance of the attacks being conducted against the two armies and, given the overall number of formations at the disposal of the Army Group, is unavoidable."[21]

An official telegram from Ludendorff arrived later during the evening:

Signal, received 9.20 pm 16 October.
Generalleutnant von Kuhl <u>Personal</u>

I see from signal Ia 1112 of 16 October that the assessments of the Army Group and Second Army are diverging and that, in the opinion of the Army Group, the measures taken by Second Army are not always appropriate to the situation and that Second Army keeps changing its view as to the situation. I cannot otherwise explain the local reverses of Second Army. I request your view if my opinion is correct and if changing the chief of staff, who will be employed elsewhere in the General Staff, will lead to an improvement in the situation.

Signed: Ludendorff

Signal: General Ludendorff Personal.

The assessments of the Army Group and Second Army concerning the situation and the necessary steps which must be taken do not always coincide. The main reason is that, at times, Second Army believes itself to be under attack in the same strength as First Army and therefore demands equivalent deployment of forces. This leads to friction concerning the measures to be applied. These differences make it more difficult for the Army Group to produce an accurate picture of the situation based on Second Army reports. Cooperation with the otherwise able and hard-working chief of staff suffered as a result. In my opinion, in the circumstances a change of chiefs would lead to an improvement in our collaborative efforts. As far as the assessment of the local setback on the Second Army front is concerned, consideration must be given to the fact that the situation there is far from easy and unfavourable circumstances played a part. It will never be possible totally to avoid such things."[22]

"17 Oct 16 I consider that only diversionary attacks are taking place before Second Army, because no fresh French divisions have appeared. That said, there is much gunfire and so there is always the threat of an attack. We have to accept that if we want to beat off the main attack north of the Somme. During the morning I went with the Crown Prince to Second Army at St Quentin. Once again Gallwitz had plenty of criticism: the Army Group artillery reserves are useless and he particularly attacked the *OHL* directive concerning the withdrawal to the *Siegfriedstellung* [Hindenburg Line], especially over the destruction of villages and towns. In those circumstances he would prefer to give up command. Finally, and in the presence of Mende

(Liaison Officer of *OHL* to the Army Group) and Faupel (Ia Second Army), he spoke very disparagingly about Ludendorff's conduct of the war, which did not make a good impression.[23]

Within a few days, the die having been cast, Ludendorff moved to arrange for the change in the chief of staff Second Army. Recalling the situation later, Gallwitz wrote,

"We received a surprise. Oberst von Bronsart, my all round, well trained, active and vigorous chief of staff has been posted to a quiet position with Armee-Abteilung Strantz and Oberst Wild, the chief there, is to come here. I received a letter from Ludendorff in which he stated that he wanted to use the outstanding Oberst Wild on a main battlefront. Although that sounded plausible, I am too long in the tooth not to recognise the deception. General von Kuhl, whom I telephoned, purported to be very surprised. However, he mentioned a conversation with Ludendorff concerning command and control within Second Army. From Bronsart I heard that Kuhl had complained to him earlier about problems he had with Second Army, together with the disapproval of the leading lights of the Army Group over the frank remarks I made during their visit of 17 October. That I can understand. I have no diplomatic skills and I always speak my mind openly."[24]

On the day the news broke, however, it prompted a furious reaction from Gallwitz and was duly recorded by von Kuhl.

"26 Oct 16 Gallwitz telephoned me in the afternoon, very worked up that Bronsart is posted to Armee Abteilung A, to be replaced by Wild. Gallwitz demanded to know the reasons. I should ask Ludendorff, who had written to him. [I replied] Wild had to be given the chance to come to a major battlefront in order to learn about large scale battles. Of course that is just a cover story. Ludendorff refused me permission to provide further information and I so informed Gallwitz. He is now going to write to Ludendorff, which is effectively pointless. He felt that if fault had been found with Second Army it impacted on him."[25]

Despite this conversation, Gallwitz did write to Ludendorff and, predictably, it got him nowhere.

"In response to my letter to Ludendorff I received a cold and uncouth rejection. Because I cannot prove anything against L. a formal complaint to

His Majesty would, for the same reason, also be unsuccessful. Given that this cannot be resolved verbally, that leaves only – a letter of resignation! Could I do it? Would it be worth it to draw opprobrium down on myself as a miserable moaner? It is no help against the powers that be. Earlier, I should never have imagined that an army commander could be treated so shabbily, but the current young influential holders of power do not lack ruthlessness."[26]

On 28 October Gallwitz visited Headquarters Army Group Crown Prince of Bavaria in what von Kuhl simply recorded as 'a personal matter'.[27] In fact he had come to complain to Crown Prince Rupprecht about the removal of Bronsart, insisting that any blame was his alone; but Rupprecht simply warned him to be more careful about what he said in future. However, both were in agreement that in time of war consideration for the feelings of others was not in the ascendant. Gallwitz did not like it, considered his position yet again, let off steam in his diary, but soldiered on, disgruntled, until the December crisis at Verdun saw him recalled to take over Fifth Army under the orders of Army Group German Crown Prince. At that he requested the services of Bronsart once more and Ludendorff acquiesced after a brief delay.

It was not just at the highest levels of command that the pressures of the battle made themselves felt. There were major issues to deal with at trench level as well. After less than two months, the demands on manpower reserves caused by severe casualties at Verdun and the Somme were leading to dangerous compromises and dilution in quality in order to generate the numbers required to continue the battle. On paper, infantry regiments in the 400 series and divisions from 201st Infantry Division onwards had the same value as any other in the order of battle. In fact, they hid numerous deficiencies, which were of great consequence on the Somme, where for much of the battle the German army relied on its individual qualitative advantage to offset Allied numerical superiority. One example that came to the notice of Headquarters First Army in early September concerned problems within one of the regiments of 204th Infantry Division, which was only raised on 10 June 1916, and was to have deployed as part of 89 Reserve Infantry Brigade (207th Infantry Division) to Mouquet Farm on 10 September. On 9 September, Oberst von Loßberg wrote to Army Group Crown Prince of Bavaria about it.

"According to a report by its commander, Infantry Regiment 413, posted with 89 Reserve Infantry Brigade, only has a trench strength of 1,900 men (including NCOs). Of these, only 440 have battle experience, 1,000 are from the 1917 year group and the remainder are untrained *Landsturm*.

"The machine gun company is also not fully operational. As a result, the Army is unwilling to deploy it on a front where there is serious fighting and it has been made available to Group Stein [XIV Reserve Corps] for employment on a quiet front. Army Headquarters hopes in this way to allow this regiment time to develop and continue its training. Group Stein will now be in a position to withdraw two battalions in need of rest into Army reserve."[28]

The regiment itself admitted in its history that most of its officers were only 'g.v.' [*Garnisonsverwendungsfähig* = rear area duties only] and that its deployment at that juncture to the Somme was, 'something that not one man in the entire regiment would have believed to be possible, but it was a fact ... it was not that we feared the prospect of battle, rather that we totally lacked experience in comparison with the 'old' regiments.'[29] In the event their 'acclimatisation' period when they were split into two groups, each comprising one and a half battalions, was far from straightforward. One group was sent to 2nd Guards Reserve Division, the other to 52nd Infantry Division between Gommecourt and Serre. There was little opportunity for any sort of systematic training, because they were kept hard at work on repairing the positions they were sent to man and, in the wake of the loss of Gueudecourt, Lesboeufs and Morval on 26 September, as an emergency measure the regiment was rushed into the line in the so-called *Grévillers Stellung*, between the *Below Stellung* and the Warlencourt – Irles road. Swept up into a battle for which they were ill prepared, their casualties were predictably heavy every time they clashed with British attackers and, by the time they were relieved, they had lost a total of thirty officers and 613 other ranks.[30]

It was not just amongst the newly created formations that there were problems. By September divisions which had been involved in heavy fighting during the early days, usually suffering crippling losses, had been reinforced and sent back for second tours. 7th Infantry Division, which had fought around Martinpuich between 12 and 25 July, returned in mid-September to Courcelette. It was far too soon and its regiments paid a high price. Writing home the following month, Leutnant Wolfgang von Vormann of Infantry Regiment 26 summed up the difficulties with complete precision.

"We have been terribly mauled once more, even worse than the last time. It is hardly to be wondered at, because then we were a superb unit, welded together by the experience we gained during the hard days of small-scale actions we had fought around the slag heaps of Saint Pierre. Commanders and men knew and trusted one another absolutely. This time we were simply a mob of soldiers. We received good reinforcements from Germany, but the interval between the first and second deployments was just too short. We lacked the proven junior commanders: NCOs and officers, who could hold the troops together. We enjoyed good success this time too, but we were not brilliant. We beat off about ten attacks, causing the British huge casualties, but we had to yield five hundred metres of ground. By then we were at the end of our tether, but we were relieved just in time…"[31]

He might have been writing to Loßberg who, on 26 September, addressed this very point in a report to Army Group Crown Prince of Bavaria.

"Raw numerical superiority can only be balanced by the superior quality of the individual soldier and his training. Our infantrymen are unanimous that in close quarter battle they are better than both the British and the French. However, the High Command must be quite clear that its make up and training is not as it was earlier. The training and leadership ability amongst both officers and NCOs is becoming ever poorer. It is not a lack of willingness; rather a lack of knowledge of the individual – and mostly very young – personalities whose own training and, consequently, skill in training and command in battle is deficient. It will be hard to improve the situation as the war continues. It must simply be taken into account and the conduct of the war and command in battle must be adjusted accordingly. It must be assumed that our enemies are faced with same situation. Therefore, victory will go to the side which makes best use of its resources in soldiers, matériel and ammunition and understands how to deploy them most skilfully."[32]

Generalleutnant von Stetten, commander II Bavarian Corps, reflecting on the outcome of the 15 September battles between Martinpuich and Flers, raised a number of similar serious concerns with his divisional commanders and proposed several measures to counter them.

"The divisional reports on the way the events of 15 and 16 September unfurled paint an impressive picture of outstanding performances and gallant deeds, but also reveal several weaknesses which, in their totality, caused the British attack to be successful … From all the reports there is no doubt that, in the truest sense of the word, the enemy artillery completely neutralised our infantry. Almost all their efforts were then devoted to protecting themselves from the effect of the enemy artillery … every new trench dug during the night was immediately subject to drum fire. As a result, the infantry sought sanctuary in craters in order, as far as possible, to remain unobserved. So developed what is known as a 'Somme Position', namely shell craters, with some protection improvised and connected by shallow, wide trenches. I believe we must find a way of coming to terms with this situation. No order, no matter how severe, can make a man do something which, from his experience, he knows will put his life at increased risk. It is clear that this type of 'position' has very serious disadvantages, both for the cohesiveness of the troops as well as the self-reliance of the individual man.

"It is pointless to close our eyes to the fact that during the Battle of the Somme the internal structure of particular units has been seriously weakened; otherwise, despite all losses, it would have been impossible for forward companies on the day of battle to have been down to forty to sixty riflemen ... Because under battle conditions as difficult as those on the Somme there will always be weak links who know, with greater or lesser skill, exactly how to remove themselves, in future consideration will have to be given to the organisation of a stricter system of policing immediately behind the front; one which will concentrate in particular on the cellars of adjacent built up areas and dugouts close to batteries, [engineer] parks and medical posts. In actual fact, during the battle the dugouts by the engineer parks and medical facilities seem to have acted like powerful magnets ...

"The striving to avoid being detected did not merely prevent the preparation of normal defences; rather it had the consequence that almost all the troops withdrew from any form of fighting. For a long time, excessive reliance on hand grenades has pushed the use of the rifle dangerously into the background. On the Somme, to this has been added such a concern that to shoot is to risk positions being betrayed that fire has not been opened, even when valuable targets have appeared. During the night 14/15 dense masses were observed moving from the rear to fill up the forward trenches. They were not fired at. Large assemblies of troops were seen being fed in the open. They, too, were not fired at ... The following statement by an officer is significant, 'It was fortunate that there were no hand grenades available, so the men had[33] to shoot.' ...

"Next to inadequate shooting and frequent failures of machine guns, another very unpleasant matter emerged; one which cannot be passed over in silence. Alongside brilliant examples of endurance, all too often there was a regrettable lack of courage to do battle, a lack of willpower such that if a man had to die at least he would sell his life as dearly as possible. This was the spirit that was engendered in his heroic little band by Oberleutnant Sturm and described in his own words, 'The shout, 'Here they come!' caused all to forget [the danger]. In the place of a depressed mood came the joy of battle, which harked back to the day of Mörchingen [Morhange].'[34]

This spirit is lacking in many fighting units and, unfortunately, it must be said, amongst their commanders. With little or no resistance, they simply surrendered and accepted the fate of being captured.

"The understanding of what being taken prisoner means to a soldier has undergone grievous change during the course of positional warfare. Of course instances can occur in the current style of warfare that make this sad fate unavoidable. Nevertheless, every soldier – and even more every officer – must have it drilled into him that to fall unwounded into the hands of the enemy is somewhat shameful and all too easily leaves an enduring stain on his character."[35]

Stetten then went on to advocate more realistic and aggressive training, a greater emphasis on patrolling and small scale actions to educate and improve the fighting spirit of his men; but the overwhelming impression left by the paper is the evidence of poor morale caused by the incessant pressure being imposed on the forward troops by the relentless battle of matériel. As ever, it is one thing to identify problems, quite another to rectify them swiftly. Oberst Ludwig Herthies, temporarily in command of Bavarian 7 Infantry Brigade, Bavarian 4th Infantry Division, prior to his confirmation in post and promotion to Generalmajor in December 1916, spent a day in late October watching units of his brigade training. What he observed displeased him greatly and he lost no time in sending a sharply worded letter to Oberst Wilhelm von Haasy, commanding Bavarian Reserve Infantry Regiment 5. He began by laying down two main points. First, all company commanders were to be in possession of a precise training programme seen and approved by his commanding officer and deviations from it were not permitted unless caused by events, such as enemy air attack and, second, properly qualified and experienced officers were to be present to direct training and provide advice.

"It is the business of battalion commanding officers", he wrote, "by means of skilful grouping of the exercising companies, purposefully and effectively to make use of the directing and advisory skills of the active officers. In future there must be no question of a repetition of that which I observed for a long time today; namely a young, completely inexperienced, reserve leutnant and company commander, accompanied by very average NCOs, waste materials, time and energy in a really useless way, which achieved nothing of training value. These young company commanders simply cannot[36] direct training, because they have never learnt how to. Therefore, they must be given a properly organised programme of instruction and, directed and advised by a properly appointed officer, learn how to direct exercises.

> "I noticed that men were standing around for two hours during live firing, then at long last simply firing three rounds. During these two hours there was not the slightest activity. This utter waste of time, given the current situation, must be condemned in the strongest terms. The very next time that I come across any such thing, I shall have to punish the director of the exercise most severely."[37]

Herthies then went on to lay down precisely how marching troops were to be disciplined and commanded. There was to be no slackness and singing was to be encouraged. The regimental commander, who was also ordered to sign off all exercise instructions in future prior to forwarding them to brigade headquarters, lost no time in adding his further instructions and sending them to his battalion commanders. It does appear that this reprimand led to improvements, but the fact that it had to be written speaks volumes about the ways losses had begun seriously to dilute the quality of the German army. Even as late as 28 December 1916, Herthies was writing once more to all formations of Bavarian 7 Infantry Brigade. This time he gave both officers and men good marks for effort, 'Once again I repeat my personal, full recognition of all officers for their total commitment to improving the training of the men under difficult conditions.'[38] Nevertheless, he found it necessary to draw attention to a wide range of areas where improvement was still needed.

Crisis at Sailly Sailissel

As autumn began, if there was one place on the battlefield where the defence was to be put to the greatest test and where it came closest to breaking, that was Sailly-Sailissel. Having completed one tour on the Somme in July near Biaches and after spending two months on the Aisne absorbing reinforcements, Infantry Regiment 160, together with the remainder of 15th Infantry Division, was sent back to the Somme on 25 September. In a valedictory message, its corps commander, General der Infanterie Julius Riemann, wrote,

> "The eyes of the Fatherland, of the entire world, are directed at the part of the front where you are to be deployed. As I see you depart, I have complete trust that the heroes of Biaches and the Ancre will add fresh glory to former deeds and that the newly formed elements will strive to match the old formations. My heartiest best wishes and those of the entire VIII Corps go with you."[39]

Three days later, on 28 September, the division was pitched straight into the bitter fighting just southwest of Sailly Sailissel, where it manned the *Quer-Riegel* from

St Pierre Vaast Wood northwest towards Morval. Things did not go well for the 'heroes of Biaches and the Ancre'. In fact, as a formation, theirs was subsequently judged to be one of the biggest collective failures of the entire battle. On 13 October, Generalleutnant von Kuhl noted in his diary,

"The 15th Division (VIII [Corps]) has failed completely and has been returned with protests to Seventh Army ... There was serious indiscipline in the 15th Division, which did not go forward into the positions. Böhn, in whose group they were deployed, states that he has never come across such terrible troops."[40]

On the return of the division to Seventh Army, its commander, Generalleutnant Freiherr Raitz von Frentz, and its General Staff officer were both sacked and Infantry Regiment 186 was rapidly replaced by Infantry Regiment 69.[41] What had gone wrong?

The first point to make is that the divisional structure had been subject to radical change in 1916. On mobilisation in 1914 it comprised 29 and 80 Infantry Brigades, with Infantry Regiments 25 and 161 and Infantry Regiments 65 and 160 respectively. On the formation of 185th Infantry Division on 19 June 1916 as part of the expansion of the number of divisions, it lost Infantry Regiments 65 and 161 to the new formation then, when 208th Infantry Division was raised on 29 August, Infantry Regiment 25 departed as well. This left only Infantry Regiment 160 of the original four – and it had taken a severe mauling in the desperate July battles. Posted in from 185th Infantry Division was Infantry Regiment 186, itself a wartime construction; then the newly raised Infantry Regiment 389 arrived to form the third regiment of 80 Infantry Brigade. Unfortunately, this regiment left no history and its records were destroyed during the bombing of the Prussian archives in Potsdam in April 1945. However, it may reasonably be assumed that in its make up it was very similar to Infantry Regiment 413, whose deficiencies have already been described.

As a result of the pressure on manpower, this hastily constructed, makeshift, division could hardly be described, even on paper, as a first class fighting formation, yet it was placed at an absolutely critical part of the battlefield. North of the Somme, despite an acute shortage of ammunition for the heavy artillery in particular,[42] formations of the French Sixth Army had been exerting enormous pressure in an attempt to break through the German defences and thus outflank Péronne. As a compromise and in line with the latest offensive policy produced by Foch, the attacks towards Sailly-Saillisel were phased with distinct gaps between major assaults. It was a French version of what the British would later refer to as 'bite and hold' and it proved to be an effective way of maintaining high operational tempo and pressure on the defence.[43] However, the period 25 September – 6 October saw almost continuous heavy fighting so, no sooner had 15th Infantry Division taken over the two defensive lines at the end of September than, first *Quer Riegel* and then *Busse Riegel* (known to the French Army as the *Tranchée de Prilip/Tranchée des Portes de Fer/Tranchée de Negotin* and *Tranchée de Carlsbad/Tranchée de Teplitz*, respectively) were attacked and captured or evacuated.

Given that Infantry Regiment 160 was the most experienced and robust of the three regiments, its description of its readiness for action and the way the situation around Sailly developed is very interesting.

"It was not without serious misgivings that the experienced soldiers of the regiment viewed this deployment. The heavy blood-letting of Biaches had still not been overcome, because only a small proportion of the replacements that had arrived in the meantime could be described as good. Even unmistakeably unreliable men were sent to the front this time. The new 5th Company had still not completely developed into a battle-ready sub unit. Whilst the training of the newly formed machine gun companies and, to some extent, their equipment, had still not still not peaked, the consequent loss to the [rifle] companies of their best NCOs and men was damaging. The feldwebels were banned from going forward into the positions and their deputies had a very difficult task. In contrast to Biaches, where there were numerous officer platoon commanders, [this time] apart from the company commanders, only one other officer per company deployed forward. This was because numerous special groups were required, each of which had to be allocated officers and the best men.

"A large working party was formed from older men and, unfortunately, the vitally important carrying party and runners, commanded by Hauptmann Ott, was initially made up of older men or those not fully fit. This had serious consequences later. The regimental staff was weakened with the departure to division[al headquarters] of its tried and tested adjutant ... and the health of Oberst von Buddenbrock was very poor. Within the divisional staff there were once more individuals who took these factors into as little consideration as was the case earlier in the Battle of the Somme, when the regiment was subordinated to the Liebert Division."[44]

Regardless of the difficulties the division faced and the risk of deploying it at such a place, the decision was made and it was sent forward, under attack by a constant rain of shells all the way to the front line. Leutnant Matthei, adjutant 1st Battalion, later described the relief of 2nd Battalion Reserve Infantry Regiment 234, which had been the first formation to occupy the *Quer Riegel* after 51st Reserve Division had been forced out of Combles.[45]

"The march forward was by companies, initially in a northwesterly direction towards Le Mesnil. Just beyond Le Mesnil the road to Saillisel was under very heavy enemy harassing fire, which landed in amongst the companies. Due to the huge amount of traffic on this road – teams of horses, guns, field kitchens, ambulances all rushed along the same route – and the shelling, elements of the companies got split up. The village of Sailissel looked like a witch's kitchen and was passed as quickly as possible. The way on beyond it, the road from Sailissel to Frégicourt Farm, was under the heaviest drum fire. The [battalion] staff was caught by a sudden concentration of fire on this road which cost it a considerable number of casualties, including Reserve Leutnant Hans Spieker, who was killed. The companies occupied the position as arranged and the staff moved to the left flank of 3rd Company, but there was no staff there to be relieved. By 3.00 am the takeover was complete.

"When it became light the battalion situation was as follows: The position ran from the Saillisel – Frégicourt road in a wide arc to the south and west … The battalion left flank linked up with Infantry Regiment 389 at the road. The road itself was not blocked; there was no sign of an obstacle. The right flank of 3rd Company was extremely poorly constructed. The trench was flattened in many places and in parts was only linked together by sight across a shallow depression towards Infantry Regiment 162 [17th Reserve Division]. As a whole the entire position was no more than knee deep and in places not dug at all. There were the beginnings of about ten dugouts in the entire sector. If they had been exploited to the full they might have provided rudimentary cover for up to fifty men. Most of the men had to dig out small holes to equip themselves with cover. There was no cover at all for sentries … The entire area between Sailly and the position was constantly under the heaviest fire. The weather was rainy and contact to the rear by day was almost impossible."

Infantry Regiment 186, moving forward to occupy the position manned by Infantry Regiment 149 and Infantry Regiment 368 at the southern end of the *Quer Riegel*, also ran into immense problems immediately. The French had infiltrated part of the Infantry Regiment 149 position. This was completely unknown to the Infantry Regiment 149 commander, who was unaware of the fact until a patrol led by Vizefeldwebel Echtermeyer of Infantry Regiment 186, intended to locate the precise front line locations, appeared with the news. Despite the presence of this nest of resistance, the relief went ahead, though it was impossible for 1st and 2nd Companies to link up because of it. Initial attempts to remove the nest failed so, for the time being, the French had a foothold in an important part of the German lines.[46] There was permanent French pressure against the entire line over the next few days, which were marked by frequent attacks and hasty counter-attacks. Even worse, there was never any let up in the amount of shelling and attacks from the air that were transforming the entire area into a moonscape of craters. The resupply and rationing system broke down, leaving the entire garrison of the front line exhausted, hungry and above all thirsty, which made the fate of the wounded waiting for evacuation quite appalling.

The nerves of the entire garrison were badly affected as the numbers of casualties continued to rise then, on 1 October, came the first catastrophe. The French had been observed moving their guns forward into the large hollow between Combles and Bois d'Anderlu to the south of the village that morning then, at 5.00 pm, from a balloon manned by Luftschiffer Abteilung 7, came a report that for the past hour the French had been moving assault troops forward towards Morval. Accompanied by a storm of gunfire, they succeeded in breaking in to the position of Infantry Regiment 389, though information did not reach Infantry Regiment 160 until 11.00 pm. Immediate steps were taken to reinforce the *Busse Stellung* but clarification did not arrive until 6.00 am, when a message from Leutnant Rothert, commanding 1st Company, dated 11.40 pm the previous evening, was finally delivered. By then the French had had seven hours to consolidate the positions they had overrun so that a counter-attack mounted with a few handfuls of exhausted men had no chance of success. Blocking positions were set up and manned by hand grenade sections. Those remaining of Infantry Regiment 389, including the commanding officer of 1st Battalion (Rittmeister von Diezelsky) and the battalion staff of 2nd Battalion under Hauptmann Bressem, pulled back to the *Busse Stellung* and, once it was full, into Sailly itself.[47] The only exceptions were surviving elements of its 2nd Battalion, who dug in about 500 metres in rear of the *Quer Riegel*.

Meanwhile 1st Battalion Infantry Regiment 160 attempted to spread itself along as much of the *Quer Riegel* as possible and to hold until it was relieved, something which had been due during the night 2/3 October in any case. Such was the confusion and lack of clarity at divisional level that not only was the request to expedite the relief ignored, permission was not granted to go ahead with the routine relief. Effectively the defence was splintering dangerously, command and control was faltering badly and there was a total failure to get food, drink and ammunition forward. The carrying parties often could not find their way through the mass of craters and were frequently shelled, so that in some instances, when the fire was lifted, they could not even find their loads in the dark.

Much the same situation persisted for the next two days. The situation forward became increasingly untenable, the effort to maintain a presence in the *Quer Riegel* impossible for exhausted men who had had nothing to eat or drink for days. The commander on the spot, Oberleutnant Adam, sent appeals for flares, sustenance and relief. The occasional message did get through to Sailly with a delay of twelve hours or more, but all attempts to bring succour failed. During the night 3/4 October a complete and strong patrol, loaded with water, cigarettes and flares, disappeared without trace, almost certainly yet another victim to the intense shelling. Lacking any information or instructions, but knowing that his men were at the end of their tether – out of ammunition and with most of their weapons unserviceable – Adam gave the order to withdraw, knowing that it would be impossible to defend against a further assault.

At a subsequent court martial, his conduct was held to be entirely justified and he was acquitted but, at the time, his action, which crossed an attempt at a counter attack towards the French break in on the *Quer Riegel*, unleashed fury at divisional and corps level. The commander of the projected counter-attack, Leutnant von Pelser-Berensberg, subsequently provided an account of scenes of death, destruction and confusion that are almost beyond comprehension.

"I moved forward at the head of my company. To begin with it was fairly quiet. Not until we had passed Mesnil did the shells begin to land right and left. The slow pace of the weary soldiers increased. Just before Sailly it got really bad. The track was terribly shot up. Here lay dead horses, there a wrecked wagon, split in two. By the side of the road lay piles of ammunition thrown down hastily. Huge shell craters had ripped up the entire road. Everywhere and from everywhere shells rained down, many exploding close to us. The way forward was sheer Hell. We had to rush through five separate defensive fire zones before we reached the front line or what was meant to be it. I got everyone successfully to the start line (a chain of shell holes about 200 metres west of Sailly). There we encountered a fresh piece of bad luck. The company was poised and waiting in the shell holes for the order to attack. Suddenly figures appeared in the darkness. It was our front line garrison, who had just evacuated their position!

"What was I to do? I was supposed to attack on the left, but there was now nobody on the right. Because that seemed mad to me, I rushed back through the defensive fire to the battalion, which was housed with three other battalion staffs in a cellar in the village of Sailissel. After much to-ing and fro-ing the assault order was confirmed! So it was off forwards once more through artillery fire that continually grew in strength. Once again I arrived in one piece. It was high time; the artillery fire was even heavier. I was only able to gather around me and lead towards the enemy those men who had been at the head of the company with me. For five or six hundred metres all went smoothly."[48]

Vizefeldwebel Rehnelt, who had to assume command of 10th Company when Leutnant von Pelser-Berensburg was hit on the head and wounded – only his helmet saved him – added,

"The enemy was not located where higher command assumed that they were and where for several days our artillery had searched for them. Instead they had worked their way another four hundred metres towards us and dug in. So it happened that our assault force bumped into them unexpectedly and came under machine gun fire from troops which were holding out some distance from where they were meant to be. The attack stalled in this fire."[49]

This latest debacle, for as such it was seen at corps level, was enough for General der Infanterie von Boehn, commander IX Reserve Corps, so he ordered the immediate withdrawal of the remnants of 15th Infantry Division on 6 October. As far as he was concerned the divisional performance had been lamentably poor and he took the unusual step of addressing the officers of Infantry Regiment 160 in Gouzeaucourt, delivering what was described as, 'a speech of undeserved harshness'.[50] The divisional commander added his own condemnatory remarks subsequently in front of the entire regiment. Subsequently, in a meeting Hauptmann von Stuckrad energetically defended the action by Oberleutnant Adam, finally convincing Generalleutnant von Frentz that the evacuation of the *Quer Riegel* had been correct.

Infantry Regiment 160 lost 1,000 men and a third of its already reduced number of officers and senior NCOs in action and also had to evacuate for medical reasons so many officers and men after relief that it was down to 270 men fit for duty when it left Sailly-Sailissel. It was extremely resentful of the way it had been treated, believing that a most serious slur had been cast over the regiment on the basis of unjustifiable complaints and that General von Boehn had been led astray in his assessments by false reporting emanating from observation balloon crews. Certainly there seems to have been some initial overreaction, because subsequently there was quite a generous allocation of medals, including a high order to its commander. In retrospect it does seem to have been hard done by; that too much had been demanded of it too soon after its previous tour of duty on the Somme. Whatever the truth, it remains a demonstration of how close the German army was coming to breaking in the face of unrelenting French pressure. Men were being pushed to the limit of their endurance and beyond and the agony of the fighting in this critical sector still ground on.

SITUATION BAVARIAN IR1 14 OCTOBER

It was not just on the Somme battlefield itself that the consequences of the heavy fighting there were being felt. On 15 October General der Artillerie Richard von Schubert, commanding Seventh Army in the Aisne sector, brought a piece of disturbing news to the attention of Crown Prince Rupprecht.

"As a result of lapses in discipline affecting Infantry Regiment 190, 16th Reserve Division, in particular the discovery that forbidden trench to trench fraternisation with the French has been occurring and that the disappearance of three Musketiers is associated with it, Headquarters XI Corps has requested Supreme Headquarters to arrange for the removal of the regimental commander, Oberstleutnant Ritter und Edler von Rogister, previously commander Uhlan Regiment 15. So far no decision has been received.

"During its first tour of duty on the Somme, Infantry Regiment 190 had extraordinarily heavy casualties and has had to accept very extensive and not entirely high quality replacements. It will receive a new commander on the day of removal and posting."[51]

This must have come as a severe blow to both Rogister and the regiment which had fought with great distinction around La Boisselle and Contalmaison in early July and Longueval in the middle of that month. However, previous good service counted for nothing in the circumstances and three days later a follow up Seventh Army communication arrived at Army Group headquarters in Cambrai.

"In connection with the report of 15 October, Army Headquarters announces that from 16th of this month the former commander of Infantry Regiment 190, Oberstleutnant Ritter und Edler von Rogister, has been posted as commander Dragoon Regiment 7 and has been replaced by Major Schütz, in peacetime a member of Infantry Regiment 131 and currently serving in Reserve Infantry Regiment 88."[52]

It was another example of an exemplary punishment meted out in an attempt to restore the extremely rigid discipline deemed necessary if the German army was to survive the pressure of the battle. So Rogister was dismissed but, simultaneously, to the north, events were reaching crisis point in the Sailly-Saillisel – St Pierre Vaast sector. Ground had been yielded by 15th Infantry Division, gaps had appeared in the defensive front so that both 16th Infantry and later 1st Bavarian Infantry Division, which relieved 17th Reserve Division, inherited a confused and highly threatening situation when they were moved forward hastily into positions virtually on the outskirts of Sailly-Saillisel. Sensing the opportunity to break through, the French redoubled their efforts to get forward and, to that end, so much artillery fire was directed into the area just south of the ruins which marked the site of the straggling village that it was simply not possible most of the time to occupy it. Later the existence of this gap was to lead to a major row between Infantry Regiment 68 and Bavarian Infantry Regiment 2.

In an attempt to eliminate French thrusts into Sailly, both Infantry Regiments 68 and 28 threw in repeated counter attacks but, in so doing, their losses had risen to such an extent that their ability to resist and maintain the necessary links with the Bavarians to the south was critically reduced. By 15 October the French 152nd Infantry Regiment had forced its way in to the village. There then followed forty eight hours of incessant close quarter battle by day and night until, on 17 October, the French were in possession of the entire former built up area of Sailly. It was such a setback that Infantry Regiment 68 post war devoted a very large section of its history to explaining that tactical confusion, unclear orders and friendly fire landing on them had placed them in an impossible situation.

The Bavarian 1st Infantry Division was furious about the situation and then and there in the field systematically set about collating all possible information so as to demonstrate that this major setback was all the fault of the Prussians. Of course, there was never any love lost between these contingents, but if the notes supplied by Leutnant Nirschl, commanding 9th Company Bavarian Infantry Regiment 2, are even close to the truth, their frustration is easy to understand.

"12 Oct 16–11.45 pm. According to the briefing officer from Infantry Regiment 76, Infantry Regiment 68 should link up with my right flank on the road Sailly – Morval. I have already deployed almost a complete platoon north of this road, but the gap is still not closed."

13 Oct 16–10.30 pm. According to the statement of the officer from [Reserve] Infantry Regiment 76 who handed over to me, my right flank should extend as far as the road Sailly – Morval. I have now extended two hundred metres to the right, because Infantry Regiment 68 refuses to move its left flank as far as the road on the grounds that the gap is being fired on by their own artillery. They definitely have enough men to fill the gap and close up to the road.

14 Oct 16–8.45 pm. It is urgently imperative in the interests of justice that the neighbouring regiment be prevailed upon to reoccupy the section which their predecessors vacated irregularly.

15 Oct 16–8.30 pm. A breakthrough occurred in the area of Infantry Regiment 68. After the attack only two sections were still to the right of us. It has now been established that Infantry Regiment 68 is only occupying the line as far as two hundred metres to the right of us. Apparently link up is complete again throughout Infantry Regiment 68.

15 Oct 16–9.50 pm. Contact with Infantry Regiment 68 exists. It is located a further two hundred metres to the right of our right flank. It is not clear if the gap has been closed once more.

15 Oct 16–11.45 pm. It has just been reported to me that Infantry Regiment 68 has once again evacuated the sector adjoining us to the right. I am about to have it temporarily re-occupied by a platoon (2nd Platoon 11th Company. A liaison team from this platoon is with me), but urgently request that Infantry Regiment 68 be persuaded to relieve the Platoon this evening. It is an area where I suffered the majority of my casualties yesterday (immediately to the north of the road Sailly – Morval). The morale of the men of Infantry Regiment 68, who at 7.00 pm this evening were still in this sector of trench, gradually deteriorated. Some of them had to be forced at pistol point to continue.

16 Oct 16–2.30 am. The French have pushed into the Prussian gap and are pressing on my right flank. The entire wood behind is said to be occupied by the French, who pulled back there from the village of Sailly. I refuse to accept responsibility that the position of my right flank can still be held.

16 Oct 16–11.30 pm. Various men of Infantry Regiment 68 fraternised with the enemy and were finally moved away as prisoners."[53]

As has been mentioned, the village fell completely into French hands the following day. Leutnant Märklin, of 6th Company Bavarian Infantry Regiment 2, had numerous caustic comments about the Infantry Regiment 68 performance that day.

"17 Oct 16–10.00 am. One company and two machine guns of Infantry Regiment 68 have just launched an attack on the French nest of resistance along the Bapaume-Péronne road south of Sailly. The men of Infantry Regiment 68 have no officer in charge of them; the machine guns are being commanded by an Offizierstellvertreter.

17 Oct 16–10.20 am. Detachments of the company of Infantry Regiment 68 which attacked are streaming backwards in disorder. The commander has apparently lost control over his men.

17 Oct 16–10.30 am. It appears that Infantry Regiment 68 has completely run away to the rear.

17 Oct 16–11.00 am. An order from the commander of our neighbouring battalion of Infantry Regiment 68 has just arrived at the Infantry Regiment 68 machine gun that is subordinated to us, 'The Prussian machine guns are to pull back as soon as the Infantry Regiment 68 battalion withdraws'. Such an order, which was also overheard by our men, has had a sorry effect, to put it no more strongly.

17 Oct 16–12.00 am. Patrols sent out in a north westerly direction could not make contact with Infantry Regiment 68."[54]

In truth too much had been asked of the men of 16th Infantry Division. They had been in the line by then for nine days, subject to the worst that the French Sixth Army could direct at them. During the first few days of their deployment their performance had been sufficiently distinguished as to merit a unit citation but they should have been pulled out of the line prior to 15 October. Unfortunately this was not possible and the consequent demands were beyond the capacity of the men to meet them. That said, 16th Infantry Division remained in the line for several more days, though its ability to contribute to the subsequent counter-attacks was very slight; in fact it compromised the ability of the Bavarians to rectify the situation. The corps commander, General der Infanterie von Boehn, gave orders in person for one of these attacks, warning that if it was not successful on 19 October it would have to be repeated the following day. Commanded by 1 Bavarian Infantry Brigade and timed to begin at 8.00 pm, by which time it would have been pitch black, it was to have been a converging attack with Infantry Regiment 28 of 16th Infantry Division assaulting from the north. However, it never even began. All attempts to find the Infantry Regiment 28 men failed to produce a link up. When, eventually, contact was made with the brigade by Headquarters Infantry Regiment 28, they simply stated that,

"Infantry Regiment 28 is not in a position to attack; it is completely exhausted. The men are wading over knee deep in mud. The hand grenades are caked in mud and unusable. Due to the darkness and enemy artillery fire, the companies which were to have participated have been split up and become entangled with each other. The French arrived in Sailly in considerable strength on 19 October ... [They] have created strong positions on the western side of Sailly and have moved a great many machine guns into position."[55]

The situation following the fall of Sailly was extremely serious, as was the inability of the weakened defenders to be able to recapture it. As proof that this was regarded as a full blown crisis, by mid-morning on 20 October Generals von Below and von Boehn, accompanied by Oberst von Loßberg, had descended on 1st Bavarian Infantry Division. The atmosphere was extremely tense; the mood of the senior delegation unforgiving. There was simply too much at stake. The divisional commander, Generalleutnant Ritter von Schoch, included a detailed account of the meeting in his after action report.

"The total failure of Infantry Regiment 28 was not mentioned at all. General von Below took exception to the fact that the division had not despatched officers of its own forward to carry out a reconnaissance of the situation, that had still not been clarified. I retorted that I did not do that because liaison officers from [Bavarian] 1 Infantry Brigade were already located with the regiments and because I had given the task to the Army's own storm troop reconnaissance officers. (The fact that these officers would make such a hash of their mission was not something that I could assume in advance.) My presentation that first of all artillery preparation would have to be effective was approved, as was my request that the interaction between 1st Bavarian Infantry Division and 16th Infantry Division should be the subject of orders[56] by the Group. Experience had shown that trying to negotiate agreements was extremely time-consuming and that it was very difficult to come to a viable result.

"Oberst von Loßberg was not in agreement with the order that the companies located on the west side of Sailly should give up a certain amount of ground. The orders, which had not yet got through, were to be countermanded. The companies were to hold on close to Sailly; first, to prevent the French from capturing the important hill to the west of Sailly and, second, because the position near Sailly made a very suitable start line for the attack on the western portion of the village. In response to my objection that in this situation effective artillery preparation would not be possible, it was stated that the beaten zone of the guns would not be too great if batteries with new equipment were employed and that our own troops would just have to accept the risk of some stray shells.

"The fact that the situation of forward companies, which already had enemy in positions to their rear, would be quite untenable, especially when the pitiable men were also going to be shot at by our own artillery, was something that apparently Herr von Loßberg[57] simply did not want to discuss. I still hoped silently that the two companies had long since pulled back their seriously threatened left flank as soon as they observed the occupation of the western edge of Sailly ... Finally, General von Below gave orders that, following thorough artillery bombardment, the attack on Sailly was to be carried out by means of simultaneous advances from the east, north and west ... Thus the Army had reverted to my proposal of 17 October."[58]

In the event, for various reasons the attack fizzled out almost as soon as it began at 5.30 pm on 21 October, but somehow the defenders, by now largely relieved, clung on. Sailly, though important, only constituted part of the defences. The remaining ruins of Sailissel continued to be in German hands for some time to come and in and around St Pierre Vaast Wood, where the fighting was utterly brutal, the defenders stood firm in the face of all attacks, providing an anchor point which prevented the German position from collapsing. All the defenders could do by now was to hang on grimly to that which they held and senior commanders simply had to accept that no more could be done with the troops available. At no point in the battle had the Allies come closer to a decisive break through, but somehow the defenders had prevented it. Crown Prince Rupprecht's diary entry for 24 October reads,

"From the point of view of artillery observation, it would be a good thing if at least the northern section of Sailly could be recaptured. Such an attempt could not be made until after the arrival of XV Army Corps. Both General von Below and General von Boehn share the view that the power of attack of our troops has been greatly reduced and that the lack of officers means that there is no future prospect of raising it."[59]

At the beginning of November, General der Infanterie von Boehn, whose corps had been responsible for the High Wood area from 24 July – 10 August, then the Sailly sector for five weeks from 29 September, produced some trenchant comments about the deleterious effect the Battle of the Somme was having on the divisions engaged there. The document itself is undated, but von Kuhl makes mention of it in his diary. '7 November. I have sent Ludendorff an important position paper by Böhn [sic.] concerning training, battleworthiness etc.',[60] so it

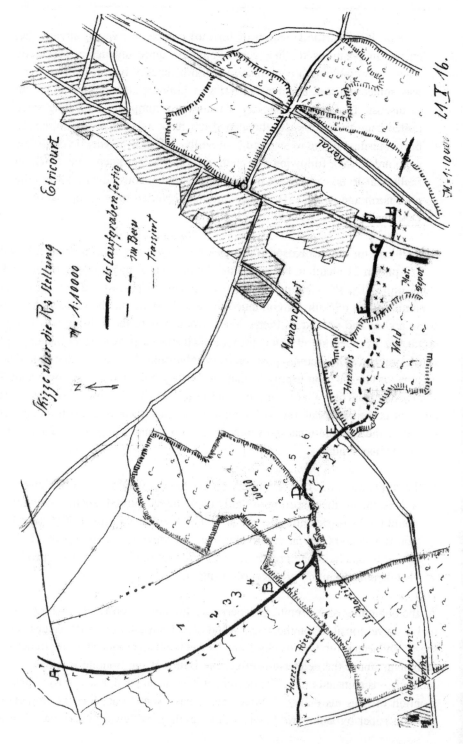

GOUVERNEMENT FARM AREA 21 OCTOBER

was obviously written and forwarded to army group headquarters shortly after he and his staff were relieved by General der Infanterie von Deimling's XV Corps.

"During the entire major Franco-British offensive, for the most part our counter-strokes and counter-attacks failed. This begs the question as to the cause of this on the German infantry that, previously, was irresistible in the attack. It is quite certain that it is difficult and costly to cross the zone where enemy defensive fire is landing, but it is not impossible, as proven by our successful attacks at Verdun and, amongst other operations, the attacks of IX Reserve Corps around Vimy. I believe that the reason lies in the fact that now the quality of the troops is no longer first class.

"As a result of the huge losses, poor quality Landsturm and badly trained replacements have had to be deployed. Discipline, which can only be maintained in positional warfare by the application of the utmost energy, has suffered badly and generally has not been properly inculcated in the latest reinforcements. Naturally this could be countered if trained, energetic, junior leaders were available to us, but they are precisely what we lack. In the best of cases the battalion commanders are junior *Hauptleute* [captains], the company commanders almost exclusively young reserve officers. It is obvious that we cannot expect the same from such loosely bound units than we were used to from our infantry.

"As commander of a Group during my two tours of duty on the Somme, I had six different divisions, in addition to my own corps, under command. In all cases I gained more or less the same impression; namely that none of them were in a position to conduct a successful attack. I am convinced that the same would apply to most of the corps along the Western Front. It is necessary to visualise how hard a task the lower levels of command have in preparing an attack in positional warfare. Just to ready the troops demands not only courage but great prudence, training and energy. Our young, inexperienced, leaders just do not possess these characteristics in sufficient measure ...

"I can only look forward with concern to a third year of war ... the attacking power of our opponents has not yet been damaged ... That which we hoped for in the French army at Verdun is happening here. Our troops are being ground down ... It seems at least questionable if the army will be equal next spring to the major battles *OHL* expects our enemies in the west to launch. It is certainly not in the condition it was at the start of the offensive this year. Decisive are not only the huge losses of leaders and men, but also the downward pressure on morale. There is a vast difference between troops who suffer bloody losses in an attack but get forward, or those, such as here, who have just been targets for enemy shells. There is a limit to even the greatest heroism. In my considered opinion the situation is so serious that it is imperative to counter it. It is vital to look at the matter absolutely realistically. I consider it my duty to raise the subject and am not afraid to do so for fear of being suspected of pessimism or inopportune weakness."[61]

Boehn then went on to demand more machine guns, 'We can never have too many of them', and to call for a radical overhaul of the entire training system, making use in Germany of experienced men recovering from wounds or those medically downgraded and for a return to the rigid discipline that previously had been part and parcel of the preparation of recruits.

"[Currently] young men arrive in the field, mostly completely untrained and lacking military bearing. It is no wonder, therefore, that in the trenches they quickly lose all sense of discipline or order. The view that our old and proven drills can be replaced by something else is fundamentally false ... Although, through strenuous efforts, the condition of the army can doubtless be improved, it will not reach the heights of 1915 or even 1916 all the time the war lasts. Even the most intensive training of young officers will not replace the ability and experience of the officers and NCOs who have fallen. Men need something to which they can cling in difficult situations. Doubtless that could to some extent be provided by brave and unshakeable young NCOs or soldiers, but they can never replace long service leaders with experience of war."[62]

That in a nutshell is what the Battle of the Somme cost the German army. The fact that it was nevertheless able to fight on for another two years is remarkable.

Notes

1. BA/MA RH61/50652 *Kriegstagebuch von Kuhl* pp. 24–25.
2. *ibid.* p. 25.
3. In other words, to make the deployed divisions with only three organic regiments up to four regiments strong, it was necessary to strip formations out of the divisions back in reserve.
4. Gallwitz *Erleben im Westen* p. 117.
5. *Kuhl op. cit.* pp. 25–26.
6. *ibid.* p. 26.
7. Jung Quoted in *Max von Gallwitz* p. 75.
8. *Kuhl op. cit.* p. 26.
9. *ibid.* pp. 26–27.
10. Gallwitz *op.cit.* p. 121.
11. *Kuhl op. cit.* p. 27.

12. Quoted Jung *op. cit.* p. 75.
13. Gallwitz *op. cit.* p. 121.
14. This is a reference to General der Kavallerie Ludwig Freiherr von Gebsattel, commander III Bavarian Corps, that was deployed in the Gueudecourt area from 18 September – 2 October 1916.
15. *Kuhl op. cit.* pp. 27–28.
16. Gallwitz *op. cit.* p. 129.
17. *ibid.* p. 130.
18. *Kuhl op. cit.* p. 28.
19. *ibid.* p. 29.
20. *ibid.* p. 30.
21. *Kriegsarchiv Munich* HGr Rupprecht Bd. 126 *HGr Rupprecht 16/10 an OHL Beurteilung der Lage.*
22. *ibid.* pp. 31–32.
23. *ibid.* p. 32.
24. Gallwitz *op. cit.* p. 133.
25. *Kuhl op. cit.* p. 34.
26. Quoted Jung *op. cit.* p. 76.
27. *Kuhl op. cit.* p. 34.
28. *Kriegsarchiv Munich* HGr Rupprecht Bd. 15 *Armeeoberkommando 1 Abt. Ia Nr 698 geh.* dated 9.9.1916.
29. Scheer History Infantry Regiment 413 p. 6.
30. *ibid.* p. 15.
31. Vormann: History Infantry Regiment 26 Band 3 pp. 603–604
32. *Kriegsarchiv Munich* HGr Rupprecht Bd. 216 *Armeeoberkommando 1 Abt. Ia Nr. 934 geh.* dated 26.9.1916. It is, of course, worthy of mention that at this time the British army, too, was concerned that its soldiers were also tending to rely excessively on hand and rifle grenades and neglecting their shooting. A concentrated training effort had to be conducted constantly to try to correct the problem.
33. Original emphasis.
34. This is a reference to the very bloody Battle of Morhange, in the Moselle region near to Luxembourg, which occurred on 19 and 20 August 1914 during the Battle of the Frontiers.
35. *Kriegsarchiv Munich* Infanterie-Divisionen (WK) 2355 *No. 292/21479 Generalkommando II A.K. An die Herren Kommandeure der 3. Und 4.I.D. Betreff: Schlacht an der Somme* dated 16.11.16.
36. Original emphasis.
37. *Kriegsarchiv Munich* 5. Res. Inf. Regt. (WK) 3 *No. 3913 7. Inf. Brigade. An 5. R.I.R.* dated 24.10.16.
38. *Kriegsarchiv Munich* 5. Res. Inf. Regt. (WK) 3 *Nr. 4842 7. bayer. Inf. Brigade. An: 5., 9.IR. RIR 5 Bemerkungen anläßlich der Komp.-Besichtigungen* dated 28.12.16.
39. History Infantry Regiment 160 pp. 129–130.
40. *Kuhl op. cit.* p. 30.
41. History Infantry Regiment 160 p. 147.
42. FOH pp. 154–157 Between 12 and 24 September, when the battles northeast of Combles were raging, some types of 155 mm artillery were restricted to thirty six shells per gun per day.
43. Krause *The Evolution of French Tactics 1914–16* in *The Battle of the Somme*, ed. Matthias Stohn pp. 210–212.

44. History Infantry Regiment 160 pp131–132.
45. History Reserve Infantry Regiment 234 pp. 228–240.
46. Neubrunner History Infantry Regiment 186 p. 75.
47. History Infantry Regiment 160 p. 138.
48. *ibid.* pp. 141–142.
49. *ibid.* p142.
50. *ibid.* p. 145.
51. *Kriegsarchiv Munich* HGr Rupprecht Bd 68 *Oberkommando der 7. Armee IIa. Nr. 372 Pers.* Dated 15.10.16.
52. *Kriegsarchiv Munich* HGr Rupprecht Bd 68 *7. Armee. Armee-Oberkommando. IIa Nr. 372 Pers.* Dated 18. October 1916.
53. *Kriegsarchiv Munich* 2 Infantry Regiment Bd 7 *Gefechtsbericht über die Kämpfe des 2. Infanterieregiments um Sailly vom 12.10. abends, bis 19.10 morg.* dated 4.11.1916.
54. *ibid.*
55. *Kriegsarchiv Munich* Infanterie-Divisionen (WK) 859 *1. Bay. Infanterie-Division Der Kampf um Sailly (15.10.1916 – 21.10.1916)* dated 20 November 1916.
56. Original emphasis.
57. The use of 'Herr' in this instance was an intentionally derogatory way of referring to Loßberg.
58. *ibid.*
59. Kronprinz Rupprecht: *'Mein Kriegstagebuch' II Band* p. 52
60. *Kuhl op. cit.* p. 35.
61. *Kriegsarchiv Munich* HGr Rupprecht Bd 68 *Abschrift [Betrachtung] v. Boehn* Undated
62. *ibid.*

CHAPTER 8

Pyrrhic Victory or Bloody Stalemate?

By mid-October the German defence was under extreme pressure all over the battlefield. As has been noted, on the Morval – Rancourt – Sailly Sailissel front the French army had come close to a breakthrough. In the Thiepval-Grandcourt sector, the British 25th Division captured Stuff Redoubt on 9 October; then Schwaben Redoubt, for so long the focus of fierce fighting, fell to the 39th Division on 14 October. Though fighting here continued undiminished for several days, the German defence never managed to regain the lost ground. On average one division per day had to be relieved, frequently by inferior formations hastily assembled and inadequately prepared. Never had catastrophic defeat seemed closer but, despite all Allied efforts, the defence never broke – why?

Numerous factors came into play, but none was more important than a significant change in the weather. Even at the height of summer, on 1 July, the ground around Thiepval was described as 'unbelievably muddy'.[1] Now, three and a half months later, the shell-torn battlefield was already a quagmire, then it began to rain seriously. It rained on 15, 17 and 18 October then, on 19th, there was heavy rain. A brief pause was followed by more rain on 23, 25, 26 and 27 October and three exceedingly wet days on 28 – 30 October.[2] The quagmire became a complete swamp, movement of any description was almost impossible and the fighting degenerated into local small scale actions which were not going to alter the course of the battle in any significant way. A year later, on 12 October 1917, Crown Prince Rupprecht made a diary entry referring to the situation during the Third Battle of Ypres, 'The weather has taken a sudden turn. Happily, it has turned to rain, which is our most effective ally.'[3]

He could have made the same point in autumn 1916, because there was a measurable, immediate, benefit to the defence. Commenting in his diary on 30 October, Rupprecht stated, 'The very moderate fighting of the past few days makes it possible, in accordance with the wishes of *OHL*, to leave certain divisions of First Army in their positions for longer than fourteen days'.[4] This development may well have been welcome as far as *OHL*, desperately juggling manpower, was concerned, but it was extraordinarily hard on those units directly involved. This point had been recognised as early as September at Rupprecht's headquarters. In a report of 27 September it stated,

"Arrangements must be made for regular reliefs. In general troops cannot hold out for longer than fourteen days. The virtual total air superiority which the enemy enjoyed until recently, their artillery – superior in both numbers and accuracy – and the extraordinary quantity of ammunition available to them, has made it possible for them to wreck our positions completely, cause us heavy casualties and interfere with our ability to develop our positions. The troops are sheltering in shell holes without obstacles or dugouts. All communications are broken, our [essential] movement between positions and the rear is causing heavy casualties, whilst getting rations and water forward to the front line is extremely difficult. Frequently the stink of corpses at the front makes it impossible for the men to eat and they cannot sleep either. If troops are kept in the positions for longer than their strength can bear, their powers of resistance diminish extraordinarily rapidly."[5]

To this Ludendorff had replied,

"I am not unaware of the disadvantages accruing from lengthy stays by troops in the positions or the problems caused by the regular fourteen day reliefs of the divisions. Bearing in mind the total strength available to us, the principle must be to keep the troops in their allocated sectors for as long as possible without allowing them to be worn down completely. This will vary considerably from sector to sector along the battlefront."[6]

So much for the official line at the highest levels. However, the policy proved to be difficult to implement, not least because of the psychological effect on the formations involved. The very fact of the rapid turnover of divisions meant that a general assumption had grown up that tours of duty would always be strictly limited in duration. In an attempt to counter this and to be seen to be trying to implement Ludendorff's directions, Commander First Army was forced to write to all corps and divisional commanders of formations either in the line or preparing to be redeployed to the Somme.

"As a result of interviews with officers, NCOs and men, the following deplorable report has reached army headquarters:
    "Personnel manning the positions have been telling their successors at the moment of relief that each division will only be deployed for twelve days – four days in the front line, four days in support and four days in reserve.

"This cycle is regarded as 'The Law of the Battle of the Somme'[7] and, if events turn out differently, the troops become despondent, cannot recognise the necessity for it and so feel themselves to be disadvantaged.

"All corps and divisions are to counter this notion vigorously. All troops are to man their allocated positions, holding on and carrying out their duty with a will until their relief is ordered. Whoever permits any other attitude to prevail has forgotten where his duty lies. The overall situation demands that the troops give their all, in order to postpone the date of their relief to the greatest extent possible.

Signed: von Below
General der Infanterie"[8]

So much for the prescribed approach astride the Somme. As always, the implementation of policy came down to the leadership and man management of the officers and NCOs of the front line units. Elsewhere along the Western Front, the pressure on manpower had become so intense that Ludendorff had to direct all manner of undesirable emergency measures in order to ensure that the supply of reinforcements to the Somme could be maintained throughout the autumn.

"The continuing hard battles on the Somme front will, for the foreseeable future, demand the supply of formations in as good condition as possible from all armies along the Western Front", he wrote. "Every possible means of saving on the deployment of troops and the demands placed on them will therefore be necessary ... I request that all subordinated armies and corps check to see where this can possibly be done in conformity with our overall requirements. Every unnecessarily occupied sap head, the holding of advanced sections of trench when the situation does not beyond doubt demand it, is a pointless use of forces which could be better employed on other tasks.

"The same applies to holding positions or sections of positions in swampy or flooded areas where, because of all manner of illnesses, our strength is reduced in far too great a way. Wherever, after careful consideration of the abovementioned type of cases, the situation permits, the trenches concerned, having been levelled, should be given up or only manned with outposts so as to make better use of our forces."[9]

Messages such as this serve to illustrate what a toll the Battles of Verdun and the Somme were taking on the pool of German manpower and what grave concerns were developing at *OHL*. At the beginning of October the momentous decision was taken to call up the class of 1898 in November, only four months after that of 1897, itself a full eighteen months ahead of the usual time.[10] Acutely aware of the need to conserve manpower and munitions, Generalfeldmarschall von Hindenburg himself intervened in the operational decision making process in early November. In the wake of an unsuccessful attempt by Group Deimling (XV Corps) to retake Sailly, following a bombardment lasting several days and a two day battle 1–2 November and then further minor Allied attacks between Le Sars and Rancourt, First Army proposed to renew the attack against Sailly.[11] This bid had to be staffed up to *OHL* because of the need for an allotment of ammunition on a large scale, but *OHL* balked and Hindenburg signalled Army Group Crown Prince of Bavaria on 7 November.

"After the recent heavy, though successful [*sic.*] battles, in consideration of the need to maintain the fighting ability of XV Corps, I cannot refrain from expressing my serious reservations about a renewal of the attack on Sailly. Only if all the preconditions for a real success are there and if the tactical situation absolutely demands it, do I consider it appropriate. I request that the Army Group tasks First Army in the light of these points to re-examine, in detail, the necessity for the attack and to inform me in a timely manner about the First Army intentions and its justification for them."[12]

The plan was scrapped and the Army Group replied by signal the following day:

"There is no intention of renewing the attack on Sailly. On the other hand, on 5 November the enemy pushed forward a very narrow, but deep, penetration between the southern edge of Sailissel and the northern edge of St Pierre Vaast Wood almost up to Gouvernement Farm. Both Headquarters First Army and Group Garnier [V Reserve Corps] are of the opinion that it cannot be allowed to remain like that or both St Pierre Vaast Wood and Sailissel will be seriously threatened from a flank and could not be defended in the long term. Following discussions, the Army Group shares this opinion. The counter-attack is to be carried out by two battalions of 111th Infantry Division. This will be practised on a training area and will be conducted, following careful preparation, under the direction of General von Garnier. Detailed reconnaissance is currently underway."[13]

This so-called Operation Hannover was carried out by elements of Fusilier Regiment 73, assisted by the divisional storm troop, during the afternoon of 15 November and was a complete success. 300 members of the French XX Corps were captured and the original line was restored.[14] This success seems to have come as an almighty relief to the entire chain of command. Messages of congratulations arrived from Hindenburg himself, together with others from Crown Prince Rupprecht, the commanders of XII Corps, V Reserve Corps, 111th Infantry Division, 16th Reserve Division and commander 221 Infantry Brigade, who contented himself with, 'Three cheers for Fusilier Regiment 73 for its outstanding feat of arms at St Pierre Vaast Wood on 15 November1916'.

Meanwhile, events on the British side were moving rapidly towards the final major action, namely the Battle of the Ancre. Ludendorff's reaction to its launch was interesting, 'On 13 November', he wrote, 'the British forced their way into our positions astride the Ancre – an especially severe blow because we had not envisaged any such thing possible, particularly not there where our troops were still manning good positions.'[15] Quite why Ludendorff thought in this way is far from clear, given that intelligence about developments in this sector had been accumulating for several days and were reported on regularly. Reflecting on the issue, Crown Prince Rupprecht made several relevant diary entries.

18th October
"It is becoming ever clearer that enemy attacks are to be expected between Gommecourt and the Ancre. The enemy have deployed three powerful divisions on that front, have begun to range in their heavy batteries and have moved up thirty batteries of field guns near to the line Gommecourt-Serre."

28th October
"Four, rather than the earlier three, divisions have been identified between Gommecourt and the Ancre. Artillery fire has increased in this sector. There are heavy concentrations every morning, obviously with the aim of getting our troops accustomed to the practice, so that one day they may be surprised when the usual barrage is followed by an attack."

2nd November
"General von Below stated [during a morning conference] that he was expecting an attack along the Gommecourt-Ancre sector, because the enemy had smashed all the trenches along this line…It is striking that the enemy is digging in vigorously on the high ground near Courcelette, Martinpuich and to the west of Delville Wood. This could well indicate that the enemy only intends to carry out an offensive with limited objectives, to capture our positions from Gommecourt to Bapaume and is considering spending the winter in these positions, security being provided by the trench line which has been begun from Courcelette to Delville Wood."[16]

Reacting to the accumulation of intelligence indicators, First Army reiterated its policy on holding ground and improving defensive positions as early as 22 October, when General von Below signed an 'officers only' order on the subject. It left no room for flexibility on behalf of the recipients, but then all decisions to yield ground voluntarily had long since been retained at army level.

> "South of the Ancre Group A [Group Fuchs = XIV Reserve Corps] is to make the enemy fight for every foot of ground. As far as the fighting strength of the troops permits, the current positions are to be driven forward and improved.
>
> "Additional stop lines are to be constructed in rear of the forward positions. Initially they are to provide cover for reserves held forward, but gradually they are to be developed into continuous positions. Above all in this connection, in the rear area of 5th Ersatz Division there is to be produced a further series of defensive positions, in order to make any thrust by the enemy against the line Miraumont – Pys time consuming and costly in casualties.
>
> "It is probable that simultaneously with their thrusts against the Ancre Line St Pierre Divion – Warlencourt the enemy will launch an attack north of the Ancre. For this battle I also order that every step of the way is to be defended, regardless of expected enfilade fire from the south."[17]

The increasingly likely possibility of a major attack also found its way into the Army Group appreciation of the situation forwarded to *OHL* on 30 October. 'From captured documents it appears that the objectives for the individual battalions of the 63rd Division, deployed north of the Ancre, have been laid out graphically.'[18] Other intelligence accumulated as 13 November drew closer, but tactical surprise was nevertheless achieved when the Hawthorn Ridge mine was blown at 6.45 am German time just to the west of the village of Beaumont Hamel. Loßberg subsequently blamed the dense fog for the artillery defensive fire coming down too late and thus permitting the attackers to make swift gains in places.[19] There were, however, other factors at work. The first and most important was the fact that the defenders from 12th Infantry Division had already been in the line for days on end in terrible weather and the positions, which had once been of a very high standard, were badly damaged. The fact was, too, that the large quantities of machine guns that wreaked havoc here on 1 July were no longer available and the ones that were were hampered by very poor visibility. This in turn had a significant effect on the way the attack ultimately unfolded.

Infantry Regiment 62, typical of all the defending formations and now manning positions either side of Beaumont Hamel, was at a very low ebb. Coughs and colds were universal and the battlefield was so smashed up that, operating in mud over knee deep, carrying parties found it impossible to keep the forward troops adequately supplied with food, drinks and ammunition, or to arrange the necessary casualty evacuation as the losses mounted in the face of increasing British bombardment. By 7 November the telephone links were all destroyed; the trenches and obstacles more or less swept away. Furthermore, British progress along the Thiepval ridge meant that large stretches of the German trenches between Y Ravine and the Ancre could now be engaged accurately by enfilade fire from the guns. Given that Infantry Regiment 62 entered the line at the end of October with company strengths already down to eighty to ninety riflemen, casualties by 10 November, amounting to thirty eight killed and 134 wounded, had a considerable impact on its fighting ability.[20] Its 9th Company, operating adjacent to Reserve Infantry Regiment 55 (which had been in the line since early September) down towards the Ancre, was hit especially hard during the afternoon of 12 November by a gas shoot. It should have been relieved, as indeed should all the forward troops, but there were no reserves at hand. In consequence, when the attack came in it was conducted by fresh troops against a relative handful of exhausted, hungry and soaking wet defenders, ill with colds, laryngitis and stomach complaints.

It should have been a walkover, but it was not. Pressure built up against Beaumont Hamel, then there was an early breakthrough in the sector near the Ancre manned by Reserve Infantry Regiment 55, followed by a thrust towards the village from the direction of St Pierre Divion,[21] but fighting went on until 4.00 pm, when the last of the defenders, some thirty survivors of 12th Company Infantry Regiment 62, surrendered, completely out of ammunition.[22] The action ended with a victory for the British 51st (Highland) Division, but at a cost of 2,500 casualties, almost forty five percent of those engaged. The Battle of the Ancre straggled on for another five days, supported at times by tanks, until it spluttered to a halt in an appalling sea of mud on Redan Ridge, which provided a dismal backdrop for a winter of unrelieved misery for both sides until the German army pulled back to the *Siegfried Stellung* [Hindenburg Line] the following March.

Of course the official ending of the main battle did not mean that everything fell silent. There were small scale attacks on Redan Ridge from time to time. There were, for example, attempts on Soden Redoubt near Serre by 32nd Division on 23 November and 7th Division on 11 January 1917 and the artillery fire was incessant, leading to the worst single incident of the war for Bavarian Reserve Infantry Regiment 1 of 1st Bavarian Reserve Division.

"The position the regiment occupied on the Ancre", wrote the regimental historian, "was the most desolate the regiment experienced in the entire war ... During the Battle of the Somme the riverbed of the Ancre was totally destroyed, so the entire area was now flooded. Heavy rainfall in late December and the constant bad weather throughout the deployment turned the whole place into a sea of mud. Whilst in Flanders at the end of 1917 it was always possible to find some solid ground, here it was simply not possible. It was necessary to test the going with every step in order to avoid falling chest deep into a crater and all movement without a stick was quite impossible. The trenches had all collapsed and were only recognisable here and there. The sentries stood up to their knees in mud. Only some of the dugouts were usable and they were partly flooded. The mud that kept flowing into them had to be bailed out all the time ... movement and orientation was extraordinarily difficult, all buildings had been totally smashed and the only signposts by day were occasional tree stumps. By night the difficulties were beyond description ...

"The enemy fire was intended to destroy us completely. Through the use of almost exclusively heavy calibre shells, the British brought down continuous destructive fire, rising to drum fire at times on the positions, the supports and the rear areas ... Sentries who lacked all protection from the fire were buried alive several times some days, but the most dangerous was fire directed at our dugouts and observed by enemy airmen. In two days, twelve 2nd Battalion dugouts were wrecked, forcing the occupants to crowd into the remaining seven ... This led to the worst disaster and greatest loss of life in a single incident. The two entrances to a dug out which held most of 8th Company were collapsed by accurate gunfire. Hearing cries for help, neighbouring sections ran to the rescue but the British, having spotted them, drove them back with shrapnel fire. Despite a night long search it proved impossible to locate the dugout and when dawn broke the sea of mud had engulfed the entire place. Two officers and forty eight men succumbed in an appalling manner to the ingress of liquid mud."[23]

It is small wonder that desertions were a problem when troops were left for days on end exposed to the worst that the weather could throw at them. Describing the conditions in mid-December, Reserve Leutnant Schröder of Fusilier Regiment 35 wrote:

"It was a constant tough battle against rain, snow, mud and more mud. The battle line was dug along the line of shell craters, which filled up with water. All day long the men stood in the morass, their roof nothing more than tent halves. Their rifles, caked with filth and unusable, served as tent poles. The elements were a stronger force than discipline or the will of the commanders. The boots of many men were simply sucked off their feet and remained lost and beyond recovery in the mud. Many wore a look of total despair. Each platoon had to stick this out for forty eight hours at a time: an eternity. I arranged for cognac, as much as I could get my hands on, to be brought forward for the troops. I took a bottle and went from man to man, talking to them and consoling them with thoughts of relief. Was it any wonder, however, that one morning a sentry post was empty, that all that was left were two rifles and knapsacks? We commanders were content if we could just get our men to stick it out. Effective defence of the position was simply out of the question. It was fortunate that it was hardly better for those opposite. When the rain was simply too awful to bear, then peace reigned for a few hours in the two lines and friend and foe climbed out of their holes, at least to have a good stretch."[24]

On 12 December Oberstleutnant Hoderlein, commanding Bavarian Infantry Regiment 4, wrote officially to Generalmajor von Reck, commanding Bavarian Infantry Brigade 8, about the toll on his men.

"The battalions have forwarded reports concerning the current state of health and I feel it my duty to bring these to your attention. The regiment has now been in the line without relief since 26th November. Because of the adverse weather all types of colds, chills and gastro-intestinal illnesses have appeared. Despite every effort to improve the lot of the troops, it has proved impossible to counter these illnesses or to prevent them from spreading. The freezing wet and cold weather, wet dugouts, work in flooded trenches with mud a metre deep, extremely strenuous carrying duties to transport rations and trench stores, frequently over bottomless tracks across country, or through mud-filled trenches and not rarely in the face of extremely heavy enemy artillery fire, are all causes for the increased incidence of chills and hence illness, as is saturated clothing, underwear and boots which never dry out. The strength of officers and men in the front line has been greatly degraded by such illnesses. Warm food and the issue of red wine and *Schnaps* are insufficient to counteract the essential warmth they need."[25]

One week later, the regiment having been kept in the line for an entire month by then, Hoderlein returned to the subject.

"Even though there has not been a notable increase of men being evacuated sick, the condition of the troops in the position has deteriorated markedly. The lengthy period of duty has had a considerable effect upon their physical and mental strength. The morale of the officers, NCOs and men is generally sound, despite the fact that all are exhibiting signs of complete exhaustion, which is doing nothing to lift spirits. Good food is contributing to morale; it is certainly encouraging men to hang on in their positions and to give of their best. Today is the twenty eighth day of this tour of duty and, with the exception of the three companies pulled back in reserve, the cramped dugouts mean that in all that time the men have only been able rest in a sitting position. The dugouts are damp and wet. The mens' uniforms, especially boots and trousers, are soaking wet and covered with mud, so that leather and cloth are beginning to rot on the man. It is impossible to clean anything on the position. Almost the entire regiment, from the youngest soldier to the most senior officer, is lousy and covered with matted filth. Every single man has a cold; only the severity varies. The current conditions are such that the duties a man has to perform with a carrying party or when digging trenches are extraordinarily hard, because men sink up to their knees with every step, frequently only being able to extract themselves at the price of their boots.[26]

Not only did these extended tours of duty put at risk the ability of the troops deployed to defend vigorously against probing attacks, Reserve Stabsarzt Dr Roeder, the medical officer of Infantry Regiment 88 holding the line near Grandcourt, pulled no punches when he warned of the consequences of the *OHL* policy.

"In my previous report I stated my fear that because of the continuing extremely bad weather conditions in this sector, if the same troops continue to be committed here, then a great many of those still on the position are likely to have to be permanently invalided out of the army. Many of the men are having to stand up to their knees in water. Because of the constant wet conditions, the dugouts are extremely unhealthy places, which lead to serious lung disease, rheumatism in the joints and to kidney infections. I can already prove on the basis of the sick list, which has still not diminished in size, that a large number of such illnesses has already appeared. In my capacity as a doctor I must make it quite clear that if the battalions which are currently deployed have to remain in their current positions, the consequence will be a considerable diminution in their value as fighting troops."[27]

Given the endless pressure on manpower, risks continued to be run by the High Command and the troops were kept in forward positions for periods that were in many cases beyond their capacity to endure. Throughout the battle the men had on the whole performed most creditably. However, the foul weather, the strain and the utter exhaustion suffered by those manning the front line meant that by the following month the rate of desertion had risen alarmingly. Following the capture of a junior British officer in an abortive attack on Soden Redoubt near Serre on 11 January, his interrogator reported that Second Lieutenant TW Doke of 1st Battalion South Staffordshire Regiment (91 Brigade, 7th Division) had stated that:

> "In recent days there had been no need to capture prisoners to find out about your deployments, because there had been deserters on most days. On the evening of the day before yesterday [10 January], fifteen men came over. A few days earlier it had been one officer and seventeen men, then another two officers and twenty men. The officer added that it seemed that the division opposite them – he thought the 38th or 33rd Division – was at the end of its tether. He added that these individuals never admitted to desertion; stating instead that they had got lost. The British, however, were in no doubt that they were deserters."[28]

This report was staffed rapidly up the chain of command and First Army directed 4th Infantry Division to conduct an immediate investigation and to report back without delay. By 14 January a reply had been prepared by Hauptmann von Papen, its General Staff Officer, who also interrogated the prisoner. Having commented favourably about Noke's reliability as a witness, Papen reported that, 'Of the missing of 33rd Infantry Division, only on the evening before his capture did the prisoner personally[29] witness the desertion by fifteen men. As far as he could remember, they were from Infantry Regiment 138.'[30] This made the statements of Noke very plausible and rang alarm bells on the German side. His recollection was a near-miss for Infantry Regiment 135 which, together with Infantry Regiments 98 and 130, made up 33rd Infantry Division – all of whose regiments were from Lorraine and already of suspect loyalty. Papen also added that, in his opinion, the apparently accurate knowledge of the German positions on the part of the British attackers could well be ascribed to information provided by deserters, in particular by, 'a machine gun feldwebel who deserted, together with his runner. He was carrying a map carefully marked with every machine gun position and dugout. It could not be confirmed if the man was Bavarian, but the officer repeatedly expressed his glee at, 'such an extraordinarily useful prisoner'.'[31]

On 24 January Loßberg passed the First Army assessment up to Army Group Crown Prince of Bavaria, reporting,

"The number of missing from 33rd Infantry Division and 14th Bavarian Infantry Division from 18 December–8 January amounted to one officer, two offizierstellvertreters and seventy nine men from 33rd Infantry Division and forty seven men from 14th Bavarian Infantry Division (which included a day of battle on 6 January). According to its report, 33rd Infantry Division believes that the high numbers are due to the poor condition of the ground and the effect of constant enemy artillery fire on positions under development leading to errors [in navigation]. Army Headquarters and the Group are of the opinion, however, that these fully recognised difficulties cannot be the only explanation for these high figures."[32]

Apart from setting up a formal enquiry, little more could be done. It was, nevertheless, indicative of poor morale and another manifestation of the toll imposed on the German army by the hard attritional fighting of 1916 and the insistence by *OHL* that formations be kept in the line for the maximum time possible, in order to reduce turbulence and the necessity to keep producing an endless succession of reinforcing divisions.

While the battle was still in its final stages, Ludendorff took the decision to direct the consolidation of the great mass of after-action reports into one final document. This was intended to capture all the lessons learned and distil them into an authoritative basis for future doctrinal development. The Battle of the Somme generated a huge amount of paperwork in the form of documentation from all levels of command. In many cases the surviving archives contain contributions from company level right up to that of Army Group Crown Prince of Bavaria. This was not a new process. Reporting of this type was standard throughout the contingents of the German army from the earliest days of the war, but the process was refined more and more as time went by until, during 1916, reports, especially those of divisional level and above, contained not only straightforward descriptions but also analysis of weaknesses, failures, measures taken to counter the problems and recommendations for future work.

Naturally, with such a variety of inputs, many differing strands of opinion can be detected but, repeatedly, the same themes tended to be addressed and it is these which were most prominent in the final paper produced. Prior to that, of course, numerous tactical notes and instructions had been issued based on the contents of earlier reports. There may well have been exchanges of this information informally, so as to spread the knowledge gained as swiftly as possible, but it is difficult to be sure. There do not appear to have been any standard distribution lists in use and the reports available for study seem only to have been addressed to the originator's superior headquarters. However, once consolidated, it is certain that there was wide scale distribution of the processed work subsequently. This is proved by the high level reaction to the capture of a copy of a corps after action report. When its loss became known, General von Kuhl, chief of staff to Army Group Crown Prince of Bavaria, wrote to all the armies under its command on 11 October:

"A report by Headquarters IV Corps concerning experiences gained on the Somme has fallen into British hands and is currently being published in the British press.

"First Army is requested to explain which report is involved and how it came to fall into British hands.[33]

"A renewed order is to be issued to all commanders, banning the taking of such documents to forward command posts or the front line."[34]

The following day, on behalf of General von Below, Oberst von Loßberg replied:

"It was a copy of a document published by Headquarters IV Corps, entitled, 'Experiences of IV Corps from the Battle of the Somme in July 1916' ... This document, classified Secret, was distributed on 2 August 1916 down to battalion level[35] as a basis for training and organisation. [Addressees] were explicitly directed not to take it into the front line. Nevertheless, it cannot be ruled out that a copy found its way into a battalion command post, there to fall into enemy hands. It is impossible to be more precise, because large numbers of copies were also distributed to corps and divisions deployed on the Somme by the headquarters of First and Sixth Armies."[36]

The procedures which emerged from this process largely determined how the German army would be reconfigured to face the certainty of a continuation of the Allied offensive. This was expected to begin as soon as the weather in spring 1917 had improved sufficiently to permit operations to be resumed on a large scale. After some consideration, Ludendorff tasked Headquarters First Army directly with the job. It was a huge undertaking, as Oberst Fritz von Loßberg later recalled.

"Already in November headquarters First Army was ordered by *OHL* to gather together in a position paper all the lessons learned when the Battle of the Somme was being fought. This would then be distributed to all the other armies. Having briefed the commander, I got down to work at once with the officers of the staff. By the end of January 1917 the paper was ready. I divided the lessons into, first, a part dealing with tactics and, second, all matters relating to administration, service support and equipment. Each specialist area was the responsibility of a subject matter expert on the staff, who developed particular sections in accordance with my guidance. Every day I spent several hours discussing the detail with the specialists. Because of the fact that even after the battle I visited the front every morning and frequently during the afternoons as well, I was able to get very little sleep at this time either."[37]

The final report was issued in two separate parts, tactics being allocated 228 paragraphs whilst at 195 paragraphs the second section, concerning administrative and logistic matters, was almost as long. It is a seriously important piece of analytical writing, with barely a wasted word and is well worth considering in some detail, because it provided the framework which informed German command and control and defensive tactics for much of the remainder of the war. It was, explained Loßberg, to be read in conjunction with Part 8 of the pamphlet, 'Principles for Command and Control of the Defensive Battle in Positional Warfare', already issued on the orders of Ludendorff.[38] He then went on to add that complete knowledge of the 'Principles' by the reader was assumed and that discussion of matters such as flexible defence in depth and combined arms tactics that it contained would be related strictly to experiences gained on the Somme. The key sections covered were: 'Infantry and Machine Guns', 'Artillery', 'Intelligence', 'Aircraft and Anti-Aircraft Guns'; and there were shorter parts devoted to such matters as engineering, searchlights, flamethrowers, grenade launchers and gas. In a way which was typically and ruthlessly self-critical, each main section was divided into three parts: I. Reasons for early failures; II. Measures by which improvements were made gradually and, III. Experiences and Lessons Learned. The declared objective was to build up a picture of precisely how the battle developed, in order to provide valuable insights to commanders who might in future find themselves and their formations in a similar situation.

One of the most fundamental aspects of the work concerned the infantry: how and where to deploy it and what tactics to employ, so as to maximise its value on the battlefield whilst, simultaneously, avoiding the extremely heavy casualties suffered during the early weeks of the battle. As early as 24 July the Guards Reserve Corps, operating in the Barleux-Estrées sector, had issued a tactical note to all subordinate formations and units that drew attention to the need to avoid unnecessary casualties.

"The front line is not to be too strongly occupied, in order to minimise to the greatest extent possible losses from artillery fire ... Reserves must not be deployed prematurely, otherwise the front line will be too densely occupied and the lack or insufficiency of cover will cause the casualty rate to rise unnecessarily.'[39]

At the end of his tour of duty in the Martinpuich sector between 15 and 29 September, Generalmajor von Petersdorff, commanding 50th Reserve Division, was even more specific in comments made in his after action report.

"Above all I wish to put forward the principle that it is the duty of all commanders to determine how they can meet the demands of the battle with as little commitment of infantry as possible. The fewer infantrymen deployed into areas under enemy artillery fire the better and the lower the casualties will be. It is not the least important aspect of the art of command to be able to calculate the precise numbers required to be equal to the battle situation. However, these minimal forces must be kept fresh. Relief after not too long a period makes this possible ...

"The proof of the essential correctness of this principle may be seen from the following fact: newly deployed companies have a battle strength of 160 men or more. After a few days this reduces to one hundred men or fewer. The size of the sector is unchanged and it is held just as successfully as it was on the day of deployment. It is essential, however, that the troops are steadfast and confident in their ability ...

"The throwing in of battalions and regiments is particularly detrimental. The very expression, 'throwing in' conceals faulty thinking. Passing rear areas behind the battlefront – often kilometres deep – which are covered by artillery fire demands proper consideration, frequently even reconnaissance. Each example of uncertainty or over-hastiness during deployment costs casualties and, generally, additional time. It must not be ignored that the battle does not begin for the infantry only once they arrive in the trenches. Negotiating the enemy artillery fire is already a part of the battle and not the easiest."[40]

Generalleutnant Endres, who commanded 5th Bavarian Infantry Division at Ginchy from 6 to 18 September, identified very clearly where the solution to these problems might lie, writing,

"The very high wastage rate is above all caused by our lack of deployment in depth.[41] If our sectors were narrower and troops were placed more deeply, we should be able to conduct reliefs and so preserve our forces. Of decisive importance for the subsequent use of forces was the removal the very same day that my division had to take over a third regimental sector of four battalions for other purposes.

"This meant that it was impossible to arrange reliefs. The ability of the troops to resist melted away in view of the fact that the first of the battalions moved into position on the night 6/7 September and were deployed until the night 18/19 September. It must also be borne in mind that occupying the Second Line or acting as supports is no less strenuous and wearing to morale than is the case for the First Line."[42]

Variations or expansion of these ideas may be found in a great many other after action reports, but it was Loßberg in his *Erfahrungen der 1. Armee in der Sommeschlacht* [First Army Experiences during the Battle of the Somme] who first spelt out exactly what caused the problems to arise and what was done to mitigate them. He began by noting that, 'The reason for our initial failure was not so much purely an infantry matter; but was due rather more to the mass that the enemy brought to bear, especially in aviation and artillery. We could not come anywhere near to countering these factors immediately.' He then explained further:

> "When the battle opened the telephone links that had operated well during quiet periods were immediately destroyed and only small quantities of optical and wireless equipment were available. The resulting inefficient communications meant that higher headquarters and cooperation with other arms were cut off and the infantry, fighting hard, were frequently on their own resources for hours or days at a time or, acting without knowledge of the situation, reserves would be despatched forward, packing the front line. The result was unnecessary casualties and was damaging to morale."[43]

Other factors were at work of course. Loßberg once more:

> "The limited number of troops available at the beginning meant that the wide sectors lacked sufficient deployment in depth. This led to a feeling of insecurity amongst commanders and led them – in an effort to hold the front line trench at all costs – not infrequently to reinforce the forward lines prematurely, to cram them unnecessarily full and, on the other hand, leave trenches to the rear unmanned. The lack of depth in the infantry positions was matched by an absence of positions to the rear or working parties to construct them."

Gradually as the battle went on and definitely once Hindenberg and Ludendorff took over from Falkenhayn, matters improved. Increases in artillery pieces and shells, large reinforcements of aircraft and anti-aircraft forces improved infantry morale considerably; not before time, as the battle reached new heights of intensity in late September and October. However, the greatest assistance to the fighting troops was achieved by simply increasing the number of divisions, which enabled group commanders to make each sector narrower and so helped to produce the necessary depth that was universally regarded as essential.

The other major consideration in all these after action reports was the artillery. The demands at Verdun meant that when the battle opened, despite endless requests by General von Below, the artillery was much too weak. It was numerically and qualitatively utterly inferior to that of the Allies. To the lack of modern heavy guns came major shortages of ammunition and means of observation, especially from the air, where Allied air superiority virtually ruled out the use of spotting aircraft. Balloons, which were in any case also vastly outnumbered, were also constantly being attacked, so yet again the infantry suffered as a result and, inevitably, the defence was driven backwards.

That in itself was a negative factor; but it also meant that not only were there parallel severe losses of guns and equipment, some of the terrain lost would have been ideally suited to the placement of artillery reinforcements once they eventually began to arrive. As it was, units and formations arriving in the battle area tended, just as was the case for the infantry, to be thrust into the most critical places where in general there were no prepared gun positions, so these had to be improvised under fire, a highly unsatisfactory situation. In many cases infantry divisions arrived without their organic artillery; in others, to boost the number of guns, artillery units were held back when the infantry was relieved. This meant in turn that infantry – artillery communications and liaison often left much to be desired, so fire support suffered.

Philosophically, there was also a never fully resolved argument about the best use of the heavier calibre weapons. The hard pressed infantry wanted as much defensive fire support as possible, especially when they were under direct attack; but if heavy guns and howitzers were used for this purpose counter-battery fire suffered. As has been discussed in previous chapters, there was a large amount of correspondence about this and directives were issued from on high condemning over-reliance on defensive fire shoots, both because it tended to use up large amounts of precious shells, but also because it was somewhat inflexible. If the enemy did not happen to be passing through a zone when the task was fired, it was completely ineffective.

Of course as has already been mentioned, observation and target acquisition was, at times, near impossible; the farcical situation facing the artillery commander at Pozières in late July, discussed in Chapter 5, being a prime example of the problem. Nevertheless, the issue was addressed squarely by Loßberg.

"Systematic counter-battery fire and also bombardment of enemy forming up places when the attacking troops were assembled there did not generally happen.[44] As far as the troops were concerned, the main saviour for the defence was exclusively constant resort to artillery defensive fire. Especially at the beginning of the battle, it was not appreciated that defensive fire provided by the artillery was simply a protective measure to prevent the enemy from entering a particular strip of terrain forward of our positions. If the enemy did not enter one of these areas or was not surprised there, it did them no damage. In other words, despite the expenditure of huge quantities of ammunition, equipment and human effort, it provided no guaranteed successful damage to the attackers."[45]

Gradually things improved, though mainly after the replacement of Falkenhayn. More guns and howitzers, particularly heavy ones, were deployed, together with increases in aircraft and balloons. When these were coupled to improvements in communications, survey and ammunition resupply, the results were generally striking. Possibly the greatest change came in much closer liaison between infantry and artillery and the subordination of the latter, mainly at divisional level, meaning that limited resources were employed to much greater effect. 1st Bavarian Infantry Division, deployed between Sailly Sailissel and St Pierre Vaast Wood and involved in the desperate battles during the first half of October, paid great attention to this matter as its commander, Generalleutnant Ritter von Schoch, made clear subsequently.

"The divisional artillery commander was in the same village, the commander of the heavy artillery in the same building, as the divisional staff. In this way close cooperation was guaranteed with the artillery commander, to whom there was a dedicated telephone link. There was always a liaison officer of the field artillery co-located with each battalion commander and a liaison officer from the heavy artillery with each regimental staff. Only lack of room meant that it was not possible to place one with the forward battalion commanders. The placement of artillery liaison officers at battalion level proved to be very effective. In order to ensure that they were able to pass information swiftly to the artillery commander, they had to be supplied with carrier pigeons and also given access to the infantry messenger relay system. In addition, from time to time the artillery commander sent reconnaissance officers forward to the front line and they returned with full reports over the precise location of our own and the enemy front lines. It is of the greatest importance to ensure that the artillery is constantly updated with exact information about our own front line and that of neighbouring units. Everything possible must be done to ensure this in order to rule out any misunderstandings with the artillery that could lead to fire coming down on our own lines ...

"Subordination of the field and heavy artillery to the division to carry out all tasks in support of the infantry proved to be most effective. Only in this way are the closest touch and swiftest cooperation between infantry and artillery guaranteed. On the other hand, it never led to problems when the group [i.e. corps] artillery commander temporarily made use of the heavy artillery for counter-battery fire or as part of a larger artillery grouping for particular tasks."[46]

That being said, the extreme pressure to which the defence was being subject made it impossible even at this late stage in the battle to maintain the desired clear delineation of roles between the heavy and field artillery which so exercised the chain of command. Schoch once more:

"A fundamental separation of the heavy artillery, reserving some for counter-battery fire and some for infantry support, was not possible. On the contrary it proved to be expedient, according to the situation and the limitations imposed by the weather on observation, to employ either the entire heavy artillery, or part of it, for counter-battery fire, or to bring fire down on the enemy positions. This policy had to be adopted because there was an insufficient number of heavy batteries in the divisional sector to permit the simultaneous conduct of the two tasks. In order to produce defensive fire, every single battery had to be tasked; for destructive fire, all the howitzer batteries were required. It was a serious disadvantage that at such moments of extreme tactical tension the heavy artillery, with the exception of one or two batteries, had to be taken off counter-battery fire, so that the enemy batteries, completely undisturbed, could bring down fire on our infantry and artillery, whilst also engaging targets in No Man's Land and producing harassing fire on the main approach routes."[47]

He then concluded with some obvious remarks, calling for further reinforcements of heavy artillery, a requirement which was easy to state but harder to achieve. It also appears to have been an area underplayed by Loßberg in his section concerning the artillery. Having listed a whole series of ways in which efficiency had been improved, he continued:

"The result of all these measures soon showed in a realisation amongst the troops that defensive fire becomes of lesser importance if counter-battery fire can be conducted systematically ... sharper alertness by the troops means that enemy attacks can be suppressed as they develop and in this way minimise the need for unnecessary demands for defensive fire. The artillery performs better the more it is supported by the infantry, especially in establishing the precise placement of both our and the enemy front lines."[48]

Of course the more reliance was placed on elastic area defence, frequently from crater field positions, the more important close and thorough liaison between the two arms became and the harder it was to produce. The German army had no choice but to try to come to terms with the use of craters, but it was clearly through gritted teeth. Whilst accepting that this type of defence was hard for the enemy to define and difficult to attack, nevertheless, in every other regard it was extremely disadvantageous. The concerns of Generalleutnant von Stetten, II Bavarian Corps, were quoted in Chapter 7. These and others were repeated at greater length by Loßberg,[50] but the most succinct criticism came from General der Kavallerie Freiherr Marschall in his *Hinweise fuer die Gefechtsfuehrung in der Verteidigung* [Advice for command and control in the defensive battle]. 'Fighting from shell holes puts a stop to any command and control. We cannot abandon the use of continuous positions.'[50]

Every effort was made to stick to the use of carefully sited and constructed positions, a policy that reached its most refined form with the construction of the *Siegfried Stellung* [Hindenburg Line] from Neuville Vitasse to Missy, east of Soissons, during late 1916 and early 1917, but it was equally obvious that any battle which followed a prolonged heavy bombardment was going to be conducted from craters, so Loßberg included several recommendations in the *Erfahrungen*.[51] The defence was to be conducted actively and feature plenty of patrols and raids. Every effort was to be made to push the front line forward in order to close up on the enemy and neutralise the Allied superiority in artillery. The system of deeply echeloning the defence, with each regiment maintaining one battalion forward in the front line, one in support and one 'resting' in reserve, was to be formally adopted throughout the army. The tactic had been developed as the Battle of the Somme dragged on and had proved to be successful, once, following the assumption of command by Hindenburg and Ludendorff, adequate reinforcements of all types had been made available; a great improvement and a change in policy fully acknowledged by Loßberg.

"All the time that General von Falkenhayn was chief of staff, command and control of the battle from *OHL* through every level down to platoon commander was extremely problematic. During the first part of the battle reinforcements were only made available at the very last minute to continue the heavy fighting. This meant that our fighting divisions were bled so dry that they could only recover very slowly once they had been withdrawn.

At hardly any time during Falkenhayn's time did First Army have access to a usable army reserve. The then *OHL* even considered – admittedly only temporarily – whether it could withdraw troops from the Somme front. Once Hindenburg and Ludendorff were placed in command, the situation changed instantly. Reserves were always available in a timely manner to permit reliefs to take place. The artillery was strengthened from central army reserves, permitting defensive fire widths to be reduced from 400 to 200 metres per battery. This meant considerably improved support for the front line troops in the defence and especially for counter-attacks. In the final part of the battle the allocation of aircraft spotting for the artillery and a squadron of fighters in every divisional sector led to a decisive improvement in the performance of our guns."[52]

One of the greatest changes made was permitting a certain degree of elasticity in the defence. Under Falkenhayn there was an absolute obligation to defend the front line, as though losing any part of it was a totally unacceptable disgrace. The German official historian summarised his stance thus:

'The first principle of positional warfare has to be not to yield a single foot of ground and, if a foot of ground is lost, to launch an immediate counter-attack with all forces, down to the last man'.[53]

Needless to say there was much criticism both at the time and subsequently about this policy from both junior and senior commentators. Leutnant Ernst Jünger of Fusilier Regiment 73 condemned it thus:

"It was the days at Guillemont that first made me aware of the overwhelming effects of the war of material. We had to adapt ourselves to an entirely new phase of war. The communications between the artillery and the liaison officers were utterly crippled by the terrific fire. Despatch riders failed to get through the hail of metal, and telephone lines were no sooner laid than they were shot to pieces... There was a zone of a kilometre behind the front line where explosives held absolute sway... Every hand's-breadth of ground had been churned up again and again; trees had been uprooted, smashed and ground to touchwood, the houses blown to bits and turned to dust; hills had been levelled and the arable land made a desert... The terrible losses, out of all proportion to the breadth of front attacked, were principally due to the old Prussian obstinacy with which the tactics of the line were pursued to their logical conclusion. One battalion after another was crowded up into a front line already over-manned, and in a few hours pounded to bits. It was a long while before the folly of contesting worthless strips of ground was recognised. It was finally given up and the principle of a mobile defence adopted... Thus it was that there were never again such bitterly-contested engagements as those that for weeks together were fought out round shell-shot woods or undecipherable ruins."[54]

Ludendorff, from his loftier perspective, came to more or less the same conclusion shortly after his meeting with the chiefs of staff in early September.

"That which I learned in Cambrai about our infantry, its equipment and tactics was extremely valuable for me. It was certain that the infantry was fighting too narrowly and rigidly. They were clinging on to ground far too much and the consequence was high casualty rates. Deep dugouts and cellars were too often fatal mantraps. The use of the rifle had been forgotten. The hand grenade had become the primary weapon and the equipment of the infantry with machine guns and other direct fire weapons had fallen way behind the measures which the enemy had taken. Initially the Field Marshal and I could only ask that, in principle, the front line positions be more thinly manned, the deep mined dugouts be destroyed and that all trenches or areas of terrain not essential for the overall defence be relinquished if their rigid defence meant that particularly heavy casualties would have to be endured. We would tackle the further questions concerning training and equipment of the infantry at a later stage."[55]

Naturally these thoughts were crystallised by Loßberg in the *Erfahrungen*; but although the defensive tactics to be adopted along the Western Front in 1917 visualised the full use of narrow but deep defensive zones, Loßberg, for various reasons, mainly doubts about the ability of the post 1916 army, led by young and inexperienced officers, to be able to master the demands of totally flexible battlefield tactics, remained wedded to the concept of rigidity in defence. As a result, he emphasised the primacy of the front line defined by higher authority, retained the power of decision voluntarily to relinquish ground at high level and denied any initiative in this matter to the deployed ground holding troops.

"In all circumstances", he wrote (his emphasis), **"we must hold firmly to the concept that, despite the adoption of 'area defences', the battle is for the front line and, in the event that it is overrun, the front line is what must be fought for."**

> "In principle, every formation must fight to retain the front line of the defensive sector allocated to it. Voluntary surrender of a position or part of a position can lead to the most serious consequences for neighbouring troops. The voluntary abandonment of positions may only occur after permission has been granted by a senior commander with a grasp of the consequences for neighbouring troops and the other arms (artillery)."[56]

Having gone on to discuss the question of troops moving forward, to the side, or to the rear to escape heavy shelling, he concluded that, of all the options, the worst and potentially most dangerous was to pull back, emphasising yet again that the Battle of the Somme was conducted on the basis that, 'Every single man had to fight for the place he was deployed. Only over his dead body was the enemy permitted to advance.'[57] However, he also accepted that there would be enemy break-ins and incursions which were to be dealt with, either through immediate counter-strokes, launched on the orders of the commander on the spot, or more deliberate, carefully prepared, counter-attacks. Out of this thinking was born the system of ground holding divisions backed by *Eingreif* divisions held out of artillery range, but able to advance rapidly to conduct meeting engagements against tiring Allied thrusts and so restore the original front line positions.

If these were to be the tactics which, based on the latest experience, were to be used to defend against the expected Allied offensives in the spring of 1917, how were the lessons to be disseminated? All the recent publications were distributed on a wide scale but, in addition, courses were run at a training area near Valenciennes during the early months of the new year. Selected for this important role was the outstanding 27th Infantry Division from Württemberg, commanded by the vigorous and thoughtful Generalleutnant Otto von Moser. The division had established its reputation during the defence of the Guillemont sector against all attacks for three weeks in August 1916. In his diary entry for 1 January 1917, Moser greeted the task with enthusiasm.

> "A doubly pleasant new year's surprise: the Star to the Order of the Red Eagle Second Class with Swords for Guillemont and news that I have been selected to command a 'Training and Demonstration Division'. That is to say, I am to conduct a practical test on a training area near Solesmes, with a division reinforced to full war establishment, of the recent *OHL* publication 'Principles for the Conduct of the Defensive Battle', produced on the basis of 1916 battle experiences. Simultaneously, I am to present these principles at Solesmes to large numbers of divisional commanders, artillery commanders and General Staff officers. For me this posting means relief from the terrible monotony of positional warfare and an escape from

the destruction associated with the *Alberich* operation, with which I have no sympathy. It will be an honourable, if difficult, duty, whose performance will demand all the energy I can bring to bear."[58]

Moser's comment about *Alberich*, the withdrawal to the *Siegfried Stellung/* Hindenburg Line and associated scorched earth policy is interesting. Serious reservations about the wanton destruction involved were shared by others, including Crown Prince Rupprecht and General von Gallwitz, both of whom considered resigning because of their opposition to it. So it would appear as though this highly controversial operation had to be forced through by Ludendorff, despite the moral objections of those ordered to carry it out.

When it came to applying all the lessons learned, one positive outcome for the defence in April 1917 was that 27th Infantry Division, its task complete, was deployed to Bullecourt, where it fought with distinction and, putting into practice all that it had learned at Valenciennes, inflicted a stinging defeat on 4th Australian Division on 11 April; but elsewhere from 9 April the picture was mixed. In yet another demonstration of the gap between theory and practice and of the strain imposed on the entire army by the battles of Verdun and the Somme, in places, particularly in the Vimy Ridge sector, not only did the layout of the defences and placement of dugouts not correspond to the latest thinking, there was a lack of manpower and trench stores to do anything about it. Canadian pressure was incessant during the weeks leading up the assault and the bad winter weather was further hindrance, so the assault went in ultimately against a position which lacked depth, where the bulk of the dugouts were in the front line trenches and where the placement of the artillery was extremely poor. The net result was the loss of the ridge and setbacks all along the line to the south.

Once more Loßberg, granted full powers of decision by Ludendorff,[59] was rushed into action to replace the Sixth Army chief of staff and, as ever, he managed to stabilise the situation until, having introduced the new concept of *offensive Abwehr* [offensive/active defence] and insisting on its implementation in full, gradually the entire battle began to be fought in accordance with the lessons so dearly bought the previous year on the Somme. For several months the new tactics held sway, first in the later stages of the Battle of Arras, Aisne and Champagne and also during the first half of the Third Battle of Ypres, until the British large scale 'bite and hold' operations were perfected under General Plumer at the Battles of the Menin Road Ridge in late September 1917.

From the German perspective the battle of the Somme was judged in two distinct, diametrically opposing, ways. The public view expressed was that it was a success, a victory at both the tactical and strategic level for German arms and its soldiers, who were qualitatively superior to their opponents. Loßberg's published judgement was that, 'The Allied plans foundered in the face of the sacrificial, indestructible courage and faithfulness of our army. Each *Sommekämpfer* can take pride in having contributed to the fact that the greatest battle of all wars ended with enemy failure and a German victory.'[60] Even long after the war, the withdrawal to the Hindenburg Line was being portrayed positively, 'The defensive victory of the Somme meant for *OHL* a second advantage. The Germans had, albeit temporarily, ripped the initiative from the enemy's hands once more.'[61] Another well known commentator, Generalleutnant Ernst Kabisch, went so far as to state, 'The strategic success of the Battle of the Somme fell to the German side'; but he qualified this by adding, 'but it was bought with very heavy losses.'[62] – somewhere around 500,000 men killed, wounded and missing, to be as precise as is possible at this remove.

In the narrow sense that there was no Allied breakthrough and the German line, therefore, was still intact at the end of the battle, it could be judged a defensive success tactically. The defenders had held on until they were rescued by the weather but, strategically, it was the beginning of the end, as can be seen from the private exchanges of view at the time by men in a position to judge. As proved by its further outstanding defensive performances throughout 1917, however, the German army was far from a spent force; but the way it fought the Somme and the consequent costs to it meant that its days were numbered. Defeat had become a matter of time, as the gap between the resources in men and material it could deploy, measured against those of the Allies, continued to widen.

The Somme had been a time of trial without precedent. Hindenburg in his memoirs probably summed up this titanic clash as well as anyone when he wrote:

'For neither of the opposing sides was there talk of the joy of victory. Over everything lay the appalling, oppressive weight of this battlefield which, in its grim desolation, seemed to surpass even that of Verdun.'[63]

Notes

1. *Kriegsarchiv Munich* HS 1984 Wurmb *Erinnerungen an die Eroberung der Feste Schwaben.*
2. McCarthy *The Somme* pp. 137–143.
3. Kronprinz Rupprecht *Mein Kriegstagebuch II. Band* p. 271.
4. *ibid.*p 54.
5. *Kriegsarchiv Munich* HGr Rupprecht Bd. 216 *Heeresgruppe 'Kronprinz v. Bayern' Oberkommando Abt. Ia No. 609 geh. dated* 27.9.1916.
6. *Kriegsarchiv Munich* HGr Rupprecht Bd. 216 *Chef des Generalstabes des Feldheeres Ia, Ic,II Nr. 243 op. geh. Betr. Lage an der Somme dated 8.10.16.*
7. Underlined phrases were emphasised in the original.
8. *Kriegsarchiv Munich* 24. Infantry. Regiment. (WK) 3 *Armee-Oberkommando1. Ia No.1402 geh. dated 19.10.1916.*

9. *Kriegsarchiv Munich* AOK 6 Bd.165 *Chef des Generalstabes des Feldheeres Ia No. 341 geh. op. dated 5.10.1916.*

10. BA.-MA. RH61/51716 *Kriegsministerium Nr. 817/16g.clb dated 6 October 1916.*

11. Loßberg *Meine Tätigkeit* pp. 264–265.

12. *Kriegsarchiv Munich* HGr Rupprecht Bd. 14 *von Hindenburg rm l a nr 843 geh op dated 7.11.1916.*

13. *Kriegsarchiv Munich* HGr Rupprecht Bd. 14 *Heeresgruppe Kronprinz von Bayern 1 a nr 1548 geheim dated 9?11.1916*

14. Voigt History Fusilier Regiment 73 pp. 444–458

15. Ludendorff *Meine Kriegserinnerungen* p. 228.

16. Kronprinz Rupprecht *op. cit.* pp. 44–56.

17. *Hauptstaatsarchiv Stuttgart* M108 Bü 75 *Gruppe A Ia. Nr.2926 geh. Armeebefehl dated 22.10.16.*

18. *Kriegsarchiv Munich* AOK 6 Bd.126 HGr Rupprecht *30/10 7.45 nm an OHL Beurteilung der Lage.*

19. Loßberg *op. cit.* p. 265.

20. Reymann History Infantry Regiment 62 p. 117.

21. Wißmann History Reserve Infantry Regiment 55 pp. 128–132.

22. Reymann *op. cit.* pp. 134–139.

23. Schacky History Bavarian Reserve Infantry Regiment 1 pp. 47–48.

24. History Fusilier Regiment 35 p. 205.

25. *Kriegsarchiv Munich* Infantry Regiment 4 Bund 4 *Betreff: Gesundheitszustand des Regts. dated 12.12.1916.*

26. *Kriegsarchiv Munich* Infantry Regiment 4 Bund 4 *Betreff: Gesundheitszustand des Regts. dated 19.12.1916.*

27. Rogge History Infantry Regiment 88 p. 313. The frankness of this report and many other surviving examples in the German archives provides a sharp contrast with what was clearly deemed appropriate in the British army at the time. Gary Sheffield *Douglas Haig: From the Somme to Victory* pp. 191–192 describes what happened when Lieutenant GN Kirkwood RAMC, medical officer 11th Battalion Border Regiment, responding to an order to give his opinion about the fitness for continued operations of his unit, stated that it was not up to further active service for the time being following the trauma of 1 July 1916. As a result, General Gough, his army commander, sought to have him dismissed the service as, 'a source of danger'; General Haig, whilst not upholding Gough's demand, nevertheless stated that, '… this medical officer ought not to have been asked the question which he was called upon to answer'. German officers in responsible positions did not even wait to be asked a specific question; instead they frequently took the initiative to highlight pressing matters. Repeatedly, a formula such as, 'It is my duty to make clear', was followed by a precise statement of a perceived problem or weakness. Proof that such openness was valued by the entire chain of command is that some of these reports, totally unaltered, found their way right up to *OHL*; the thoughts of General Boehn quoted in chapter 7 being a prime example.

28. *Kriegsarchiv Munich* 1 R.I.B. Bd 37 *Vernehmung eines gefangenen englischen Leutnants des I. South Staffordshire Batl., 91. Brig.,7.Div, eingebracht am 11.1 bei Feste Soden dated 12. January 1917.* Doke was reported captured on 11 January 1917 and repatriated on 14 December 1918.

29. Original emphasis.

30. *Kriegsarchiv Munich* HGr Rupprecht Bd. 16 *4. Garde-Inf.-Div. Ge. St. Offz: Vernehmung eines am 11.1 bei Feste Soden engl. Offiziers des 1./S. Staff.R (7. Division) dated 14.1.1917.*
31. *ibid.*
32. *Kriegsarchiv Munich* HGr Rupprecht Bd. 16 *Armee-Oberkommando 1 Ia No. 2127 geh. Betr. Vermißte bei 33.I.D. dated 24.1.1917.*
33. On the original this sentence is marked 'only for First Army' so, presumably, Second, Sixth and Seventh Armies received a shortened version.
34. *Kriegsarchiv Munich* HGr Rupprecht Bd. 14 *Heeresgruppe 'Kronprinz von Bayern' Oberkommando Ia No. 951 geh. dated 11.10.1916.*
35. Author's emphasis.
36. *Kriegsarchiv Munich* HGr Rupprecht Bd. 14 *Armee-Ober-Kommando 1. Ia Nr. 1306 geh. Zu Ia 951 geh. dated 12 October 1916.*
37. Loßberg *op. cit.* p. 270.
38. *Kriegsarchiv Munich* Gen. Kdo. III. A.K. (WK) 1835 *Erfahrungen der 1. Armee in der Sommeschlacht* [Erfahrungen] p2.
39. *Kriegsarchiv Munich* 4 Infantry Regiment Bd 4 *Garde-Reserve-Korps Generalkomando Abt. Ia Nr. 2900: Einige Erfahrungen aus den Kämpfen an der Somme dated 24.7.1916.*
40. *Kriegsarchiv Munich* Gen. Kdo. III. A.K. (WK) 1835 *50 Reserve-Division Bericht über Erfahrungen in der Somme-Schlacht dated 20 October 1916.*
41. Original emphasis.
42. *Kriegsarchiv Munich* Gen. Kdo. III. A.K. (WK) 1835 *Bayer. 5. Infanterie-Division Betreff: Erfahrungen aus der Somme-Schlacht dated 17 October 1916.*
43. *Erfahrungen* p. 4.
44. Underlined words are emphasised in the original.
45. *Erfahrungen* p. 17.
46. *Kriegsarchiv Munich* Infanterie-Divisionen (WK) 193 *1. Bayer. Infanterie Division No. 500 Ia Betreff: Erfahrungen aus der Sommeschlacht dated 14 Oct 16.*
47. *Kriegsarchiv Munich* Infanterie-Divisionen (WK) 193 *1. Bayer. Infanterie Division No. 500 Ia Betreff: Erfahrungen aus der Sommeschlacht dated 14 Oct 16.*
48. *Erfahrungen* p. 18.
49. *Erfahrungen* p. 11.
50. *Kriegsarchiv Munich* HGr Rupprecht Bd. 216 *Garde-Reserve-Korps generalkommando Ia Nr. 5813. Geheim. Hinweise fuer die Gefechtsfuehrung in der Verteidigung auf Grund der Erfahrungen an der Somme dated 6 October 1916.*
51. *Erfahrungen* pp. 11–12.
52. Loßberg *op. cit.* p. 268.
53. GOH p. 335.
54. Jünger: *'The Storm of Steel'* pp. 107 – 110
55. Ludendorff: *'Meine Kriegserinnerungen'* p. 213
56. *Erfahrungen* p. 11.
57. *Erfahrungen* p. 12.
58. Moser *Feldzugsaufzeichnungen* p. 244.
59. Loßberg *op. cit.* pp. 280–281.
60. *Erfahrungen* p. 2.
61. Grote *Somme* p. 172.
62. Kabisch *Das Volksbuch* p. 158.
63. Hindenburg *Aus meinem Leben* p. 160.

Appendix

Selective Biographical Notes

The Battle of the Somme 1916 involved a great many commanders who may not be immediately familiar to the reader. Some of those who appear in the book are:

Below General der Infanterie Fritz Wilhelm Theodor Carl von (1853–1918) Commander First Army. General von Below was a distinguished soldier who was born into a noble family and began his career as a sekondeleutnant in Footguard Regiment 1. Selected for the Great General Staff later, he served in various appointments until his appointment as commander 1st Guards Infantry Division in 1908. In September 1912 he was promoted to general der infanterie and assumed command of XXI Corps in Saarbrücken. In 1914 his corps fought in Lorraine in the centre of Sixth Army commanded by Crown Prince Rupprecht of Bavaria then, in October, during the so-called 'Race to the Sea', it was transferred to the Arras area as part of Second Army under Generaloberst von Bülow. Despatched to East Prussia at the beginning of 1915, it was under command Tenth Army in the winter battles. In April 1915, Below was succeeded in command by General von Hutier and returned to the Western Front to assume command of Second Army, commanding it until mid July 1916 on the Somme when a reorganisation meant that he was now responsible for the battles north of the Somme as Commander First Army. The following month he was awarded the Oak Leaf to his Pour le Mérite and he continued to operate in the north until the conclusion of the *Alberich* withdrawal in March 1917. At that moment, the entire First Army headquarters was moved to the Aisne front where it was heavily involved in holding the attacks of the French Fifth Army. In June 1918 he was given command of Ninth Army, but he was already a sick man. He was relieved of his duties in August 1918 and finally retired at the end of the war. He died a short time later of a lung infection and was buried in Berlin in the *Invalidenfriedhof*.

Boehn General der Infanterie Max Ferdinand Karl von (1850–1921) Commander IX Reserve Corps. General Boehn came from a distinguished military family. His father, uncle and younger brother all became senior generals in their turn. He entered the army in 1867 as a three-year volunteer and fahnenjunker with Footguard Regiment 3 in Hanover. He was commissioned as a sekondeleutnant in March 1869 and was posted the following year to Infantry Regiment 76 in Hamburg. He fought in several actions of the Franco-Prussian War with this regiment, was wounded in the arm and received the Iron Cross Second Class and the Mecklenburg Military Service Cross Second Class for his performance. Several years at regimental duty interspersed with external appointments followed then, in 1889, having served as a company commander with Grenadier Guard Regiment 1 (Kaiser Alexander) in Berlin, he was promoted major and made adjutant of 1st Guards Infantry Division, also in Berlin. He carried out other appointments with the Guards before returning to Infantry Regiment 76 as an oberstleutnant and battalion commander in 1897, remaining there as its commander when he was promoted oberst in 1899. His career continued successfully when he was promoted Generalmajor in 1901 and sent to command 9 Infantry Brigade in Frankfurt an der Oder in 1901. Promotion to generalleutnant followed in April 1905 when he took over 18th Infantry Division in Flensburg. He was promoted general der infanterie in December 1909 and assumed the role of fortress commander at Ulm. The King of Württemberg awarded him the Grand Cross of the Order of Frederick in 1911 and he was pensioned off in September 1912.

On the outbreak of war, he was recalled out of retirement to command IX Reserve Corps. To begin with the corps was engaged in anti-invasion duties in Schleswig Holstein, but by late August 1914 had been despatched to Belgium where it was heavily and controversially involved in the sacking and burning of Louvain. It later redeployed to the Roye-Noyon sector and participated in the battles around Soissons in January 1915. In late 1915 his corps was redeployed once more to Sixth Army for the autumn battles in Artois, remaining there until it carried out a tour of duty on the Somme in mid July 1916. Service on the Somme and Flanders then alternated until, in February 1917, Boehn was appointed commander of Armeegruppe C and the following month of Seventh Army. In the battles along the Chemin des Dames in spring 1917, Boehn received the Oak Leaf to his Pour le Mérite, awarded the previous year on the Somme. In December 1917 Boehn marked fifty years of service, for which the Kaiser decorated him with the Grand Cross of the Order of the Red Eagle with Oak Leaves and Swords. Raised to Generaloberst in March 1918, his army was involved in the German offensive then in May he commanded the attack across the Chemin des Dames, during which his army advanced sixty kilometres and he was made a Knight of the Order of the Black Eagle. He briefly commanded an army group in Artois from August to October 1918 then reverted to command of what was left of Seventh Army up until the Armistice. He left the army in January 1919 and spent his brief retirement in Berlin.

Gallwitz General der Artillerie Max Karl Wilhelm von (1852–1937) Commander Second Army. General von Gallwitz entered the army on 13 August 1870 as a volunteer in Field Artillery Regiment 9 and became an officer in 1872. In 1877 he undertook a three year training course at the *Kriegsakademie* and in 1883 was appointed to the General Staff. From 1886 his career alternated between command and staff appointments and on 16 January 1890 he was appointed commander Field Artillery Regiment 27 in Mainz. After promotion to major, he became the General Staff officer of 9th Division in Glogau, Silesia [modern day Powiat Glogowski, Poland] on 22 March 1891. This was followed on 18 October 1895 by a staff appointment to VII Corps in Münster. By 1899 he was an oberst and thereafter was promoted rapidly until, having commanded 15th Infantry Division in Cologne from October 1906 – April 1911, he was made Inspector of the Field Artillery, promoted to the rank of General der Artillerie and ennobled in 1913. On the outbreak of war, he was made commander of the Guards Reserve Corps which, following the fall of Namur, was sent east and fought in the Battle of the Masurian Lakes as part of Eighth Army commanded by Hindenburg. In February 1915 he was given command of an enlarged force which later became Twelfth Army that fought in the First and Second Battles of Przasnysz, during the latter of which he achieved a breakthrough along the Narew. On 30 September 1915 he was made commander of the new Eleventh Army which, under Mackensen, played a leading role in the defeat of Serbia. He received the Pour le Mérite in July 1915 and the Oak Leaf to it in September of that same year. Returning to the Western Front in March 1916, he became the commander of *Angriffsgruppe* West which, as part of Fifth Army, conducted operations on the east bank of the Meuse. In mid July 1916 he was posted to the Somme, there to command Second Army and for a time 'Army

Group Gallwitz'. In December 1916 he assumed command of Fifth Army at Verdun and carried on in that role until the end of the war. He received the Grand Cross of the Order of the Red Eagle for his work on the Somme and in December 1917 the Order of the Black Eagle. Post war he went into politics and died during a convalescent holiday in Italy in spring 1937.

Kuhl General der Infanterie Hermann Josef von (1856–1958) Chief of Staff Sixth Army/Army Group Bavarian Crown Prince. General von Kuhl was a highly intellectual, educated man who studied philosophy, classical philology and comparative linguistics to doctoral level before joining the army in 1878 as a cadet in Infantry Regiment 53. He carried out regimental duties for ten years and was promoted oberleutnant prior to attending the Prussian *Kriegsakademie* from 1889–1892. After five years alternating between junior staff and regimental appointments, he returned as an instructor at the *Kriegsakademie* in 1897, combining these duties with that of a section chief in the General Staff. His staff career flourished under Generalfeldmarschall Alfred Graf von Schlieffen and he was promoted up to the rank of Generalmajor by 1912 and ennobled in 1913. He briefly commanded 25 Infantry Brigade in Munster from June 1913–August 1914, but his skill lay in staff duties and on mobilisation, he was made chief of staff to First Army under General der Infanterie Alexander von Kluck. Having been promoted Generalleutnant in April 1915, he was posted that September as chief of staff to General Max von Gallwitz's Twelfth Army, moving in late November 1915 as chief of staff Sixth Army under Crown Prince Rupprecht. On 28 August, the day that Army Group Bavarian Crown Prince was formed on the Somme, he was awarded the Pour le Mérite. Kuhl remained in the same post right up until the end of the war then, following the resignation of Crown Prince Rupprecht on 11 November 1918, he supervised and commanded the withdrawal of its formations to Germany and their subsequent demobilisation. Post war he became a leading historian and commentator on the war, wrote numerous books and articles and strongly represented the view that the war was lost through defeat in the field by superior numbers and materiel, rather than because the army had been 'stabbed in the back'. In addition to the receipt of numerous military decorations and honours, von Kuhl was awarded the civilian version of the Pour le Mérite for Arts and Sciences, one of very few men to be honoured with both orders.

Loßberg Oberst Fritz von (1868–1942) Chief of Staff Second/First Army. Oberst von Loßberg was a key figure in the German army throughout the First World War, rising from the rank of oberstleutnant to generalleutnant and finally becoming a general der infanterie in the Reichswehr after the war. His exceptional talents were first recognised whilst he was serving at Supreme Army Headquarters in 1915, when he briefed the Kaiser in person about the crisis in Third Army at the beginning of the Autumn Battle in Champagne and how it could be resolved. That same day he found himself posted with immediate effect as chief of staff to that army. This was a considerable honour for a newly promoted oberst and, for the next three years, he was despatched from army to army to handle one crisis after another. Possessed of the ability to reduce major operational problems to their essentials, he repeatedly brought to bear clarity of thought, dynamism and bold decision making. Although nominally working as the adviser to a series of senior field commanders, in fact, armed with the full power of command he always demanded (and was granted) by his superiors, he *de facto* assumed command positions. It was, for example, Loßberg, personally, who directed the defensive battles against the British army on the Somme, at Arras and Passchendaele. He had a very strong constitution and an extraordinary capacity for hard work and long hours. He caught up with sleep by dozing in chairs at odd moments or during his daily car journeys to the front and, at times of crisis, never spent more than four hours per day in bed. He received numerous honours and awards, including the *Pour le Mérite* and Oak Leaves to it, from all the contingents of the German army.

Soden General der Infanterie Franz Ludwig Freiherr von (1856–1945) Commander 26th Reserve Division. General von Soden joined the élite Württemberg formation, Grenadier Regiment 119, as a one year volunteer in 1873. The following January he became a fahnenjunker and was commissioned as a sekondeleutnant in February 1875. From 1880–1883 he studied at the Prussian *Kriegsakademie*, then he went as an oberleutnant to Grenadier Regiment 123 in October 1883, but as early as July the following year he was recalled and from 1 May 1886 he was posted to the General Staff in Berlin, where he was promoted hauptmann in 1888. He then spent two years on the staff of X Corps and 19th Infantry Division, before spending the period September 1891–April 1893 as a company commander with Grenadier Regiment 119. He was then appointed successively Ia (chief of staff) to 26th Infantry Division and XIII (Royal Württemberg) Corps. He then took command of 1st Battalion Infantry Regiment 83 in Kassel in 1898. He became an oberstleutnant in April 1900 and was posted as chief of staff to X Corps until February 1903, when he was appointed commander Infantry Regiment 125. He remained in that appointment until May 1906 when he became commander 51 Infantry Brigade and was promoted generalmajor that September. In January 1910 he was promoted generalleutnant and commander 26th Infantry Division until retirement in March 1911. Recalled at the outbreak of war, he was given command of 26th Reserve Division, part of XIV Reserve Corps. After fighting in the Vosges, the corps was moved north to the Somme where it remained for the next two years and played a significant part in the Battle of the Somme in summer and autumn 1916. Soden led his division with great distinction and energy, despite being aged sixty during the battle. His reinforced division famously smashed the attacks of the British VIII and X Corps on 1 July 1916. Soden was then promoted general der infanterie and given command of VII Reserve Corps in Champagne. This was another successful period of command and Soden received the Pour le Mérite in July 1917. From August to November 1917 he commanded XI Corps, then was posted to V Reserve Corps where he was simultaneously in overall command of Meuse Group (East) at Verdun. He remained in that area until the Armistice, leaving the army in January 1919. Post war he wrote several books about formations of the Army of Württemberg.

Stein General der Artillerie Hermann Christlieb Matthäus von (1854–1927) Commander XIV Reserve Corps. Confusing the issue is the fact that there were two officers during the Great War named General der Artillerie Hermann von Stein. One, a Bavarian, had a distinguished career that included a spell as divisional commander at Maurepas during August 1916. The one concerned here was a Prussian officer who joined Infantry Regiment 3 as an *Advantageur* [officer candidate] in 1873. He became a Sekondeleutnant in 1875, then attended the *Kriegsakademie* in 1886, where he was made a premierleutnant and then posted to the General Staff from 1888. He carried out regimental duty in Field Artillery Regiment 7 from September 1890, then returned to the General Staff of 34th Infantry in 1894. On promotion to major in in 1896 he was sent to the General Staff in Berlin then the following year became commander of Field Artillery Regiment 33 and was promoted to oberstleutnant. Highly thought of professionally, he was appointed head of the Mobilisation Branch of the Great General Staff in 1903. He was promoted oberst in 1905 and generalmajor in 1910. Following senior staff appointments, in April 1912 he became a generalleutnant and was posted as commander 41st Infantry Division in Deutsch-Eylau, East Prussia, where he was ennobled in 1913. At the outbreak of war he was serving again with the central staff, responsible for the overall supervision of the army reports, but by September 1914 he became commander XIV Reserve Corps, an appointment he held throughout the so-called 'Race to the Sea', after which he was redeployed to under command of Second Army and responsible for the Somme front north of the river. Having commanded in the defensive *Schwerpunkt* of the Battle of the Somme from July–October 1916, he handed over his command to Generalleutnant Georg Fuchs and served until October 1918 as the Prussian Minister of War, taking over from Generalleutnant Adolf Wild von Hohenborn, who was posted to command XVI Corps.

Bibliography

Unpublished Sources
Bundesarchiv/Militärarchiv Freiburg im Breisgau
RH61/50652 *Persönliches Kriegstagebuch des Generals der Infanterie a.D. von Kuhl.*
RH61/51716 *Kriegsministerium M.J. 14864/16. A.1. Geheim* dated 17.7.16.
RH61/51716 *Kriegsministerium Nr. 817/16g.clb dated 6 October 1916.*

Kriegsarchiv Munich
N.B. The file numbering system used by the *Kriegsarchiv* has changed recently and some of the documents here referenced were consulted under the old one. Nevertheless, the search catalogues are still arranged by formations and units, so tracing the items quoted is entirely straightforward, regardless of the actual file reference provided below.

HGr Rupprecht Bd. 14 *Heeresgruppe 'Kronprinz von Bayern' Oberkommando Ia No. 951 geh.* dated 11.10.1916.
HGr Rupprecht Bd. 14 *Armee-Ober-Kommando 1. Ia Nr. 1306 geh. Zu Ia 951 geh.* dated 12 October 1916.
HGr Rupprecht Bd. 14 *von Hindenburg rm l a nr 843 geh op dated 7.11.1916.*
HGr Rupprecht Bd. 14 *Heeresgruppe Kronprinz von Bayern l a nr 1548 geheim dated 9?11.1916*
HGr Rupprecht Bd. 15 *Armeeoberkommando 1 Abt. Ia Nr 698 geh.* dated 9.9.1916.
HGr Rupprecht Bd 16 *Chef des Generalstabes des Heeres Ia/II Nr. 35 358 op. Geheim* dated 18.09.1916.
HGr Rupprecht Bd. 16 *4. Garde-Inf.-Div. Ge. St. Offz :Vernehmung eines am 11.1 bei Feste Soden engl. Offiziers des I./S. Staff.R (7. Division) dated 14.1.1917.*
HGr Rupprecht Bd. 16 *Armee-Oberkommando 1 Ia No. 2127 geh. Betr. Vermißte bei 33.I.D. dated 24.1.1917.*
HGr Rupprecht Bd 68 *Oberkommando der 7. Armee IIa. Nr. 372 Pers.* dated 15.10.16.
HGr Rupprecht Bd 68 *7. Armee. Armee-Oberkommando. IIa Nr. 372 Pers.* dated 18.10.1916.
HGr Rupprecht Bd 68 *Abschrift [Betrachtung] v. Boehn* Undated.
HGr Rupprecht Bd 126 *HGr Rupprecht 16/10 an OHL Beurteilung der Lage.*
HGr Rupprecht Bd 126 *30/10 7.45 nm an OHL Beurteilung der Lage.*
HGr Rupprecht Bd 216 *Heeresgruppe Gallwitz Ia Nr 115 Geheim* dated 27 Jul 16.
HGr Rupprecht Bd. 216 *Armee-Ober-Kommando 1. Ia Nr. 934 geh.* dated 26 September 1916.
HGr Rupprecht Bd. 216 *Heeresgruppe 'Kronprinz v. Bayern' Oberkommando Abt. Ia No. 609 geh. Die Lage an der Somme* dated 27.9.1916.
HGr Rupprecht Bd. 216 *Chef des Generalstabes des Feldheeres II Nr. 200 op. geh. Betrachtung* dated 27.9.1916.

HGr Rupprecht Bd. 216 *Res. Inf. Regt. 74 13278 Wesentlichste Erfahrungen des Regiments aus den Kämpfen an der Somme* dated 2.10.1916.

HGr Rupprecht Bd. 216 *Garde-Reserve-Korps generalkommando Ia Nr. 5813. Geheim. Hinweise fuer die Gefechtsfuehrung in der Verteidigung auf Grund der Erfahrungen an der Somme* dated 6 October 1916.

HGr Rupprecht Bd. 216 *213. Inf. – Division I.17.x. geh. Erfahrung in der Somme-Schlacht 22.-30. IX. 16* dated 6.10.16.

HGr Rupprecht Bd. 216 *Chef des Generalstabes des Feldheeres Ia, Ic,II Nr. 243 op. geh. Betr. Lage an der Somme* dated 8.10.16.

AOK 6 Bd 3 *Kriegstagebuch 1916.*

AOK 6 Bd.165 *Chef des Generalstabes des Feldheeres Ia No. 341 geh. op.* dated 5.10.1916.

Gen. Kdo. III. A.K. (WK) 1835 *Bayer. 5. Infanterie-Division Betreff: Erfahrungen aus der Somme-Schlacht* dated 17 October 1916.

Gen. Kdo. III. A.K. (WK) 1835 *50 Reserve-Division Bericht* über *Erfahrungen in der Somme-Schlacht* dated 20 October 1916.

Gen. Kdo. III. A.K. (WK) 1835 *Erfahrungen der 1. Armee in der Sommeschlacht.* [01.1917].

Infanterie-Divisionen (WK) 193 *1. Bayer. Infanterie Division No. 500 Ia Betreff: Erfahrungen aus der Sommeschlacht* dated 14 Oct 16.

Infanterie-Divisionen (WK) 859 *1. Bay. Infanterie-Division. Der Kampf um Sailly (15.10.1916 – 21.10.1916)* dated 20.11.1916.

Infanterie-Divisionen (WK) 2355 *No. 292/21479 Generalkommando II A.K. An die Herren Kommandeure der 3. und 4.I.D. Betreff: Schlacht an der Somme* dated 16.11.16.

Infanterie-Divisionen (WK) 4131 *GenKdo XIV.R.K. Ia No. 1196 geh.* dated 3.07.1916.

Infanterie-Divisionen (WK)13704 *Chef des Generalstabes des Feldheeres Ia/II Nr. 175 gh.op. ERFAHRUNGEN DER SOMME-SCHLACHT.* dated 25.9.1916.

1 R.I.B. Bd 37 *Vernehmung eines gefangenen englischen Leutnants des I. South Staffordshire Batl., 91. Brig.,7.Div, eingebracht am 11.1 bei Feste Soden* dated 12. January 1917.

2 Infantry. Regiment. Bd 7 *Gefechtsbericht* über *die Kämpfe des 2. Infanterieregiments um Sailly vom 12.10. abends, bis 19.10 morg.* dated 4.11.1916

Infantry Regiment 4 Bd 4 *Garde-Reserve-Korps Generalkomando Abt. Ia Nr. 2900: Einige Erfahrungen aus den Kämpfen an der Somme* dated 24.7.1916.

Infantry Regiment 4 Bund 4 *Betreff: Gesundheitszustand des Regts. dated 12.12.1916.*

Infantry Regiment 4 Bund 4 *Betreff: Gesundheitszustand des Regts. dated 19.12.1916.*

9. Inf. Regt. (WK) 7 *Abschrift der Aussagen von Augenzeugen* über *die Vorgänge am 15.9.16* dated 21.9.1916

13. Inf. Regt. (WK) 13 *Armee Oberkommando 1 Ia No. 842 geh.* dated 16.9.1916

16. Inf. Regt. (WK) 3 *2. Bataillon Gefechtsbericht für die Zeit vom 1.7. Mittags bis 3.7. Mittags*

16. Inf.Regt. (WK) 24 *Bataillon Befehl vom 10.7.16 Beilage Nr. 29*

16. Inf. Regt. (WK) 3 *3. Garde-Infanterie-Division I Geheim! Divisions-Befehl* dated 12 Jul 16

16. Inf. Regt. (WK) 3 *16. Bayer. Infanterie. Regiment. An K.b.10.I.Div. Beaulencourt 15.7.1916 9,15 pm.* 16. Inf. Regt. (WK) 3 *K.4.Chev.Rgt. 'König' Stabsarzt Dr. Eber Bericht* über *den Gefechtstag Bayr. 16.Inf.R. am 14.7.1916* dated 22.11.16.

16. Inf. Regt. (WK) 3 *2. Bataillon b.16.Inf. Regts. Gefechtsbericht für die Zeit vom 1. mit 5. Juli 1916* dated 11.8.16

24. Infantry. Regiment. (WK) 3 *Armee-Oberkommando1. Ia No.1402 geh. dated 19.10.1916.*

5. R. I. R. (WK) 3 *III. / R.I.R. 5* Gefechtsbericht *des III./ R.I.R. 5 über den 15. u. 16.9.1916.*

5. Res. Inf. Regt. (WK) 3 *No 3913 7. Inf. Brigade. An 5. R.I.R.* dated 24.10.16.

5. Res. Inf. Regt. (WK) 3 *Nr. 4842 7. bayer. Inf. Brigade. An: 5., 9.IR. RIR 5 Bemerkungen anläßlich der Komp.-Besichtigungen* dated 28.12.16.

6 RIR Bd 2 Map *Verteilung der Reste des Reserve Infantry Regiment 6 1.VII.16.*

8 BRIR Bd 3. *I. Nr. 28 Regimentsbefehl 24.6.1916.*

8 BRIR Bd 4 *Gefechtsbericht d. 1. R. Komp Infantry Regiment 180 v. 1.7.16/Bericht* über *die Tätigkeit der 1. Rekr. Komp. 180 am 1. und 2. Juli 1916.*

HS 1984 Wurmb Herbert von *Erinnerungen an die Eroberung der Feste Schwaben an der Somme am 1.7.16.*

HS 2205 Bram Generalmajor *Anteil des Bayer. Res. Inf.Regts. 8 an der Somme Schlacht*

HS 2293 Brennfleck Major a.D. *Der Heldenkampf des I. Bataillons 16. Infanterie Regiments – der 14. Juli 1916.*

Hauptstaatsarchiv Stuttgart

M43/19 *Reserve-Infanterie-Regiment Nr. 99 Gefechtsbericht für die Zeit vom 24.6–30.6.16. den 17.8.1916*

M99 Bü142 *Gefechtsbericht des 10. Württ. Infanterie-Regiments Nr. 180 über die Kämpfe im Abschnitt Thiepval vom 25.9. Bis 7.10.1916* dated 4.12.1916.

M108 Bü 75 *Gruppe A Ia. Nr.2926 geh. Armeebefehl* dated 22.10.16.

M407 Bü 42/103 *III. Reserve Infantry Regiment 119 Bericht* über *die Gefechtstätigkeit den 20.7.1916.*

M410 Bü 239 *Kriegstagebuch der 52. (K.W.) Reserve Infanterie Brigade 24.6.1916 – 1.7.1916*

M410 Bü 260 *Geschichte der 52 (K.W.) Reserve-Infanterie-Brigade II. Teil Die Sommeschlacht*

Till Collection
Jochimsen Johannes Jürgen/Poser Till (Ed) *Herz im Feuer 1914 – 1921* 1961

Published Works (German: author known)
Bauer Georg *Reserve-Infanterie-Regiment Nr. 74: Die Geschichte vom Leben und Kämpfen eines deutschen Westfront-Regiments im Weltkriege 1914–1918* Oldenburg 1933

Bolze Generalmajor a.D. Walther *Das Kgl. Sächs. 7. Feldartillerie-Regiment Nr. 77* Dresden 1924

Bruchmüller Oberstleutnant a.D. Georg *Die deutsche Artillerie in den Durchbruchsschlachten des Weltkrieges* Berlin 1922

Cochenhausen General d. Art. Z.V. Dr Friedrich von *Gedanken von Clausewitz* Berlin 1943

Ehlert Hans, Epkenhans Michael & Groß Gerhard P. (Hrsg.) *Der Schlieffenplan: Analysen und Dokumente* Paderborn 2006

Etzel Generalmajor a.D. Hans *Das K.B. 9. Infanterie-Regiment Wrede* Würzburg 1927

Falkenstein Major a.D. Hans Trützschler v. *Das Anhaltische Infanterie-Regiment Nr. 93 im Weltkriege* Oldenburg 1929

Foerster Oberarchivrat Wolfgang *Graf Schlieffen und der Weltkrieg* Berlin 1925

Foerster Roland G (Hrsg) *Die Wehrpflicht: Enstehung, Erscheinungsformen und politisch-militärische Wirkung* Munich 1994

Gallwitz General der Artillerie a.D. h.c. Max v. *Erleben im Westen* Berlin 1932

Gehre Ludwig *Die deutsche Kräfterverteilung während des Weltkrieges: Eine Clausewitzstudie* Berlin 1928

Gothein Georg *Warum verloren wir den Krieg?* Deutsche Verlags-Anstalt 1919

Grote Hans Henning Freiherr *Somme* Hamburg 1941

Gruson Oberst a.D. Ernst *Das Königlich Preußische 4. Thür. Infanterie-Regiment Nr. 72 im Weltkriege* Oldenburg 1930

Guhr Generalmajor a.D. *Das 4. Schlesische Infanterie-Regiment Nr. 157 im Frieden und im Kriege 1897–1919* Zeulenroda 1934

Hasselbach Major a.D. von & Skrodzki Hptm d.Res. a.D. *Das Reserve-Infanterie-Regiment Nr. 38* Zeulenroda 1934

Helbling Generalmajor a.D. Max, Brunner Oberst a.D. Ernst Ritter von & Dittelberger Generalmajor a.D. Martin Ritter von *Das K.B. Reserve-Infanterie-Regiment Nr. 2* Munich 1926

Hindenburg Generalfeldmarschall von *Aus meinem Leben* Leipzig 1934

Hohn Reinhard *Scharnhorsts Vermächtnis* Bonn 1952

Jaud Generalmajor a.D. Karl & Weech Oberstleutnant a.D. Friedrich von *Das K.B. Reserve-Infanterie-Regiment 19* Munich 1933

Jung Jakob *Max von Gallwitz (1852–1937) General und Politiker* Osnabrück 1995

Kabisch Generalleutnant a.D. Ernst *Streitfragen des Weltkrieges 1914–1918* Stuttgart 1921

Kabisch Generalleutnant a.D. Ernst *Somme 1916* Berlin 1937

Kaiser Generalmajor a.D. Franz *Das Königl. Preuß. Infanterie-Regiment Nr. 63 (4. Oberschlesisches)* Berlin 1940

Keiser Oberstleutnant von *Geschichte des Inf.-Regts. v.d. Marwitz (8. Pomm) Nr. 61 im Weltkriege 1914–1918* Privately published 1928

Klähn Leutnant d. Res. Friedrich *Geschichte des Reserve-Infanterie-Regiments Nr. 86 im Weltkriege* Berlin 1925

Klaus Justizrat und Major a.D. Max *Das Württembergische Reserve-Feldartillerie-Regiment Nr. 26 Im Weltkrieg 1914–1918* Stuttgart 1929

Klett Fritz *Das Württembergische Reserve-Dragoner-Regiment im Weltkrieg 1914–1918* Stuttgart 1935

Knieling Lutz & Bölsche Arnold *R.I.R. 234 Ein Querschnitt durch Deutschlands Schicksalringen* Zeulenroda 1931

Krämer Max *Geschichte des Reserve-Infanterie-Regiments 245 im Weltkriege 1914/1918* Leipzig

Kuhl General der Infanterie z.D. Dr. phil. H v. *Der deutsche Generalstab in Vorbereitung und Durchführung des Weltkrieges* Berlin 1920

Kuhl General d.Inf. a.D. Hermann v. *Der Weltkrieg 1914–1918 Band I* Berlin 1929

Kümmel Leutnant d. Res. A.D. Adolf *Res.-Inf.-Regt. Nr. 91 im Weltkriege 1914–1918* Oldenburg 1926

Leistenschneider Stephan *Auftragstaktik im preußisch-deutschen Heer 1871 bis 1914* Berlin 2002

Loßberg General der Infanterie z.V. Fritz v. *Meine Tätigkeit im Weltkriege 1914–1918* Berlin 1939

Ludendorff Erich *Meine Kriegserinnerungen 1914–1918* Berlin 1919

Lutz Hauptmann Ernst Freiherr von *Das Königlich bayerische 16. Infanterie-Regiment im Kriege 1914–1918* Passau 1920

Möller Hanns *Fritz v. Below, General der Infanterie* Berlin 1939

Moos Leutnant d.R. a.D. Ernst *Das Württembergische Res.-Feld-Artillerie-Regiment Nr. 27 im Weltkrieg 1916–1918* Stuttgart 1925

Moser General Otto von *Feldzugsaufzeichnungen als Brigade- Divisionskommandeur und als kommmandierender General 1914–1918* Stuttgart 1923

Moser Generalleutnant z.D. Otto von *Ernsthafte Plaudereien über den Weltkrieg* Stuttgart 1925

Müller Major d.R. P., Fabeck Oberst a.D. H. von & Kiesel Oberstleutn. a.D. R. *Geschichte des Reserve-Infanterie-Regiments Nr. 99* Zeulenroda 1936

Neubrunner Leutnant Dr. Carl & Pfeffer Reserve Leutnant Dr. Georg *Geschichte des Infanterie-Regiments 186* Oldenburg 1926

Nollau Oberstleutnant a.D. Johannes *Geschichte des Königlich Preußischen 4. Niederschlesischen Infanterie-Regiments Nr. 51* Berlin 1931

Reinhardt Generalleutnant a.D. Ernst *Das Württembergische Reserve-Infanterie-Regiment Nr. 248 im Weltkrieg 1914–1918* Stuttgart 1924

Reymann Oberleutnant a.D. H. *Das 3. Oberschlesische Infanterie-Regiment Nr. 62 im Kriege 1914–1918* Zeulenroda 1930

Reymann Major a.D. Martin *Das Infanterie-Regiment von Alvensleben (6. Brandenbg.) Nr. 52 im Weltkriege 1914/1918* Oldenburg 1923

Ritter Oberstleutnant a.D. Holger *Geschichte des Schleswig-Holsteinischen Infanterie-Regiments Nr. 163* Hamburg 1926

Rogge Oberst a.D. Walter *Das Königl. Preuß. 2. Nassauische Infanterie-Regiment Nr. 88* Berlin 1936

Rupprecht Kronprinz *In Treue Fest: Mein Kriegstagebuch:* Volumes 1 & 2 Munich 1929

Schacky Hauptmann Siegmund Frh. Von *Das K.B. Reserve-Infanterie-Regiment Nr. 1* Munich 1924

Scheer Leutnant d.R. a.D. Carl *Das Württembergische Infanterie-Regiment Nr. 413 im Weltkrieg 1916–1918* Stuttgart 1936

Schiedt Major a.D. *Das Reserve-Infanterie-Regiment Nr. 51 im Weltkriege 1914–1918* Zeulenroda 1936

Schönfeldt Kgl. Preuß. Major a.D. Ernst von *Das Grenadier-Regiment Prinz Karl von Preußen (2. Brandenburgisches) Nr. 12 im Weltkriege.*Oldenburg 1924

Schreibershofen Major a.D. M. von *Das deutsche Heer: Bilder aus Krieg und Frieden*Berlin 1913

Schulenburg-Wolfsburg Generalmajor a.D. Graf v.d. *Geschichte des Garde-Füsilier-Regiments* Oldenburg 1926

Schwarte Generalleutnant Max *Der Weltkrieg um Ehre und Recht: Der deutsche Landkrieg Zweiter Teil* Leipzig 1923

Soden Freiherr von *Die 26. (Württembergische) Reserve-Division im Weltkrieg 1914–1918 I. Teil* Stuttgart 1939

Stein General der Artillerie z.D. Kriegsminister a.D. Dr. von *Erlebnisse und Betrachtungen aus der Zeit des Weltkrieges* Lepzig 1919

Stosch Oberstleutnant a.D. Albrecht von *Somme-Nord I. Teil Die Brennpunkte der Schlacht im Juli 1916* Oldenburg 1928

Vischer Alfred *Das 10. Württ. Infanterie-Regiment Nr. 180 in der Somme-Schlacht 1916* Stuttgart 1917

Voigt Oblt. d. Res. *Geschichte des Füsilier-Regiments Generalfeldmarschall Prinz Albrecht von Preußen (Hann.) Nr. 73* Berlin 1938

Wellmann Generalleutnant a.D. *Mit der 18. Reserve-Division in Frankreich 24. Februar 1915 bis 4. Oktober 1916* Hamburg 1925

Weniger Generalmajor a.D. Heinrich, Zobel Oberst a.D. Artur & Fels Oberst a.D. Maximilian *Das K.B. 5. Infanterie-Regiment Großherzog Ernst Ludwig von Hessen.* Munich 1929

Wißmann Oberst von *Das Reserve-Infanterie-Regt. Nr. 55 im Weltkrieg* Berlin 1929

Vormann Wolfgang von *Infanterie-Regt Fürst Leopold von Anhalt-Dessau (1. Magdeburg) Nr. 26* 1926

Wurmb Major a.D. Herbert Ritter von *Das K.B. Reserve-Infanterie-Regiment Nr. 8* Munich 1929

Published Works (German: author unknown)

Reichskriegsministerium *Der Weltkrieg Zehnter Band:Die Operationen des Jahres 1916 bis zum Wechsel in der Obersten Heeresleitung* Berlin 1936 [GOH]

Offizieren des Regiments *Das K.B. 14.Infanterie-Regiment Hartmann* Munich 1931

Verein Ehemaliger Offiziere des Regiments *Das Füsilier-Regiment Prinz Heinrich von Preußen (Brandenburgisches) Nr. 35 im Weltkriege* Berlin 1929

Offizier-Vereinigung *Geschichte des 9. Rhein. Infanterie-Regiments Nr. 160 im Weltkriege 1914–1918* Zeulenroda 1931

Militärgeschichtliches Forschungsamt *Operatives Denken und Handeln in deutschen Streitkräften im 19. Und 20. Jahrhundert* Herford 1988

Published Works (English)

Brose Eric Dorn *The Kaiser's Army: The Politics of Military Technology in Germany During the Machine Age 1870–1918* Oxford 2001

Clausewitz Carl von *On War* Pelican Books, London 1971

Dupuy Colonel Retd. T N *A Genius for War: The German Army and General Staff 1807 – 1945* London 1977

Edmonds Brigadier-General Sir James *History of the Great War. Military Operations France and Belgium 1916: 2nd July 1916 to the end of the Battle of the Somme* London 1938 [BOH]

Falkenhayn General Erich von *General Headquarters 1914–1916 and its Critical Decisions* London

Görlitz Walter *The German General Staff: Its History and Structure 1657–1945* London 1953

Howard Michael *The Franco-Prussian War: The German Invasion of France 1870–1871* London 1979

Jünger Ernst *The Storm of Steel* London 1929

Leonard Roger Ashley (Ed) *A Short Guide to Clausewitz on War* London 1967

Maddocks Graham *Montauban* Barnsley 1999

McCarthy Chris *The Somme: The Day-by-Day Account* London 1993

Pidgeon Trevor *Flers and Gueudecourt* Barnsley 2002

Prior Robin and Wilson Trevor *The Somme* London 2005

Sheffield Gary *Douglas Haig: From the Somme to Victory* London 2016

Sheffield Gary and Bourne John (Eds) *Douglas Haig: War Diaries and Letters 1914–1918* London 2005

Sheldon Jack *The German Army on Vimy Ridge 1914–1917* Barnsley 2008
Strohn Matthias (Ed.) *The Battle of the Somme* Osprey Publishing 2016
Tschuppik Karl *Ludendorff: The Tragedy of a Specialist* London 1932
Wilhelm Crown Prince *Memoirs of the Crown Prince of Germany* Naval and Military Press Reprint 2005
Zuber Terence *Inventing the Schlieffen Plan* Oxford 2002

Published Works (French)
Etat-Major de l'Armee – Service Historique *Les Armées Françaises dans la Grande Guerre Tome IV 3ᵉ Volume* Paris 1936

Index